Cherokee Heritage Trails Guidebook

CHEROKEE

HERITAGE TRAILS

is a project of the Blue Ridge Heritage Initiative

Project Director:

Beverly Patterson, North Carolina Arts Council

Published in association with the

Museum of the Cherokee Indian,

the North Carolina Arts Council,

the Tennessee Overhill Heritage Association,

the North Carolina Folklife Institute,

the Tennessee Arts Commission, and the

Blue Ridge Parkway, National Park Service

Cherokee Heritage Trails Guidebook

BARBARA R. DUNCAN & **BRETT H. RIGGS**

Published in association with

The Museum of the Cherokee Indian *by*

The University of North Carolina Press

Chapel Hill & London

Set in Charter and Meta types
by Tseng Information Systems, Inc.
Maps by Brett H. Riggs
Manufactured in the United Kingdom

The Blue Ridge Heritage Initiative gratefully acknowledges the financial
support of the following:
    National Endowment for the Arts
    North Carolina Arts Council
    North Carolina Department of Cultural Resources
    Tennessee Arts Commission
    Z. Smith Reynolds Foundation
    Appalachian Regional Commission
    American Express Corporation
    W. K. Kellogg Foundation

The paper in this book meets the guidelines for permanence and durability
of the Committee on Production Guidelines for Book Longevity of the Council
on Library Resources.

Library of Congress Cataloging-in-Publication Data
Duncan, Barbara R.
Cherokee heritage trails guidebook / Barbara R. Duncan and Brett H. Riggs.
    p. cm.
"A project of the Blue Ridge Heritage Initiative."
Includes index.
ISBN 0-8078-5457-3 (pbk.: alk. paper)
1. Cherokee Indians.   2. North Carolina—Guidebooks.   3. Tennessee—
Guidebooks.   4. Georgia—Guidebooks.   I. Riggs, Brett H.   II. Blue Ridge
Heritage Initiative.   III. Title.
E99.C5 D84   2003
975.004'755—dc21   2002151439

paper   07 06 05 04 03   5 4 3 2 1

Go Like a Child

*How would I like visitors to approach the Cherokee Heritage Trails?
I would like for them to forget that this country—the great United
States—even exists. I would like for them to go back to a time when
there was only the Creek and the Choctaw and the Chickasaw and
the Cherokee in this area. Back to a time when there were no
massive roads and cars. And to go out and to just feel, and to listen
to the voices of the past. To realize that the hawk and the eagle and
the crow that fly above these grounds have that appreciation of the
past. The fishes are the same fishes. The birds are the same birds. The
insects are the same insects. We are the only ones who've grown out
of our place.*

*We must be quiet long enough to be able to get back to the point
of appreciation. It would be good to go into these places with
reverence and with a time of silence. Then and only then can you
look around and see great mountains and their panoramic view as
the Cherokee saw them thousands of years ago. Then in the silence
you will begin to get a great appreciation for what you're sitting on
or standing on—the Earth itself. Be quiet enough long enough that
you become part of it.*

*Teach your children how to be quiet. They're born from Mother
Earth. Watch them when they're little. They love to take their shoes
off and run their little toes through the soil. They love to take their
shoes off and run in the water and in the rain.*

*We are born with the appreciation of the earth. I hope people will
go to these sites with an open mind. Go like a child.*

—Freeman Owle

CONTENTS

Cherokee Heritage Trails Guidebook

MAP 1
Cherokee
Heritage
Trails:
an
overview

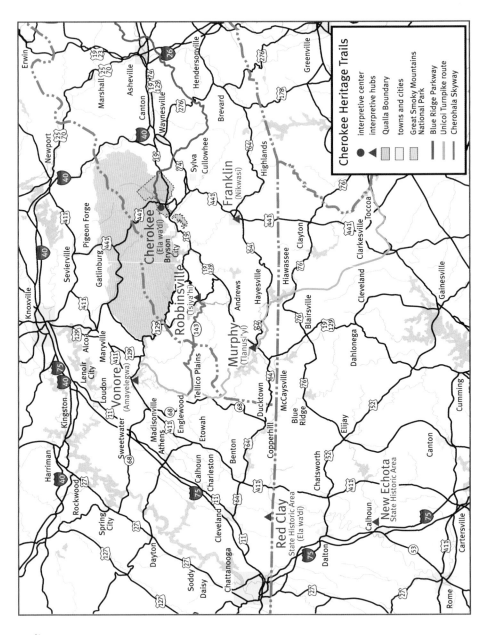

Cherokee Heritage Trails

● interpretive center
◀ interpretive hubs
    Qualla Boundary
    towns and cities
    Great Smoky Mountains
    National Park
━━━ Blue Ridge Parkway
┅┅┅ Unicoi Turnpike route
═══ Cherohala Skyway

WELCOME

The Museum of the Cherokee Indian is pleased to host the Cherokee Heritage Trails. These trails wind through the mountains of North Carolina, Tennessee, and Georgia telling the story of the Cherokee people, Ani-Kituhwa-gi. Once the Cherokee commanded much of the southern Appalachians: territory that became part of West Virginia, Virginia, North and South Carolina, Kentucky, Georgia, Tennessee, and Alabama. Today the Eastern Band of Cherokee Indians owns a remnant of those ancestral lands. But we still recognize the old Cherokee homeland.

Its physical features are still here—the rivers and ridges, the rich plant and animal life, and the beautiful Appalachian vistas. On the Cherokee Heritage Trails visitors and residents alike can explore places that were part of the original Cherokee territory: ancient sites identified by archaeologists, sites of historical events, and places of myth and legend. Some of these sites clearly interpret Cherokee history; others make more demands on the imagination.

And we, the Cherokee people, are still here. The Eastern Band of Cherokee Indians, a federally recognized tribe with more than 12,000 members, owns about 57,000 acres of tribal land in western North Carolina. More than 200,000 people are members of the Cherokee Nation in Oklahoma, and another 15,000 are members of the United Keetoowah Band, making the Cherokees the second largest tribe in the United States. While we live in the modern world of cars, television, and daily jobs, many of our members also weave baskets, make pottery, carve in wood and stone, tell stories, sing the old songs, and perform ceremonial dances. Visitors will encounter these and other Cherokee traditions at festivals and special events along the Cherokee Heritage Trails.

This book includes descriptions of Cherokee sites and events, comments from Cherokee people, photographs, and maps. The introduction provides an overview and timeline, sketching out the historical and cultural backdrop for individual sites on the trails. The chapters themselves focus on seven central locations on the trails: Cherokee, Robbinsville, Franklin, and Murphy in North Carolina, Vonore and Red Clay in Tennessee, and New

Ken Blankenship, director of the Museum of the Cherokee Indian. (Photograph by Cedric N. Chatterley)

Echota in Georgia. Sites in each area are identified as local sites or nearby sites, side trips, and scenic drives.

Descriptions of events appear at the end of each chapter, and a calendar summarizing these listings is at the end of the book. Powwows and powwow-related events are not included. Although Cherokee people participate in powwow dancing and drumming, these dances and songs come from other tribes or from the powwow traditions that evolved since World War II, and they do not represent Cherokee tradition.

But this guidebook also offers information of another kind: the voices of Cherokee people themselves. Some quotations draw on previously published materials on history and folklore, but many others come from contemporary members of the Eastern Band, including tribal elders Walker Calhoun, Emmeline Cucumber, the late Robert Bushyhead, and Jerry Wolfe, and among the younger generation, Tom Belt, Marie Junaluska, and Freeman Owle. Through their words presented here, Cherokee people themselves become your guides on these trails.

The original Cherokee homeland has been altered over the past two hundred years, with the addition of roads, towns, and new species of plants and animals; with the extinction of the chestnut tree, the elk, the Carolina parakeet, the buffalo, and others. But the shape of the hills, the flow of the rivers, and in some remote places, the landscape, remain much as Cherokees experienced them for thousands of years. We still have these features of the landscape, and we still have the Cherokee understanding of our relationship with this land preserved in stories, dances, medicine formulae, ceremonies, and customs.

Every site presented here contributes to an understanding of Cherokee history and culture and has been chosen by Cherokee people to represent our heritage to the public. These places can be safely visited without endangering the sites or violating any Cherokee religious traditions. We invite you to visit with an open mind and to let the land, the Cherokee voices, and the people themselves give you a glimpse of Cherokee ways of seeing the world. Don't be surprised if the landscape changes before you—from highways and cities to watersheds and ancient villages, from a modern world to the home of giants and little people.

Ken Blankenship, Director
Museum of the Cherokee Indian

AN INTRODUCTION TO
CHEROKEE HISTORY AND CULTURE

> It's always been my belief that we were put here in the beginning. This is our land. This is where our Creator wanted us to be, because this is where he put us. All the things here have helped us survive—the natural resources, the plants. That's how we have lived; without those things we wouldn't be here. He's blessed us with this land, and in return we should respect it, we should take care of it.
> —Marie Junaluska

The Cherokees say that they have always been here in the southern mountains, that the Creator put them here. The first man and first woman, Kanati and Selu, lived at Shining Rock Wilderness, near present-day Waynesville, and the first Cherokee village was at the Kituhwa Mound, near present-day Bryson City. They say that their language and their traditions were given to them by the Creator.

Many contemporary Cherokee people believe, as Christians, in the creation story in Genesis. Walker Calhoun said, "When Adam and Eve was without a garden, the Creator told them to fill the earth with people. And God told Adam to take care of the earth."

Many Cherokee people also believe that the Creator placed them here in the mountains, and they continue to tell Cherokee creation stories. They tell how the water beetle, *Dayunishi,* brought mud from below the waters to make the earth, and how the great buzzard shaped that earth with his wings, making the mountains of Cherokee country.

Archaeological evidence shows people living in the southern Appalachians more than eleven thousand years ago; we know them through their distinctive stone tools and their beautifully made, fluted spear points. During this time, at the end of the last Ice Age, the climate was colder, the southern Appalachians were covered with spruce and fir, and mastodons and other extinct species foraged the upland landscape. Even today, Cherokee stories tell of strange, giant animals that once roamed the mountains, hearkening back to the end of the Ice Age. Cherokee elder Jerry Wolfe recalls, "My dad always said that when the Cherokees came into this coun-

The Nantahala River, flowing through the Nantahala National Forest in western North Carolina, is a setting for Cherokee legends. (Photograph by Roger Haile)

try, into these mountains, that it was dangerous. It was a dangerous place because of all the monsters that lived here."

About ten thousand years ago, the climate grew warmer, and people adapted to a changing environment by developing new tools and new, more diverse patterns for hunting, fishing, and gathering plant foods. Archaeological sites yield different and distinctive styles of spear and dart points, and weights and sinkers for fishing nets as well as fishhooks carved from bone. People carved stone bowls from steatite (soapstone), and created mortars and pestles for grinding seeds and nuts, some of which were cultivated. People began making baskets at least ninety-five hundred years ago, and their woven, twined cords left impressions on clay hearths that survived the ages. An extensive network of trading paths followed rivers and mountain ridges.

Over the millennia, people in the southern mountains developed vil-

The Cherokee Story of Creation

The earth is a great island floating in a sea of water, and suspended at each of the cardinal points by a cord hanging down from the sky vault. When the world grows old and worn out, the people will die and the cords will break and let the earth sink down into the ocean, and all will be water again. We are afraid of this.

When all was water, the animals were above in Galunlati, the sky arch, but it was very crowded, and they were wanting more room. They wondered what was beyond the water, and at last Dayunishi, "Beaver's Grandchild" the little water beetle, offered to go and see if it could learn. It darted about in every direction over the surface of the water, but could find no place to rest. Then it dived to the bottom and came up with some soft mud, which began to grow and spread on every side until it became the island which we call the earth. It was afterward fastened to the sky with four cords, but no one remembers who did this.

At first the earth was flat and very soft and wet. The animals were anxious to get down. At last they sent out the buzzard and told him to go and make ready for them. This was the Great Buzzard, the father of all the buzzards we see now. He flew all over the earth, low down near the ground, and it was still soft. When he reached the Cherokee country, he was very tired, and his wings began to flap and strike the ground, and wherever they struck the earth there was a valley, and where they turned up again was a mountain. When the animals above saw this, they were afraid that the whole world would be mountains, so they called him back. But the Cherokee country remains full of mountains to this day.

Swimmer, Ayuini

lages, agriculture, pottery, bows and arrows, and more elaborately carved stone pipes. According to scholars, Cherokee language, part of the Iroquoian language family, became a separate, distinct language at least thirty-five hundred years ago (1500 B.C.).

More than a thousand years ago, people in the southern mountains began developing a distinctively Cherokee way of life, with patterns of belief and material culture that survive to this day. They began to focus on growing corn, whose name reflects its importance: *selu,* name of the

Jerry Wolfe, storyteller. (Photograph by Cedric N. Chatterley)

first Cherokee woman. They built permanent, well-organized villages in the midst of extensive cornfields and gardens throughout the fertile river valleys of the Cherokee country. In these villages, homes ranged around a central plaza used for dances, games, and ceremonies. At one end of the plaza, the council house, or townhouse, held the sacred fire, symbol of the Creator and embodiment of the spirit of the town. Often the townhouse stood on an earthen mound, which grew with successive, ceremonial rebuildings.

At the heart of this culture was the idea of balance, or *duyuktv,* "the right way." Men's hunting and fishing, for example, was balanced by women's farming. The rights of the individual were balanced with the good of the whole, resulting in great personal freedom within the context of responsibility to the family, clan, and tribe. The size of the townhouse reflected the size of the village because all the people of the village—men, women, children, and old people—had to fit in the townhouse in order to make decisions together. On an individual level, the physical, intellectual, and spiritual aspects of oneself were to be integrated and balanced. Thus one became a "real person": Ani-Yvwiya.

Every aspect of daily life and the physical world had spiritual significance. Ceremonies and customs maintained balance for the individual and the community. Men fasted and prayed before hunting, and then offered thanks in a ceremony after killing an animal; on returning to their village,

People in the southern Appalachians have grown gourds for thousands of years, using them for storage, birdhouses, masks, and dippers. (Photograph by Roger Haile)

they shared the meat, used all parts of the animal, and often danced to honor the animal. When gathering plants, only the fourth was taken, and a gift was left in return. Even today stories of the Little People emphasize the importance of reciprocity. Their permission must be asked before picking up anything from the woods—a stone, a feather, a leaf—and if their permission is given, a gift must be left. Entire villages fasted and purified themselves in order to give thanks before eating the new corn crop. Every day began with the going-to-water ceremony, when everyone entered a stream near their village, faced east, and prayed to the seven directions: the four cardinal points, the sky, the earth, and the center—the spirit. They gave thanks for a new day, and washed away any feelings that might separate them from their neighbors or from the Creator, emerging cleansed physically, mentally, and spiritually.

Cherokees developed and cultivated corn, beans, and squash—"the three sisters"—along with sunflowers and other crops. In addition to farming, Cherokee women continued gathering wild foods from woods and fallow fields: nuts, wild greens, fruit, and berries. Men continued hunting wild game and fishing.

Cherokee women owned their houses and fields, and passed them from mother to daughter. Cherokee women also passed their clan affiliation to their children, both male and female. A man's most important relatives were his mother, maternal grandmother, and his sisters—the women of his clan. Until he married, he lived in their houses, and when he married he moved to his wife's house. People of the same clan did not marry each

Oconaluftee River near downtown Cherokee, North Carolina.
(Photograph by Cedric N. Chatterley)

other. The clans also enforced unwritten laws regarding homicide and other social infractions. If someone was killed, his or her clan was owed a life from the clan of the killer. When this life was paid, balance was restored, and no further retribution took place. Clan members sat together at dances and ceremonies, in special sections reserved for their clan. Although oral tradition suggests that at one time there may have been as many as fourteen clans, each with its own special skills and responsibilities, today seven Cherokee clans survive: wolf, deer, bird, paint, long hair, wild potato, and blue.

The existence of gorgets carved from marine shells from the Gulf of Mexico suggests the extent of Cherokee trading practices. Worn around the neck, these round shell ornaments, about four inches in diameter, were elaborately carved with spirals, crosses, rattlesnakes, water spiders, and birds. Many of these creatures play an important role in Cherokee stories.

Clan masks in a Cherokee Fall Fair exhibit. (Photograph by Roger Haile)

Cherokees also traded mica throughout eastern North America, and received copper and pipestone from the Great Lakes region and plants and shells from the Atlantic coast.

Chunkey stones, marbles, and ball sticks indicate favorite games of the time. Smooth chunkey yards were found in villages. Stickball games were played on large cleared fields.

Archaeological evidence, early written accounts, and the oral history of the Cherokee themselves show Cherokees as a mighty nation controlling more than 140,000 square miles with a population of thirty-six thousand or more. Unified by language, traditions, and its clan system, the Cherokee nation had no centralized government or written laws. Towns governed themselves by democratic consensus, and each had its own priest, war chief, and peace chief. Cherokee people were athletic, with some men as much as six feet tall. Everything they needed they created from their environment: food, medicine, clothing, shelter, weapons, musical instruments, jewelry, and goods for trade. They practiced empirical science by observing the world around them, and then they used that knowledge combined with spiritual inspiration and practical application to create a society that used resources in a sustainable way.

Into this ever-changing but ever-balancing world came people from Eu-

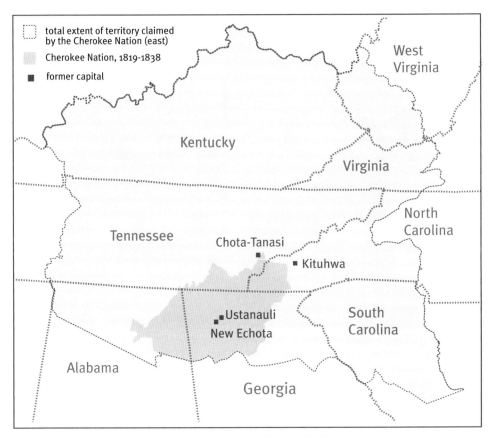

MAP 2. *Extent of the territory formerly claimed by the Cherokee Nation*

rope and Africa. In 1540, Hernando de Soto's expedition passed through the margins of Cherokee territory. Their gifts, their diseases, and their greed foreshadowed the patterns of the next three hundred years of Cherokee history. In search of gold and slaves, this army of "500 Christians," as they described themselves, executed any who would not provide them directions to the next settlement. Strangers without accurate maps or sufficient food, they raped, murdered, and demanded tribute as they crossed through the rugged mountains. According to the Spanish chroniclers on the expedition, Cherokee villages provided food: seven hundred turkeys from one village; twenty baskets of mulberries from another; and three hundred hairless dogs—supposedly a delicacy. The Cherokees, however, say that this was a joke. They say they gave the Spaniards opossums, which Cherokees do not eat because of that animal's scavenging habits.

De Soto's chroniclers commented on the impressive weaponry of Ameri-

Blow gun contest at the Cherokee Fall Fair. (Photograph by Roger Haile)

can Indians, noting that the Spanish men did not have the strength to pull their bows. Cherokee warriors could fire six or seven arrows in the time it took to load and fire one arquebus, the unreliable Spanish flintlock. Their arrows had enough power to entirely penetrate the body of a horse from hindquarters to heart. Chroniclers also marveled at the abundant game, wild foods, and cultivated crops among Native Americans of the Southeast. They, and a later expedition led by Juan Pardo in 1567, traded beads, knives, buttons, and other goods for food. Some African slaves escaped these expeditions and continued to live with Native tribes.

The Spaniards also brought devastating diseases. Like other Native Americans, the Cherokee people had no resistance to European diseases, which quickly became epidemic. Because diseases traveled ahead of de Soto's expedition, the Spaniards found some villages deserted, their entire population dead. Some scholars now estimate that 95 percent of Native Americans were killed by European diseases within a hundred and fifty years of Columbus's landing, thus enabling conquest and giving the appearance of an empty land.

After these first expeditions, with their brief contact, the Cherokees had only sporadic exposure to Europeans. They met the British in Virginia in 1634. By 1650, they had begun growing peaches and watermelons, acquired through trade. But it wasn't until the 1690s that the Cherokees began making regular contact with any Europeans. In 1693, Cherokee leaders traveled to Charlestown to complain that Cherokee people were being sold as slaves to the British, a practice that continued for thirty years after their meeting.

In the eighteenth century, the Cherokees felt the full impact of Europeans in their territory. Peaceful cultural exchange, trade goods, new technology, intermarriage between Cherokee women and British traders, and trips to England by Cherokee leaders were the positive results. Negative results included three major smallpox epidemics, each killing one-third to one-half of the Cherokee population at the time; repeated "scorched earth" military campaigns destroying dozens of Cherokee towns; and the loss of 75 percent of the Cherokee territory through treaties. The Cherokees began the century living in towns built around mounds, celebrating festivals, sharing wealth, and balancing men's and women's roles. By the end of the century, many of the old towns had been destroyed or ceded, and the federal government was pressing a Civilization Policy to make Cherokee men farmers instead of hunters and warriors, and to make women spinners and weavers rather than the successful farmers they had been.

The Cherokees began the 1700s far outnumbering the colonists, even though their population had been drastically reduced by epidemics. They ended the century vastly outnumbered, with colonists crowding tribal lands. From an estimated population of thirty-five thousand in 1685, about seven thousand survived in the mid-1760s. This population, still spread throughout the southern Appalachians, was concentrated in the Lower and Middle Towns (along the Little Tennessee River), the Valley Towns (along the Hiwassee River), and the Overhill Towns (along the Tennessee River).

During this time, the Cherokees helped the colonists by eliminating the Yamassee and Tuscarora, their neighbors and enemies, who had been the buffer between themselves and the Europeans. They also brought deerskins for trade. From 1700 to 1715, nearly a million skins were shipped from Charlestown to Europe, and the trade increased for more than fifty years. The trade brought white traders—mostly Scots—into Cherokee country; the traders often married Cherokee women.

A Cherokee man might trade fifty deerskins in a good season, and according to exchange rates set in 1716, these would buy a gun (35 deerskins), sixty bullets (2 deerskins), twenty-four flints (2 skins), one steel for striking flint (1 skin), and perhaps an axe and hoe (5 deerskins each). Cherokee women actively participated in the trade, to the surprise of the British. The corn raised by Cherokee women, and their baskets, were in great demand, and in turn they received cloth, iron pots, weapons, plows, hoes, and bells.

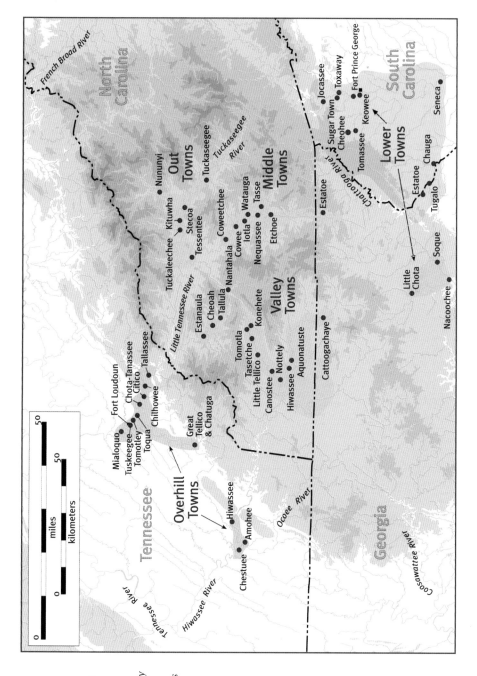

MAP 3
Cherokee
towns,
mid-
eighteenth
century,
with
present-day
state
boundaries

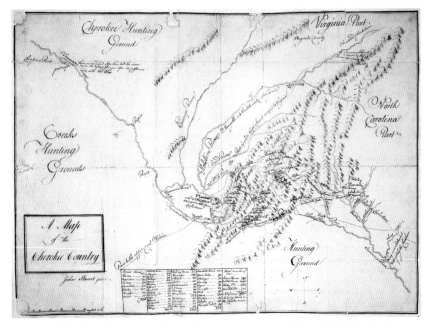

"A Map of the Cherokee Country," by John Stuart, ca. 1762. (From the British Library; courtesy of the Museum of the Cherokee Indian)

Exchange rates set eighty-four bushels of corn as the price of a calico petticoat.

During this period of trade, Cherokee men began hunting with guns as well as continuing to use bows and arrows. The Cherokees began keeping and breeding horses about 1720, soon developing large herds. Because traders used horses to carry their packs, the Cherokee word for trader was the same as the word for horse, *sogwili.*

Cherokee women, in addition to their already extensive agriculture and woodland gathering, began growing apples (from Europe), black-eyed peas (from Africa), and sweet potatoes (from the Caribbean). By mid-century, they were keeping horses, chickens, and hogs. They resisted raising cattle because the slow nature of cattle, they thought, would be imparted to anyone who ate beef, and because cattle were so destructive to gardens that they required fencing. By the end of the century, however, Cherokee households included cows as well. Cherokee Beloved Woman Nancy Ward said that she saved Lydia Bean, a white woman, from being burned at the stake because she knew how to make butter and cheese and would teach the Cherokee women to do so.

Nancy Ward and other Cherokee women attended every treaty signing in the eighteenth century. At first they asked where the white women were, but they soon learned that only white men made treaties. They continued to send greetings to the queen and to white women in Europe, while the British ridiculed the Cherokee "petticoat government."

Peaceful trade and intermarriage went on from 1700 to 1760. From 1760 to 1794, however, the Cherokees were at war. Events throughout this period gave rise to stories about Indians scalping settlers on the frontier, stories that became part of the American myth of this country's origins, a myth since dramatized in novels, Wild West shows, medicine shows, radio, and finally television and movies. These stories live on in the oral history of white frontier families as well. In reality, Cherokee actions against settlers were either part of military action directed by the British, or retaliation for murder according to Cherokee laws controlling homicide and its punishment through the clan system. Historical documents further show that Cherokee violence against settlers was matched by the violence of individuals of European descent and by their military forces. Both sides committed atrocities.

In the French and Indian War, the Cherokees allied themselves with their main trading partners, the British; soon, however, the Cherokees turned against them. In 1759, Cherokee men on their way home from aiding British forces and Virginia militia were killed in an ambush by Virginia colonists, German settlers from whom they stole horses. The unwritten Cherokee law, universally enforced by clans throughout the Cherokee nation, required a life for a life. If the murderer could not be found, then someone in his clan was executed in his place. The white people had maintained that they were all of the same clan, so the remainder of the Cherokee war party, on the way home, killed nineteen German settlers on the Yadkin River in North Carolina. From the Cherokee perspective, this ended the matter, but from the British and colonial perspectives, the Cherokees had murdered innocent settlers. Colonists retaliated against Cherokee towns, and Cherokee warriors retaliated further. The Virginians who had ambushed the Cherokees sold their scalps to the British and collected a bounty, and that turned the Cherokees against their former allies.

Early the next year a delegation of Cherokee leaders went to Charlestown to make peace. Cherokees still operated as a confederation of autonomous towns united by language, culture, and clan kinship, so they sent a delegation of town chiefs. The governor refused to meet with them and sent them under armed guard to Fort Prince George. There the peace delegation became hostages, and finally all twenty-two were killed in an uprising. As a result, in February of 1760, Cherokees led by Oconostota, Ostenaco, and Willenawaw laid siege to the British garrison at Fort Loudoun, in their

Overhill Towns, next to the capital city of Echota. Ostenaco, angered by the treachery of the British, was quoted in the *South Carolina Gazette:* "Make peace who would, I will never keep it."

In response, South Carolina mounted an expedition led by Colonel Archibald Montgomery that burned and destroyed all the Cherokee Lower Towns in upper South Carolina. Cherokee forces stopped the army at the town of Etchoe, which was on the Little Tennessee River (near present-day Otto, North Carolina), in June of 1760, and they saved the Middle Towns. Montgomery's defeat meant that relief would not be coming to Fort Loudoun, and in August, troops there surrendered, promising to give all their weaponry to the Cherokee. Before they left the fort, however, the soldiers buried their powder and shot, and threw their guns and cannon into the river. In retaliation, the Cherokees attacked the departing troops the next morning, killing one soldier for each Cherokee chief killed in South Carolina, and taking the rest prisoner. Captain John Stuart, who was well liked by the Cherokees, was taken away by Attakullaculla, who delivered him safely to Virginia.

The following year, in 1761, Colonel James Grant, formerly a lieutenant with Montgomery's expedition, mounted another campaign against the Cherokees. Again, the expedition devastated the Cherokee Lower Towns. Once again the Cherokees, led by Oconostota, brought warriors to the narrow pass below the village of Etchoe. There Grant and his troops fought for five hours against thousands of Cherokee warriors. Later Grant commented that if the Cherokees had not run out of ammunition, they would have defeated the British.

Grant pushed through into the Little Tennessee River Valley, destroying fifteen towns, more than fifteen hundred acres of crops, and killing livestock. His soldiers complained what hard work it was to cut down the huge Cherokee orchards and to destroy the well-built houses. Perhaps the most poignant comment came from Lieutenant Francis Marion, later the legendary "Swamp Fox" of the American Revolution.

> We proceeded, by Colonel Grant's orders, to burn the Indian cabins. Some of the men seemed to enjoy this cruel work, laughing heartily at the flames, but to me it appeared a shocking sight. . . . But when we came, according to our orders, to cut down the fields of corn, I could scarcely refrain from tears. Who, without grief, could see the stately stalks with broad green leaves and tasseled shocks, the staff of life, sink under our swords with all their precious load, to wither and rot untasted in their mourning fields.
>
> I saw everywhere around the footsteps of the little Indian children,

where they had lately played under the shade of their rustling corn. When we are gone, thought I, they will return, and peeping through the weeds with tearful eyes, will mark the ghastly ruin where they had so often played.

"Who did this?" they will ask their mothers, and the reply will be, "The white people did it—the Christians did it!"

And thus, for cursed mammon's sake, the followers of Christ have sowed the selfish tares of hate in the bosoms of even Pagan children.

The destruction of so many towns within two years worked a hardship on the Cherokees, who took to the woods and mountains, later rebuilding some but not all of these towns. This destruction was humbling as well: for the first time, Cherokee country had been successfully invaded by Europeans.

Following Grant's campaign of 1761, the Cherokees made peace with Great Britain. Lieutenant Henry Timberlake volunteered to visit the Cherokees to assure both sides that the peace would be kept. He stayed at Echota for three months. Then Timberlake took three Cherokee leaders—Ostenaco, Cunne Shote (Stalking Turkey), and Woyi (Pigeon) to London where they met with King George III and exchanged presents. The Cherokees and other tribes heartily approved of the king's Proclamation of 1763, which stated that colonists would not settle west of the Blue Ridge.

At the Treaty of Sycamore Shoals in 1775, Richard Henderson, a land speculator and Daniel Boone's employer, brought wagon loads of presents and whisky for the Cherokees in hopes of inducing them to sign away their hunting grounds that occupied nearly all of the present-day state of Kentucky. The prophetic remarks of Dragging Canoe, Cherokee warrior and cousin of Nancy Ward, were recorded:

Whole Indian nations have melted away like snowballs in the sun before the white man's advance. They leave scarcely a name of our people except those wrongly recorded by their destroyers. Where are the Delawares? They have been reduced to a mere shadow of their former greatness. We had hoped that the white men would not be willing to travel beyond the mountains. Now that hope is gone. They have passed the mountains and have settled upon Cherokee land. They wish to have that usurpation sanctioned by treaty. When that is gained, the same encroaching spirit will lead them upon other land of the Cherokees. New cessions will be asked. Finally the whole country, which the Cherokees and their fathers have so long occupied, will be demanded, and the remnant of Ani-Yvwiya, the Real People, once so great and formidable, will be compelled to seek refuge in some distant wilderness. There they will be permitted to stay only a short while, until they again behold the advancing banners of the same greedy host. Not being able to point out any further retreat for the miserable Cherokees, the extinction of the whole race will be proclaimed. Should we not therefore run all risks, and incur all consequences, rather than submit to further loss of our country? Such treaties may be all right for men who are too old to hunt or fight. As for me, I have my young warriors about me. We will have our lands. I have spoken.

The Cherokees, along with many other tribes, allied with the British during the American Revolution. At British direction, the Cherokees, often accompanied by Tories dressed as Indians, attacked border towns in present-day South Carolina, North Carolina, Georgia, and Tennessee. A punitive American expedition in 1776 took forces under General Griffith Rutherford to attack Cherokee villages far behind the lines of the American frontier. Colonel Andrew Williamson attacked from South Carolina, and smaller militia forces from Georgia and Virginia attacked their borders as well. Rutherford's forces alone destroyed thirty-six Cherokee towns on the Little Tennessee, Tuckaseegee, Oconaluftee, and Hiwassee Rivers, killing men, women, children, and livestock, executing prisoners and the wounded, and burning crops as well as houses. By the end of the war in 1782, some of the Cherokee towns had been burnt several times over, and women and children were living in the woods, while Cherokee warriors continued to support the British. A smallpox epidemic further devastated the Cherokees in 1783. Along with other tribes, they finally made peace.

Exceptions to the peace included the Cherokee leader Dragging Canoe, who continued to make war against the encroaching settlers until his death. Also during this time, "mountain men" and "Indian fighters," including John Sevier, attacked peaceful Cherokee villages. With the "Chickamauga Cherokees," warriors living on Chickamauga Creek near present-day Chattanooga, Dragging Canoe harassed the backcountry settlers of Tennessee. At times his cousin Nancy Ward warned white settlers of impending raids. In gratitude, the "Indian fighters" often spared her home and the town at Chota. But Dragging Canoe and the Chickamauga Cherokees persisted in military efforts to preserve Cherokee land in Tennessee until 1794, shortly after Dragging Canoe's death.

In 1789, George Washington and Secretary of War John Knox created the "Civilization Policy." This policy was supposed to solve the "Indian problem" by teaching Indians to live like white people; the policy also suggested that they intermarry with whites until their native identity disappeared completely.

In the fifty years beginning in 1789 and ending in 1839 (when the last groups on the Trail of Tears reached Oklahoma), the Cherokees made an incredible recovery from defeat and devastation. They transformed themselves into a "civilized tribe" with written language, schools, churches, farms, commercial enterprises, a written constitution, representative government, and a bilingual newspaper. Centered in what is now northwest Georgia, this remarkable transformation has been called the "Cherokee Renaissance" by historians.

Changes did not proceed smoothly or in equal measure in different parts of the Cherokee nation. Factions within the Cherokee nation disagreed about what their relationship should be to white culture and to the newly formed United States. During this period the Cherokees moved from a decentralized government with towns led by peace chiefs and war chiefs to a national council with a written constitution. Their struggle to balance autonomous units with a central government was not unlike that of the new United States. The long legal process of delineating the powers of states and the powers of the federal government directly affected the Cherokees, and they were active participants in it

During this period, 1789–1839, Cherokee women began growing cotton and flax, and they became expert spinners and weavers. Their demand for looms, cards, and spinning wheels outpaced the supplies of the Indian agents. And no wonder: native women had been weaving baskets, mats, sandals, fishing nets, sashes, and clothing for thousands of years. At issue for the federal government was whether Cherokee men would become farmers rather than hunters and warriors. The United States wanted the extensive hunting grounds of all the tribes for white settlement—with a phase of land speculation where tribal lands taken in treaty by the federal government would then be sold at a profit by the federal government, the states, and land speculators. The United States also wanted to neutralize warriors by placing them on individual farmsteads rather than in communal towns, and by making them farmers. While some Cherokee men began farming, most turned to ranging cattle and hogs in the woods, driving them to market, and they continued to hunt and fish.

The U.S. government, to promote "civilization," partially funded missionaries to the Cherokees. The Cherokees wanted their children to learn to read and write English. Missionaries offered these skills along with education in religion, farming, and domestic arts. The Moravians came in 1799, and James Vann allowed them to build Springplace Mission on his property, near present-day Chatsworth, Georgia. Presbyterian missionaries opened a school in 1804. The American Board of Commissioners for Foreign Missions sent Congregationalist ministers in 1816, who founded the Brainerd

Print shop at New Echota, Georgia. (Courtesy of New Echota State Historic Site)

Mission, whose cemetery still stands in downtown Chattanooga. The Baptists founded their first mission in 1819, for the Valley Towns, near present-day Murphy, North Carolina, on the Hiwassee River. The Methodists began sending circuit riders in 1824. During the 1820s Cherokee men started to become preachers as well, particularly in the Valley Towns. Acceptance of Christianity did not proceed smoothly. In 1811, Cherokee visionaries received messages that led to a revival of the old traditional religion for several years. From 1824 to 1827, White Path led a religious and political rebellion calling for a return to traditional ways, and laid down this cause only when it became apparent that the Cherokee nation needed to be unified in order to deal with the crisis of removal.

Cherokee government was also changing. Cherokees had been learning to get along with foreign governments since the early eighteenth century, mainly by assuming a facade of centralized authority, with "chiefs" and even "emperors." In reality, however, the Cherokee national government was made up of the headmen and elders of towns. When they met, their town had already reached consensus on an issue, and they brought that decision to the national council. Consensus and harmony were valued in national government as well as in daily life. From the late 1700s until 1817, the Cherokee national council included influential men representing all the Cherokee towns as well as young leaders of warriors. Any Cherokee could attend the meeting and speak.

Gradually this tribal council took on responsibilities formerly carried out by clans or within villages. In 1808 at Broomestown, it established a light horse police force to cut down on horse stealing and to enforce inheritance laws (particularly for property passing from men to their children). In 1810 it canceled all outstanding blood debts between clans. In 1817 it adopted a constitution creating an Executive Committee and a National Council. Articles in 1825 delineated property rights, giving Cherokee landholders the right to sell their land to anyone except a non-Cherokee. By 1828, the council adopted the Cherokee Constitution with three branches of government: executive, legislative, and judicial.

Perhaps the most remarkable accomplishment of the Cherokee Renaissance was the creation of a written language by a man who was himself illiterate. George Gist, known as Sequoyah, was born in the Overhill Towns, and was inspired to create a written form for the Cherokee language. He finally succeeded with a syllabary, which has a written symbol for each of the eighty-five syllables used to make up the Cherokee language. With the help of his daughter Ayoka, he demonstrated his system to the Cherokee council in 1821. Within months, a majority of the Cherokee nation became literate. They wrote letters to each other, began keeping records in this language, and quickly developed a printing press and bilingual newspaper. The *Cherokee Phoenix* (literally, "It has risen again") began publication in 1828 and continued until the state of Georgia stopped it in 1834 because of its anti-removal sentiments.

In spite of the dramatic changes made by Cherokees during this period, becoming "civilized" by any standard, the Cherokee nation was removed to Indian territory during the period 1838–1839, leaving only a small group on a remnant of their once-huge territory. Beginning with Thomas Jefferson's Georgia Compact of 1802, the government had urged removal of all Indians from the Southeast. The Louisiana Purchase provided a place to send them, the War of 1812 removed the British as a threat, and by 1817 the federal government was insisting the Cherokees move to Arkansas. A small group, "The Old Settlers," did so.

A clause in the treaties of 1817 and 1819 allowed Cherokee families to move off of tribal lands, claim 640 acres each, and apply for citizenship. Many families did this in Tennessee, Alabama, Georgia, and North Carolina, often remaining on their own farms or town sites in the ceded area. In the following years, only North Carolina courts upheld Cherokee claims to these lands.

Cherokee removal became inevitable when gold was discovered in Georgia in 1828 and Andrew Jackson was elected president of the United States in 1829. Georgia rapidly passed repressive laws, forbidding Cherokees to testify in court and distributing Cherokee lands to whites in a land lottery. Jackson campaigned for removal, and in 1830 Congress passed the controversial Indian Removal Act by a slim margin.

The Cherokees resisted removal with every possible political and personal means: editorials, letters, petitions, personal appeals, public speaking tours, and delegations to Washington. In response to Georgia's legislation, the Cherokee nation pursued the case all the way to the Supreme Court. In 1832 the Supreme Court ruled that the Cherokee Nation constituted a sovereign nation within the state of Georgia, subject only to federal law; this decision continues to be the basis for tribal sovereignty for all Native Americans. When John Marshall handed down this decision, Andrew Jackson is reputed to have said, "He has made his decision, now let him enforce it." Georgia's depredations continued.

In December of 1835, a small group of Cherokee leaders, unauthorized by the Cherokee nation, signed the Treaty of New Echota at Elias Boudinot's house in their newly built capital named for the old town of Echota. This "Treaty Party" consisted of Major Ridge, John Ridge, Elias Boudinot, and twenty-four other signers. Despite immediate protests from the Chero-

John Ross (1790–1866), Cherokee entrepreneur and Principal Chief of the
Cherokees during Removal, and his second wife. (Archives and Manuscripts Division,
Oklahoma Historical Society)

kee National Council, the U.S. Congress ratified this treaty in May of 1836
and gave the Cherokees two years to remove to Oklahoma.

John Ross, principal chief of the Cherokees, began efforts to halt removal. He collected sixteen thousand signatures of Cherokee people on a
petition against removal—virtually all of the nation—and took it to Washington, D.C. At home he counseled his people to continue with their daily
lives, and to continue to plant and harvest, giving no indication that they
accepted the Treaty of New Echota. Junaluska, who had saved Andrew
Jackson's life at the Battle of Horseshoe Bend, traveled to Washington to
plead the Cherokees' cause, but Jackson would not see him.

Cherokee people recorded sentiments such as the following in many
letters, speeches, and essays during this time. "We the great mass of the
people think only of the love we have to our land. For we do love the land
where we were brought up. We will never let our hold to this land go. To
let it go will be like throwing away our mother that gave us birth." Thus
wrote Aitooweyeh and Knock Down to John Ross, principal chief.

The government had been preparing for removal by conducting a census
of Cherokee households, estimating property values and carrying out geographical surveys, particularly in western North Carolina—the area consid-

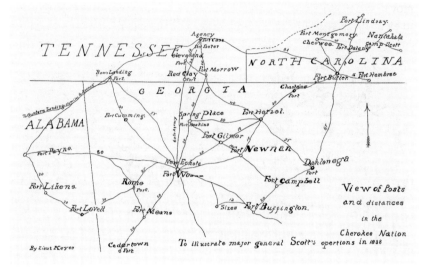

Military posts and distances in the Cherokee Nation [Georgia and neighboring states], map by Lt. E. D. Keyes, 1838. (Record Group 75, Map CA 96, National Archives, College Park, Md.)

ered most likely to provide resistance, as well as the most difficult terrain in which to conduct a military action. Soldiers began constructing garrisons throughout the Cherokee Nation.

In spite of frantic last-minute efforts in Washington, D.C., Cherokee removal began on May 24, 1838, as specified by the ratified, though fraudulent, treaty. John Ross had sent messages to every village, counseling people not to resist. He invoked both the Great Spirit and the Old Testament, saying "the desert shall rejoice and bloom as a rose." (He later surrounded his home in Indian Territory with rosebushes.)

Federal soldiers and state militia rounded up Cherokee people in Georgia, Tennessee, Alabama, and North Carolina, taking them to thirty-one "forts" throughout this area. Often looters accompanied the soldiers. From these forts and stockades, they were taken to eleven internment camps. Neither stockades nor internment camps had facilities for sanitation, cooking, or sleeping.

These primitive conditions, the abuses of local militia and soldiers, and tragic results for the first contingents who took the water routes led John Ross to appeal to President Martin Van Buren to allow him to oversee the rest of the removal, and this appeal was granted. In all, sixteen detachments of Cherokees left the East, traveling by land and by water through the summer and winter of 1838–39. Scholars now estimate that in the removal, in the stockades, on the trail, and in the first year in Oklahoma, four to eight thousand Cherokees died—one quarter to one-half the population. John Ross's wife Quatie died after giving her blanket to a sick, crying child, who survived.

One group of Cherokees remained in North Carolina, the Oconaluftee Citizen Indians. Sixty families, led by Yonaguska, Long Blanket, and Wilnota, had claimed land in their own names under the Treaties of 1817 and 1819. Yonaguska had had a vision in 1830 calling for the Cherokees to give up alcohol and stay in their homeland, saying that they could only be happy in the country where the Creator had placed them. His people followed this revitalizing vision, and by 1836 were able to successfully appeal to the North Carolina legislature to be allowed to remain on their lands, mostly near the Oconaluftee River. Petitions signed by local white men attesting to their sobriety and industriousness aided their case, as did the advocacy of Yonaguska's adopted white son, William Holland Thomas, a trader and lawyer.

During removal, three to four hundred Cherokees hid in the wooded mountains of western North Carolina, particularly on the rugged slopes of the Nantahalas and the Deep Creek watershed below Clingman's Dome (Kuwahi). Most Cherokees had been arrested in June and moved to Tennessee in July, and they had heeded Ross's counsel of nonresistance. In November of 1838, however, when only a few federal troops remained in the mountains hunting fugitives, Tsali and his family killed two soldiers who were attempting to bring them in.

Tsali and his family lived in a small hollow along the Nantahala River, near Wesser, North Carolina. The 1835 census lists six household members, all full bloods: three males over eighteen and three females over sixteen years of age. They owned two cabins, two hothouses (the *asi*), and one corncrib on thirteen acres of improved land that included thirty-six peach trees and twelve apple trees. All this was valued at $169. Tsali's neighbors were his son Lowin, with similar holdings, and Oochella (Euchella), who had once been a leader in the Cowee village where he and Tsali had lived before that land was taken in the Treaty of 1819.

Tsali and his wife, along with his sons and their wives and children, were fugitives from May to November of 1838, along with hundreds of others hiding in the rugged Nantahala area, and to the northeast on the lower slopes of Kuwahi. Soldiers who found them and brought them in say the attack was unprovoked, but Cherokee oral histories say that the soldiers offended the women and that a baby was killed accidentally. In any case, once soldiers were killed, the federal government would not rest until retribution was exacted. Troops under Colonel William S. Foster

Tsali and his sons as portrayed in Unto These Hills *outdoor drama, Cherokee, N.C.*
(Courtesy of the Cherokee Historical Association)

William Holland Thomas (1805–93) helped Cherokees obtain land in North Carolina after Removal. Portrait attributed to Jesse Atwood, ca. 1850. (Courtesy of the Museum of the Cherokee Indian)

combed the mountains in cold rainy weather for weeks with no success. William Holland Thomas, the Oconaluftee Citizen Indians, and a group under Euchella's leadership then began to aid in the search. They found Tsali. Cherokee legend says that he agreed to come in and be executed so that the other Cherokees would be allowed to stay in the mountains.

After Tsali's execution near Big Bear's farm, the Army gave up its search for Cherokees in the mountains. Euchella's band, who had been in hiding, were allowed to stay by proclamation of the U.S. Army, supported by a deposition of local white men. Whether the Army forced Euchella and Yonaguska's people to help bring in Tsali is not clear, but they certainly would not have been allowed to stay in North Carolina if they had aided Tsali. The Oconaluftee Citizen Indians under Yonaguska's leadership were allowed to continue living on their private lands along the Oconaluftee and the Tuckaseegee. Some other Cherokees living on their own deeded land also were able to stay. Those hiding in the mountains came out. Some Cherokees escaped from the Trail of Tears, or like Junaluska, walked from Indian Territory back to the mountains of western North Carolina. These people, about one thousand in all, became the ancestors of today's Eastern Band of Cherokee Indians. Among them, some still trace their ancestry back to Tsali, Euchella, Junaluska, and Yonaguska, and the stories of that time are told as though they happened yesterday.

The federal government continued to encourage the Cherokees in western North Carolina to remove to Oklahoma, but they refused to do so. Aided by William Holland Thomas, Yonaguska's adopted son and the tribe's acting chief, they managed to stay on their lands. They continued to hunt, fish, and farm in order to survive. They hired themselves out as laborers on farms owned by whites, and worked as road builders in the mountains. Some had special skills, such as the blacksmith Saloli (Squirrel) who invented a rifle mechanism that was patented. They gave their earnings to Will Thomas to buy and hold land in his name until their legal status could be established. (Other white men also assisted the Cherokees: Albert Siler in Macon County for the Sand Town Cherokees, and Gideon Morris and John Welch in Cherokee County and Graham County.) Their knowledge of medicinal plants was valued by surrounding communities. Cherokee women made and traded baskets. They lived in the townships organized by Will Thomas after removal. These townships corresponded to their representation on the tribal council: Yellow Hill, Birdtown, Painttown, Wolftown, and Big Cove. Snowbird and Tomotla, in Graham and Cherokee Counties, also were represented on the council. In every town and community, the *gadugi,* or work group, carried on the cultural values of the tribe by helping those in need, a tradition that continues today.

The federal government recognized the Eastern Band of Cherokee Indians in 1868, along with other tribes with whom they had made treaties. The Eastern Band then held a general council at Cheoah in Graham County to adopt a tribal government under a constitution and elected Flying Squirrel (Sawnook, or Sawanugi) as their first principal chief in 1870. Cherokee ownership of tribal lands as well as individual parcels became legally established. The Cherokees paid property taxes to the state of North Carolina, and under the laws of post–Civil War reconstruction, were allowed to vote. Chief Nimrod Jarrett Smith applied for legal status for the tribe as a corporation in North Carolina, which was granted in 1889.

Shortly before that, in 1887, James Mooney, a young Irish ethnologist, began work in Cherokee on behalf of the Bureau of American Ethnology. He learned the Cherokee language and collected stories, oral histories, and medicine formulas by talking with Swimmer, Will West Long, Ayasta, Suyeta, John Ax, and William Holland Thomas. Mooney's monumental *Myths of the Cherokee* and *Sacred Formulas of the Cherokee* remain the classic works on the Eastern Band. Mooney found that the Cherokee shamans used hundreds of medicinal prayer formulas as well as more than seven hundred plants, although he believed that these traditional practices were declining.

The turn of the twentieth century found about fifteen hundred Cherokees living on their individual lands and on tribal land in Swain, Jackson, Graham, Macon, and Cherokee Counties. Their legal status continued to be debated. In 1895 a federal court ruling on a tribal timber sale found that the Cherokees were wards of the federal government. Democrats, the ma-

Nimrod Jarrett Smith's daughter Lilly.
(Photograph by James Mooney, 1888;
National Anthropological Archives,
Smithsonian Institution)

jority party in North Carolina, took advantage of this ruling to deny voting rights to the Cherokees, many of whom had voted Republican in the presidential election of 1884, when the vice-presidential candidate was believed to have Native American blood. Local registrars did not allow Cherokees to vote in the elections of 1900. Cherokees continued to try to register and to vote, however. Returning veterans from World War I marched on the Swain County Courthouse but were turned away, as were Cherokee women who tried to register after the passage of the Nineteenth Amendment in 1920. Cherokees did not regain the right to vote in local, state, and federal elections until 1946, when veterans returned from World War II and demanded that right.

During the early part of the century, logging and farming provided income and subsistence, but the tribe also turned to tourism as a source of income. The first Cherokee Indian Fall Fair, in 1914, was subsidized by the tribal council specifically to encourage tourism. The opening of the Great Smoky Mountains National Park in 1934, adjacent to the Qualla Boundary, although controversial within the tribal government, was finally welcomed as a way to attract visitors, who brought a new source of income. Tourism, however, proved to be a double-edged sword. Although sales of

Doubleweave rivercane basket by Eva Wolfe. (Photograph by Rob Amberg)

baskets and beadwork encouraged the continuation and development of
those traditions, Cherokees found that they also had to change some traditions to meet the expectations of their market. Influenced by the Wild West
shows of the 1890s, by the stereotypes of patent medicine shows of the early
1900s, and by movies and finally television, visitors wanted to see natives in
Plains Indian costume. Visitors also preferred shiny black Catawba pottery
rather than the ancient stamped pottery of the Cherokees, whose potters
have only recently revived their own distinctive style. These market-driven
changes in tradition coexist with the older traditions today.

After World War II, the Cherokees formed three organizations that gave
them a voice in preserving, presenting, and marketing their own culture.
The Museum of the Cherokee Indian began with the collections of Samuel
Beck in a log cabin in 1948 and grew into a new building in 1976 and a
completely new, high-tech exhibit in 1998. Qualla Arts and Crafts Mutual,
a Cherokee crafts cooperative, set standards for quality and authenticity
in crafts traditions, and it provided a year-round market for its members'
work. Today it has more than three hundred members. The Cherokee Historical Association, in partnership with businessmen from surrounding
counties, built the Mountainside Theater and created the outdoor drama
Unto These Hills and the Oconaluftee Indian Village and Living History Museum. Millions of visitors have attended the drama, which tells the story
of the Cherokees and the Trail of Tears. The Oconaluftee Indian Village,

which re-creates a Cherokee village ca. 1750, has provided work for crafts demonstrators and informal apprenticeships for youth for more than fifty years.

The twentieth century also brought boarding schools operated by the federal government, which tried to eradicate Cherokee language and culture by separating children from their families and by using corporal punishment for speaking the language. Operated from 1892 to 1948, the boarding school in Cherokee educated several generations of Cherokee children, many of whom never taught the language to their children, so that their children would not be punished as they were. Cherokee children were also sent away to boarding schools at Carlisle, Pennsylvania, and Chilocco, Oklahoma, to the Hampton Institute in Virginia, and to the Haskell Institute in Kansas. Although the Cherokee boarding school closed in 1948, the Bureau of Indian Affairs operated schools for the Cherokees until 1990. At that time, the Eastern Band took charge of the operation and funding of their own schools, instituting courses in Cherokee culture and language in an ongoing attempt to save the Cherokee language from extinction.

Citizenship, tribal membership, and property ownership of the eastern Cherokees were influenced by events of the 1920s and 1930s. In 1924, a census of tribal members created the Baker Roll, which is the standard for membership in the Eastern Band today. All land owned by the tribe and by individual members (as defined by this roll) was placed in trust with the federal government in preparation for allotment, and at this time the federal government declared all Native Americans citizens. The state government of North Carolina maintained that these citizenship rights would be valid only when tribal lands were allotted. Allotment never took place, however, leaving the lands in trust to the federal government and Eastern Band citizenship in limbo. Finally, in 1930 the U.S. Congress passed legislation specifically giving full rights of citizenship to Cherokee Indians residing in North Carolina. Having individual and tribal lands legally held in trust enabled the Eastern Band to hold on to their lands, because they could not be sold to outsiders. Today, only tribal members can buy land from other tribal members or from the tribal land holdings. Although this has maintained the Cherokee lands, it has also slowed development, because banks are reluctant to loan money for home construction, and businesses are reluctant to build on leased land.

In the 1950s and 1960s the tribe began efforts to improve living conditions on the Qualla Boundary. Many tribal members lived in poverty, at standards well below those of surrounding counties. In 1952 a sales tax began financing the Cherokee Tribal Community Services Program, which supports a tribal police department, a fire department, and the Water and

The Eternal Flame at the Mountainside Theater in Cherokee.
(Photograph by Roger Haile)

Sewer Enterprise. In 1962 the Qualla Housing Authority began offering low cost loans for house construction. Other tribal enterprises included the Cherokee Boys Club and trout farming and trout fishing on the boundary waters. "The Cherokees" factory manufactured moccasins and souvenirs.

In 1984, the Eastern Cherokees and the Cherokee Nation formally met for the first time since removal. The "eternal flame" was brought back to North Carolina and burns at the entrance to the Mountainside Theater. Traditions of ceremonial dance have been revived through the efforts of Walker Calhoun, nephew of Will West Long. Cherokee people are struggling to recover their language, and to preserve their traditions in a cultural renaissance that began in the late twentieth century.

In 1988 the Indian Gaming Act allowed federally recognized tribes to offer games of chance on tribal lands, subject to approval by state compacts. Beginning with bingo, the tribe has expanded gaming facilities to include a casino, which opened in 1997. Because of the casino and resulting new businesses on the boundary (such as banks, restaurants, hotels, and a grocery store), full-time jobs with benefits are now available to most tribal members. Because of income to the tribe from gaming, college education is now possible for any tribal members who are interested. A kidney dialysis center has been built to serve the nearly one-third of the Eastern Band members who have diabetes. Because of new jobs as well as per capita payments from gaming proceeds, the standard of living for the Eastern Band now approaches that of people in surrounding counties.

From the time of removal to the present day, the Eastern Band of Cherokee Indians has struggled to remain together as a people on their land. A nation within the larger nation of the United States, they have sustained their own government while dealing with state and federal governments. Located in the remote and rugged mountains of western North Carolina, they have survived economically through logging, farming, tourism, and now gaming. Their spoken and written language—once considered evidence of the highest degree of civilization—was forbidden by schools for a hundred years. Yet the language survives, not only among elders, but among schoolchildren as well. Originally hunters, farmers, medicine people, artists, map makers, and musicians, the Cherokee people now also work as lawyers, doctors, social workers, teachers, opera singers, computer technicians, accountants, and in all occupations—many of them on the Qualla Boundary or nearby. While participating in the global culture of the twenty-first century, many people still practice ancient ceremonies, weave baskets, and deliberately keep alive the old traditions. Casino profits are establishing a foundation to develop guidelines for planning and controlling growth while preserving traditional culture and the environment.

Cherokee elders like Robert Bushyhead and Emmeline Cucumber often speak the Cherokee language among themselves. (Photograph by Cedric N. Chatterley)

Throughout many centuries, then, the Cherokees have balanced old and new, adapting to change while preserving the essence of what makes them Cherokee: respect for each other and for the earth; caring for the elders and for youth; treating each day as a gift; preserving harmony through humor and through prayers; speaking the language, singing the songs, dancing to honor the Creator.

And in 1997 the Eastern Band bought back more than three hundred acres of land, the Kituhwa village site, home of the first Cherokee village, the town that defined them as a people, Ani-Kituhwa-gi.

Marie Junaluska said, "I think we need to preserve Kituhwa because it was the mother town. We're searching to find a way to preserve it without digging it up. To me that's a very sacred place. It's a very peaceful place. If you ever go there, you can feel the peace. The spirit that was there a long time ago is still there.

"There was also a mound there at Kituhwa that you can still see a little bit of today. And we're in the process of building it back up. Every year the children go there and take a small portion of dirt and place it on the mound."

Balancing old and new, the Cherokees have come full circle—back to their origins. Join them on the Cherokee Heritage Trails.

Notes on Pronouncing Words in the Cherokee Language

Vowels:
A is pronounced as the short a in father
E is pronounced as the long a in say
I is pronounced as the long e in see
O is pronounced as the long o in no
U is pronounced as oo in fool
V is pronounced nasally as a short u, as in uh-huh

Consonants:
Usually pronounced as in English
In the Eastern dialect K is pronounced as G, so Kituhwa is "Giduhwa"

A TIMELINE OF CHEROKEE HISTORY

10000 B.C.–8000 B.C.
    Stone tools, small groups traveling to seasonal campsites in the southern Appalachians

8000 B.C.–1000 B.C.
    Semipermanent villages, baskets, fish hooks, atlatl, cooking bowls, early cultivation of wild plants

1000 B.C.–A.D. 900
    Settled villages, corn and agriculture, pottery

A.D. 900–1600
    Cherokee towns with mounds

1540	De Soto expedition, first contact with Europeans
1731	Cherokee leaders to London with Cuming
1738	Smallpox epidemic
1756	French and Indian War
1760–61	Montgomery and Grant expeditions—the Cherokee War
1762	Cherokee leaders to London with Timberlake
1763	King George's Proclamation
1776	Revolutionary War
1783	Smallpox epidemic
1794	End of Dragging Canoe's war
1808	Broomestown Council
1814	Cherokees aid Jackson at Battle of Horseshoe Bend
1821	Cherokee Council approves Sequoyah's syllabary
1828	*Cherokee Phoenix* begins publication
	Gold discovered in Georgia
1830	Indian Removal Act passed
1832	Supreme Court rules on sovereignty
1835	Treaty of New Echota signed
1836	Treaty of New Echota ratified by Congress
1838–39	Removal and Trail of Tears
1861–65	Thomas Legion fights with Confederacy

1868	Eastern Band recognized by federal government, has voting rights, pays property taxes
1870	First principal chief of Eastern Band elected
1889	North Carolina recognizes Eastern Band as legal corporation
1893	First boarding school
1917–18	Cherokee men serve in military in World War I
1924	Lands held by Cherokee individuals taken and held in trust by federal government; Baker Roll
1941–46	Cherokee men serve in military in World War II
1946	Cherokee men and women allowed to register to vote
1948	Boarding school closes in Cherokee, North Carolina
1948–49	*Unto These Hills,* Oconaluftee Indian Village, Qualla Arts and Crafts Mutual, and Museum of the Cherokee Indian founded
1984	First Joint Council of Eastern and Western Cherokees since removal
1988	Indian Gaming Act followed by Cherokee Bingo
1990	Eastern Band begins operating their own schools
1996	Eastern Band elects first woman principal chief
	Eastern Band opens casino
1997	Eastern Band purchases Kituhwa Mound

TRAVELING THE TRAILS

Cherokee Heritage Trails sometimes lead to remote areas. As you travel, you can cruise on four-lane highways or you can choose to explore the wild places of the southern Appalachians where cell phones may not work, where fast food franchises are few and far between, and where gas stations do not light up the night sky on every corner. Whether you consider this a blessing or a curse, be prepared.

Seven central locations along the trails offer accommodations, fuel, food, and areas where cell phones will function. If you are choosing to explore Cherokee Heritage Trails in the backcountry along scenic drives and side trips, be sure to fuel your car, get supplies, and make any necessary calls at these locations. They include Cherokee, Robbinsville, Franklin, and Murphy, North Carolina; Vonore and Red Clay (Chattanooga area), Tennessee; and Calhoun, Georgia. Chapters in this guidebook correspond to these geographical centers.

The most remote driving tours include the Unicoi Turnpike from Murphy, North Carolina, to Vonore, Tennessee, and the Overhills Driving Loop. The Unicoi Turnpike was used to take Cherokee people from their homes to begin the Trail of Tears, and in places the original road remains visible as wagon ruts in the ground alongside the paved or gravel road. The Overhills Driving Loop tours through the backcountry locations of original Cherokee town sites in Tennessee.

Other connecting routes include scenic highways whose curving two-lane blacktops range from the venerable Blue Ridge Parkway to the newly constructed Cherohala Skyway. Many of the Cherokee Heritage Trails routes follow state-designated Scenic Byways, as they roll through pastoral farmland or dramatic scenes like the Cullasaja Gorge, near Franklin, North Carolina.

If you want to travel by means other than automobile, you can bike, canoe, kayak, ride horseback, or hike throughout the Cherokee homeland territory. Accommodations range from luxury hotels to comfortable cabins to primitive camping in roadless wilderness areas.

Cherokee People Today
Cherokee, North Carolina

The land to me is very sacred, and we should all think of it as being sacred—any land, all land out there. I believe the Creator put us here, on this land, and this land gives us life. It gives us all the things we need to live. It gives us so many blessings.

In the spring, we have the wild greens. All the different kinds. And then the berries start—strawberries, and then blackberries, blueberries, raspberries. And then when the berries are done, in the fall, the nuts come in—hickory, walnut, butternut—all the kinds you could want. And if we plant a garden, the land gives us so much—corn, beans, squash. Anything we plant grows more than we can put away, so that we have to give it to the neighbors. We can feed a whole neighborhood on what we grow in the garden. Being a Cherokee Indian, that's what I was raised with, living off the land.

And that's why I believe that all land is sacred. Because the Creator gave it to us, and gave us so many blessings. And we should treat it with respect.

—Marie Junaluska

Cherokee and the Qualla Boundary provide unique opportunities to visit Cherokee people where they live, work, and raise their families. In this nation within a nation, about eight thousand members of the Eastern Band maintain their culture and their communities on a small remnant of their ancestral homelands. Despite entrance signs and a North Carolina historical marker describing this as the "Cherokee Indian Reservation," this land is not technically a reservation because the Cherokee people themselves own the land, which the federal government holds in trust.

For the Cherokee people, living together here remains vitally important to maintaining their identity. Here the elders still speak Cherokee language with each other, and they visit the schools to speak it with students. Community groups prepare "Indian dinners" to sell to benefit a family with a sick child, or the basketball team. In the spring, people gather ramps—

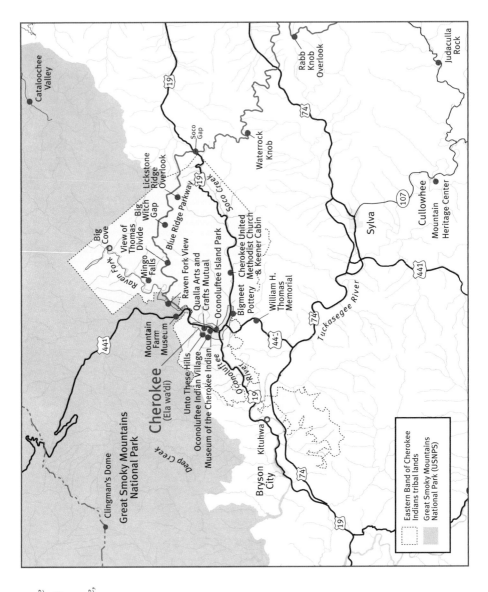

MAP 4
*Cherokee
Heritage
Trails,
Cherokee,
N.C.*

Cataloochee
Valley

Rabb
Knob
Overlook

Judaculla
Rock

Soco
Gap

Waterrock
Knob

Big
Cove

View of
Thomas
Divide

Lickstone
Ridge
Overlook

Big
Witch
Gap

Mingo
Falls

Blue Ridge Parkway

Raven Fork View

Qualla Arts and
Crafts Mutual

Oconoluftee Island Park

Bigmeet   Cherokee United
Pottery   Methodist Church
           & Keener Cabin

William H.
Thomas
Memorial

Cullowhee

Mountain
Heritage Center

Sylva

Clingman's Dome

Great Smoky Mountains
National Park

Mountain
Farm Museum

Cherokee
(Ela wa'di)

Unto These Hills

Oconoluftee Indian Village

Museum of the Cherokee Indian

Deep Creek

Tuckasegee River

Bryson
City

Kituhwa

Eastern Band of Cherokee
Indians tribal lands

Great Smoky Mountains
National Park (USNPS)

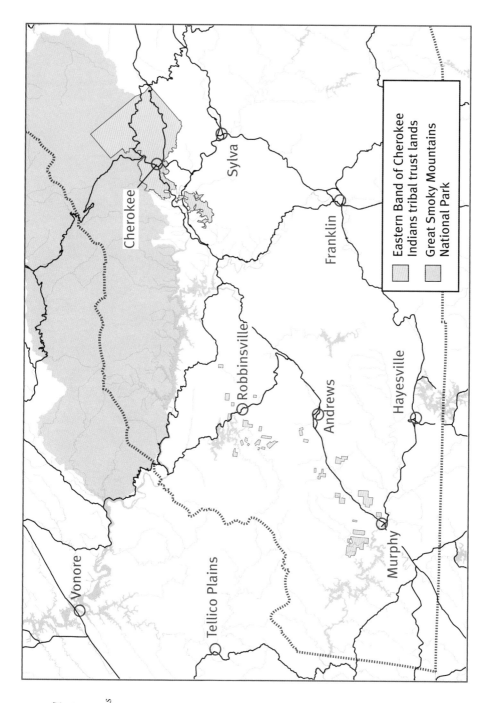

MAP 5
Cherokee
lands and
the Great
Smoky
Mountains
National
Park,
1990

Vonore

Tellico Plains

Robbinsville

Andrews

Hayesville

Murphy

Cherokee

Sylva

Franklin

Eastern Band of Cherokee
Indians tribal trust lands

Great Smoky Mountains
National Park

Qualla Boundary—the Land

How did the Cherokees hold onto this 100-square-mile fragment of their original 140,000-square-mile territory? Hundreds of Cherokees owned land in their own names before removal in 1838, and some of these parcels became part of today's tribal land. Other parcels were acquired by Cherokees who remained here after removal in 1838, working and buying land with their own money. Doubtful of their legal status after the turmoil of removal, the Cherokees asked a white man, William Holland Thomas, to hold their land in his name until the state of North Carolina gave the Cherokees legal status and a self-governing charter in 1889. Then, in 1924, the federal government placed this land in a trust.

Cherokee tribal lands cannot be sold to nontribal members. Today, Cherokee individuals own land, and they can sell, exchange, or lease it to other members of the Eastern Band, with the approval of the tribal government. Individuals can also pass their property on to their heirs. If land is leased to nontribal members for business purposes, then a percentage of proceeds must be paid to the tribal government. Cherokee people can own property elsewhere under the same terms as other U.S. citizens, and they do not have to live on tribal lands. About three thousand members of the Eastern Band live in communities surrounding the Qualla Boundary and in other states.

Today, about 50,000 acres of the Cherokee land are located near the town of Cherokee, adjacent to the Great Smoky Mountains National Park. Another large parcel of 2,250 acres remains in Graham County, about sixty miles away, and this is the home of the Snowbird community; about four hundred members of the Eastern Band live on these lands. Other Cherokee land lies further south—5,575 acres scattered throughout Cherokee County, near the old Cherokee communities and homesteads of Marble, Grape Creek, and Hanging Dog—home to about five hundred tribal members.

a wild leek—in places known for generations. People turn out to support football, basketball, wrestling, and baseball as well as stickball teams. Traditional volunteer work groups, or *gadugi,* help community members who need a garden turned, a roof fixed, a grave dug. Almost everyone attends church, and some attend traditional stomp dances on sacred grounds. Relatives who have moved away always come back to visit, and Cherokee pro-

Goingback Chiltosky carved the Tribal Seal of the Eastern Band of
Cherokee Indians that appears on the Tribal Council House in Cherokee.
(Photograph by Cedric N. Chatterley)

And where did the Qualla Boundary get its name? From "Quallatown," a small settlement that once stood on Shoal Creek near the
mouth of Soco Creek, where it enters the Oconaluftee River (now the
junction of the US 441 Bypass and 441 Business). Known as "Indian
town" in the early 1800s, it became Quallatown when a post office was
established there in 1839 and it was named for Kwali, or Polly, an older
Cherokee woman who lived nearby. At that time, Quallatown included a
store operated by William H. Thomas, the Indian agency where Thomas
conducted business, a blacksmith shop, and several nearby homesteads.

fessionals who have "worked away" all their lives return home to retire,
adding their skills and experience back into the community. Townships created after removal still have their own churches, community buildings, and
tribal council representatives: Yellow Hill, Birdtown, Wolftown, Painttown,
and Big Cove. (Snowbird and Tomotla, in Graham County and Cherokee
County, also have representatives on the tribal council.)

In Cherokee, tribal members work as bankers, business owners, man-
agers, police officers, EMTs, schoolteachers, nurses, homemakers, and

Citrus Bigwitch with fresh ramps at the Cherokee Ramp Festival. (Photograph by Roger Haile)

clerks, as well as basket makers and storytellers. Day by day they continue to balance modern life with Cherokee traditions. Many individuals dedicate their lives to carrying on Cherokee traditions and passing them to the next generation. The whole community remains close-knit despite the presence of millions of visitors every year from fifty U.S. states and dozens of foreign countries. In fact, the Cherokee community continues to welcome visitors—not just a legacy from a century of tourism, but a heritage from the oldest Cherokee values: respecting differences and including outsiders.

In Cherokee, the Museum of the Cherokee Indian serves as the main interpretive center for Cherokee Heritage Trails. Its exhibit tells the story of the Cherokee people and provides an overview for those traveling on the Cherokee Heritage Trails. The Oconaluftee Indian Village Living History Museum presents a Cherokee village frozen in time at 1750, where Cherokee people demonstrate basket making, pottery, flint knapping, beadwork, weaving, the blowgun, and dugout canoe making. The Bigmeet Pottery and Qualla Arts and Crafts Mutual (a crafts cooperative) present the work of local artists as well as exhibits about crafts. In downtown Cherokee, the Oconaluftee Island Park provides a peaceful walking trail with interpretive media installations speaking for the trees in Cherokee language and in English.

A mile or so north of town, the Keener Cabin stands—the oldest remaining building on a Cherokee site in North Carolina. South of town, at Campground Cemetery, a marker commemorates the life of William Hol-

The Museum of the Cherokee Indian. (Photograph by Barbara Duncan)

land Thomas, white chief and advocate for the Eastern Band in the nineteenth century. Up Big Cove, Mingo Falls can be visited by those willing to hike.

Rewarding side trips from Cherokee include mounds, mountaintops, hidden valleys, and mysterious rocks. West of Cherokee, the Kituhwa Mound, original village of the Cherokee, lies along the Tuckaseegee River. A few miles away, in the Great Smoky Mountains National Park, Deep Creek drains the southern slopes of Clingman's Dome. Over one ridge to the east, the Oconaluftee River rushes down the slopes of Clingman's Dome to the Mountain Farm Museum, where a hiking trail winds along its banks. Farther afield, in Jackson County, the petroglyphs of Judaculla Rock continue to mystify visitors and scholars alike. In Haywood County, a trip to Cataloochee Valley, part of the Great Smoky Mountains National Park, takes you back to settlements at the turn of the century. Nearby, Cataloochee Ranch offers Cherokee programs along with food and lodging.

Engineered and designed more than fifty years ago as the ultimate scenic drive, the Blue Ridge Parkway continues to provide panoramic backcountry vistas. From Cherokee to Spruce Pine, the parkway visits sites significant in Cherokee history and culture and offers the traveler commanding views, off-road hikes, museums, and folk art.

Events on the Qualla Boundary include the Cherokee Fall Fair, started in 1914; the Ramp Festival, held every April; Cherokee Voices Festival held in June at the Museum of the Cherokee Indian; and the outdoor drama *Unto These Hills.* Mountain Heritage Day at Western Carolina University features Cherokee crafts people and storytellers along with Appalachian traditions.

Among the many shops in the town of Cherokee, some are owned and operated by Cherokee people and have a high proportion of authentic Cherokee artwork and crafts. Bear Meet's Den and Bigmeet Pottery are both on US 19. In town, the Qualla Arts and Crafts Mutual, Museum of the Cherokee Indian, F.B.I. Traders, Holiday Inn Gallery, Medicine Man Craft Shop, Trail of Tears Gallery, and Waterwheel Crafts offer locally made products.

Fishing, hiking, camping, climbing, mountain biking, and horseback riding can all be enjoyed here. Trout fishing on Boundary waters, in ponds, and in the Great Smoky Mountains National Park yields rainbow trout, brown trout, and occasionally the rare speckled trout. Hundreds of miles of hiking trails wind through the Great Smoky Mountains National Park, and at overlooks on the Blue Ridge Parkway, short loop trails explore the heights. Many campgrounds provide facilities near Cherokee, and camping is allowed in certain areas of the national park. Many hiking trails also permit mountain biking. Outfitters offer horseback riding at Deep Creek and Cataloochee Ranch.

SITES IN CHEROKEE

■ Museum of the Cherokee Indian

We're trying to educate and entertain. With our new exhibit, children stop and listen and learn as they go through. After visitors tour the museum, they will know who the Cherokee are, and why we are still here.

— Ken Blankenship, museum director and member of the
Eastern Band of Cherokee Indians

The Museum of the Cherokee Indian, a nonprofit organization located on the Qualla Boundary, tells the story of the Cherokee people and sets the scene for the Cherokee Heritage Trails. Here the Cherokee community presents its perspective on its own history and culture. The museum's high-tech exhibit, installed in 1998, takes the visitor from eleven thousand years ago to the present. Cherokee people were involved in creating the exhibit: elders as well as scholars consulted on the script; life-size figures were created from full-body casts of local people; and many of the

Eastern Band Cherokees served as models for life-size figures in the
Museum of the Cherokee Indian exhibit featuring three Cherokee chiefs.
(Photograph by Cedric N. Chatterley)

voices in the audio portions of the exhibit are those of tribal members. This award-winning exhibit combines artifacts with interactive technology, special effects, and colorful graphics.

Cherokee people make up most of the employees and Board of Directors of the museum, and more than a hundred Cherokee artists sell their work in the museum gift shop: baskets, pottery, blowguns, wood carvings, decorated gourds, beadwork, jewelry, and reproductions of artifacts like gorgets, buckskin bags, and masks. Audio CD's and tapes by local Cherokee musicians and storytellers are sold here, along with other Native American music. Books by local artists, historians, and storytellers form part of the extensive selection of books on Cherokee history, culture, language, and genealogy, as well as books on other tribes and Native Americans in

Duyuktv

The Cherokee word duyuktv *means "the right way." This philosophy of seeking balance in the world and embracing harmony has always been at the core of Cherokee spirituality. For the Cherokees, living "the right way" meant being in balance. To be sick was to be out of balance— either physically, mentally, or spiritually.*

Being in balance meant being responsible for one's actions and remembering the good of the whole—the family, the tribe, and the earth. Duyuktv *means taking only what is needed and living in harmony with nature.*

Exhibit panel in the lobby of the Museum of the Cherokee Indian

general. Among the videos sold here are those produced by the museum and aired on public television: "The Principal People" and "Plants and the Cherokee."

At the Cherokee Voices Festival in June, Cherokee people demonstrate crafts, tell stories, perform music, and do traditional dance. Elders who do not usually travel long distances to festivals often participate in this museum-sponsored event. Throughout the summer and fall, Cherokee artists and crafts people exhibit and demonstrate inside the museum. In addition to public events, the museum sponsors classes taught by Cherokee master artists for Cherokee youth and adults in order to help preserve and perpetuate the language, music, basket making, and other traditions.

Through its new Education Department, the museum offers classes and educational seminars, with the goal of improving teaching about the Cherokee and other Native Americans. All educational offerings combine experiences with Cherokee people with academic learning. A summer institute for teachers on Cherokee history and culture is taught annually, and workshops have been provided for universities, school systems, visiting groups, and the National Park Service. In its "Cherokee Experience Programs," the museum arranges lectures, hands-on workshops, field trips to Cherokee sites, food, and performances tailored to the interests of visiting groups. The National Endowment for the Humanities awarded the museum a challenge grant to create an endowment to support education programs, which the museum is continuing to build.

Melissa Maney teaching a pottery workshop at the Museum.
(Photograph by Cedric N. Chatterley)

Founded in 1948, in a log cabin, the museum's purpose is to "preserve and perpetuate the history, culture, and stories of the Cherokee." Its archive serves as a research center for many scholars and organizations (but does not do genealogical research). Its collections include rare books, manuscript materials from the removal period, the William Holland Thomas collection, thousands of black-and-white photographs from the late 1800s and early 1900s, and microfilm of all documents on the Cherokee from foreign archives. Research may be conducted by appointment. Since 1976 the museum has published the *Journal of Cherokee Studies,* the first peer-reviewed journal dedicated to a single tribe.

CONTACT: Ken Blankenship, Executive Director, Museum of the Cherokee Indian, 589 Tsali Blvd., P.O. Box 1599, Cherokee, NC 28719, 828-497-3481, <www.cherokeemuseum.org>

HOURS: Open daily at 9:00 A.M. except on Thanksgiving, Christmas, and New Year's Day. There is an admission charge for exhibits; the gift shop is free.

LOCATION: At the intersection of US 441 and Drama Road

Qualla Arts and Crafts Mutual features the work of local Cherokee artists.
(Photograph by Roger Haile)

■ Qualla Arts and Crafts Mutual

I feel that the Qualla Co-op has played a large part in the continuation and preservation of
the native Cherokee crafts by giving an outlet, creating a place to market those crafts
which would otherwise have perished.

— Freeman Owle, storyteller and stone carver

The Qualla Arts and Crafts Mutual sells only the best quality crafts,
handmade with natural materials by Cherokee people. Here you will find
meticulously made baskets, pottery, woodcarving, beadwork, jewelry, dolls,
blowguns, and other items. But the crafts cooperative is more than another
crafts store. For more than fifty years, it has provided year-round income
for Cherokee artists by buying their work during the winter as well as during the summer tourist season. Profits are shared with all co-op members,
who must be enrolled in the Eastern Band. The co-op has helped Cherokee traditions survive, and has held high standards for their quality. In the
process, it has become one of the most successful Native American crafts
cooperatives in the country.

In addition to the sales area, an exhibit room provides information on
crafts traditions through displays of materials, photographs of the process

of creation, and examples of work. The Qualla co-op is a nonprofit organization that has been active in supporting crafts throughout the region as a member of the Southern Highlands Craft Guild and one of the founding members of Handmade in America. Its work and its members have been documented in three videos: "Cherokee Basketmakers," "Cherokee Woodcarvers," and "Cherokee Potters."

CONTACT: Qualla Arts and Crafts Mutual, Inc., P.O. Box 310, Cherokee, NC 28719, 828-497-3103
HOURS: Open daily from 9:00 A.M. until 5:00 P.M.
LOCATION: US 441 and Drama Road in downtown Cherokee

■ Oconaluftee Indian Village and Living History Museum

The crafts are inherent with the Eastern Band of the Cherokee. And we used to have craft families: certain families would make baskets, and other families would make pottery, and they stuck to that one craft.

— Mollie Blankenship

The Oconaluftee Indian Village and Living History Museum portrays an eighteenth-century Cherokee village on a large site on the mountainside above the town of Cherokee. Cherokee people demonstrate carving, weaving, pottery, dugout canoe making, flint knapping, blowgun making, and other traditional crafts as they would have been done in the 1700s. They work in a setting of natural beauty and authentic reconstructions of Cherokee architecture. Guides lead visitors along the village's paths, among streams and rhododendrons, to houses constructed of woven saplings plastered with mud, early log cabins, and brush arbors. Their tour includes stops at a council house and dance grounds, where guides lecture on Cherokee history, culture, language, government, and traditions. When the hour-long tour is finished, you can also visit a nineteenth-century cabin and Cherokee garden.

Delighting thousands of visitors annually, from kindergartners through senior citizens, "The Village," as it is locally known, makes history come alive. Its interpretation of Cherokee culture by contemporary Cherokee people is based on both scholarly research and Cherokee oral tradition. Since it opened in 1948, the village has provided employment to a significant number of Cherokee people who are skilled in traditional arts and crafts. It also provides employment for Cherokee high school students as guides, who learn in detail about Cherokee tradition through their training and through informal apprenticeships with the elders who also work here.

Indian Dinners

"Indian dinners" have become a tradition in themselves over the years. Enjoyed by the local Cherokee community as well as outsiders, an Indian dinner usually includes fried chicken, potatoes, hominy, cabbage, wild greens, bean bread with fatback, herb tea, and fruit cobbler. These represent long-standing Cherokee foodways, which are different from "powwow chow" with its ubiquitous and delicious fry bread. These traditional Cherokee foods and preparation methods have long influenced southern cooking and Appalachian fare. What would we do without beans and cornbread?

Today's Indian dinners balance unique Cherokee traditions with food familiar to most Americans. Fried chicken represents wild turkey and other game (and the frying technique comes from African Americans in the South). Potatoes, domesticated by Native American horticulturists in South America, have long been a standard in the southern mountains. Hominy, usually associated with southern cooking, was actually developed by Cherokee women who leached water through hardwood ashes to create lye, in which they soaked their Cherokee corn—a genetically unique maize developed over centuries. A specially woven basket facilitated rinsing the hominy in running water. Wild greens, picked in season, go with the meal: ramps and sochan in the spring, sweet cane and creasies in the summer. The unique Cherokee bean bread is formed from unbolted corn meal and cooked pinto beans, then wrapped in corn husks and boiled like a dumpling, resulting in a solid cake. Most people season their bean bread with a little bit of grease from fried fatback. In the fall, chestnut bread is made in the same way, using chestnuts instead of beans, sweetened with maple syrup, and wrapped in hickory leaves. Herb tea varies with the season—sassafras in the spring, spicewood and mint in the summer. Fruit cobblers also change with the season, but blackberry dumplings remain a favorite year-round.

Many Cherokee women prepare these foods at home for their families. When someone in the community needs money for medical costs or a sports team needs to travel, women work together to prepare these meals for sale at lunchtime events, advertised in the local paper and by word of mouth. In recent years, the Cherokee chapter of the North American Indian Women's Association has been making Indian dinners for visiting groups and festivals to help fund their activities and cultural projects.

A side dish of ramps and potatoes with a traditional meal that includes a serving of bean bread and fatback. (Photograph by Roger Haile)

Children take turns pounding corn.
(Photograph by Murray Lee)

CONTACT: Manager, Oconaluftee Indian Village, Cherokee Historical
    Association, P.O. Box 398, Cherokee, NC 28719, 828-497-2315 or
    828-497-2111
HOURS: Open daily from 9:00 A.M. until 5:00 P.M., May through the end
    of October. Admission charge, restrooms, concessions, souvenirs.
LOCATION: On Drama Road, just past the Mountainside Theater

■ Bigmeet Pottery

When you walk into Bigmeet Pottery, you see portraits of the Principal Chiefs of the Eastern Band, along with a century of crafts made by
local people. Louise Bigmeet Maney and her husband John Henry Maney
created this pottery studio, retail shop, and exhibit space. Louise passed
away in 2001, and was designated a "beloved woman" posthumously by
the Eastern Band. Louise's family members were potters for generations.
Her great-grandmother, Iwi Catolster, was photographed making pottery
by M. R. Harrington for the Smithsonian near the turn of the twentieth
century.

The Bigmeet Pottery features pottery that is burnished to a smooth finish
on the outside, and incised with lines in geometric patterns, or impressed
with textures from peach pits and other materials. Unglazed, the pots are

Photographs of Cherokee Principal Chiefs line a wall at Bigmeet Pottery.
(Photograph by Cedric N. Chatterley)

fired in an open fire, rather than a kiln. The pottery takes on a black finish if softwoods are burned, and retains the color of the clay if hardwoods
are burned. Recently, the Maneys began incising the Sequoyah syllabary
on pots.

Louise Bigmeet Maney received the North Carolina Folk Heritage Award
for her work with pottery, and for her work in maintaining traditions within
the community. She was a mother and grandmother, actively involved with
her family. In addition to doing research for her museum, she served as
president of the Cherokee Chapter of the North American Indian Women's
Association (NAIWA), and with her local chapter often prepared "Indian
dinners" for educational groups and festivals. She was president of the
Painttown Community Association, whose community building stands just
behind the pottery.

CONTACT: Bigmeet Pottery, P.O. Box 583, Cherokee, NC 28719,
    828-497-9544. Call anytime before 9:00 P.M.
HOURS: Generally open Monday through Saturday from 10:00 A.M. until
    5:00 P.M., but hours are subject to change. Call ahead to confirm hours
    or to make an appointment.
LOCATION: US 19 North, just north of intersection with US 441 in
    downtown Cherokee

■ Talking Trees at Oconaluftee Island Park

When the animals and plants were first made—we do not know by whom—they were told to watch and keep awake for seven nights, just as young men now fast and keep awake when they pray to their medicine. They tried to do this, and nearly all were awake through the first night, but the next night several dropped off to sleep, and the third night others were asleep, and then others, until, on the seventh night, of all the animals, only the owl, the panther, and one or two more were still awake. To these were given the power to see and to go about in the dark, and to make prey of the birds and the animals which must sleep at night.

Of the trees, only the cedar, the pine, the spruce, the holly, and the laurel were awake to the end, and to them it was given to be always green and to be the greatest for medicine, but to the others it was said: "Because you have not endured to the end, you shall lose your hair every winter."

—Tagwadihi, "Catawba-killer" of Cheoah

(Collected by James Mooney, ca. 1890; in *Myths of the Cherokee*)

In the middle of downtown Cherokee, the Oconaluftee Island Park has become a haven for walking, wading, picnicking, and just sitting by the river. All summer, children build dams and dikes of river stones out from the shore to make wading pools, and then the winter rains and spring floods wash the stones back to the shoreline, ready for another season of creative rock piling. In addition to the natural magic of water, sun, and river stones, this park has talking trees.

Created by the Eastern Band and the agricultural extension office, Talking Trees at Oconaluftee Island Park gives voice to the trees through audio installations on a walking trail around the island. The push of a button activates voices in Cherokee and English speaking for the black cherry, yellow poplar, Carolina silverbell, shortleaf pine, sycamore, butternut, red maple, flowering dogwood, and the river itself. Traditional Cherokee religion teaches that all living things are our relatives and can speak to us in a spiritual sense. Here one can enjoy the stories of trees as well as walking, picnicking under the gazebo, or just sitting with one's feet in the river.

CONTACT: Cherokee Reservation Cooperative Extension Office, P.O. Box 456, Cherokee, NC 28719, 828-497-3521
HOURS: Open daily from 8:00 A.M. until 10:00 P.M. Free admission, restrooms.
LOCATION: On US 441 North, just past intersection with Business 19 from downtown Cherokee, located across from Cherokee Elementary School

Chiefing in Cherokee

Chief Henry, perhaps the most photographed and best known of the "chiefs," of downtown Cherokee, works in Saunooke Village amid ice cream shops, restaurants, gift shops, and live bears.

"Want to take a picture?" he says. A sign says "Chief Henry: photos $5. With your camera, tips." I say I'm from the museum and present my card. "How's business? My business is down 40 percent this year," he comments like the local businessman that he is. Not only do Henry and others make money from having their pictures taken, they attract business to nearby shops he has built: Chief Henry's Mini-Golf, Chief Henry's Moccasins, and Chief Henry's Gift Shop.

Chief Henry spies grandparents and children approaching; he welcomes them with eye contact, outstretched arms and a smile. "Want to get your picture made?" he asks. The granddaughter starts to cry. Chief Henry acts immediately, as skilled as any preschool teacher or lion tamer: "Stand up here on the stool with your grandpa. Do you like ice cream? Do you like french fries?" With the mention of ice cream, the toddler stops crying, and she is almost smiling by the time her grandpa stands next to her and grandma snaps the picture. They walk away happy.

"Get up there Royce," calls an aunt to a little boy, and Royce stands in front of Chief Henry. Cameras click and film rolls. Royce (4) and Madeline (2) are with aunts and grandparents from McComb, Mississippi. Grandpa hands Chief Henry some bills, which he tucks away in his regalia.

A tourist walks up and asks Chief Henry, otherwise known as Henry Lambert, where to get good apples. He gives directions. "Do you answer many questions?" I ask Henry. "Oh, I'm a walking information booth," he says. "I've answered more questions than the Chamber of Commerce."

A couple approaches, camera in hand. "Want to get your picture made?" asks Henry, motioning the woman to come stand next to him. He puts his arm around her as her husband takes a picture. Then she and Henry start mugging. "Eat your heart out, honey," she says to her husband, and then Chief Henry kisses her on the cheek. All three are laughing, and her husband is snapping photos.

Bill and Loretta Graham are from Arcadia, Missouri, and yes they

Henry Lambert chiefing in Cherokee. (© 2000 Steve Wall)

are married, they tell Chief Henry, for thirty-three years. "I have to ask," Henry says, "because sometimes people have borrowed someone for the weekend, you know. One time a man came up to me—I said hello because I'd seen him before—and he gave me ten dollars to not remember who he was with." We all laugh.

"Do you see the same people again?" I ask. "Oh yes," Henry says. "I've had five generations of the same family get their pictures made with me. Meet them on their honeymoon, and then they keep coming back."

"I put on the feathers in 1948," Chief Henry said, "and I never looked back."

For many visitors, having their picture taken with a "chief" on the streets of Cherokee is their first experience with a real Native American. Beginning in the early twentieth century, a public influenced by Wild West shows, medicine shows, and silent westerns expected to see all Native Americans in Plains Indian dress. Cherokee people invited to demonstrate "authentic" traditions in Atlanta in the 1930s arrived to find their tipis waiting. Some audiences today still expect any "real Indian" to be wearing lots of feathers.

Most Eastern Band Cherokees today know that the "chiefs" represent the public's expectations more than Cherokee tradition, and are non-judgmental about these efforts to connect with visitors. When the public became more educated about Native American traditions, following the popularity of the movie "Dances With Wolves" several of the downtown "chiefs" began wearing clothing more true to the Cherokees' traditions. They now attract visitors also.

Want to get your picture made?

SITES NEAR CHEROKEE

■ Mingo Falls

Now, in Big Cove we have several areas—areas that are called by English names, and they differ in the Cherokee language. Mingo Falls was a logging area many years ago and I understand, someone mentioned, that some loggers from West Virginia had logged—cut timber up on that property. And of course it has the falls. And the falls didn't have a name when the loggers went in. And they said, "Those falls look like Mingo Falls that is in West Virginia." And they called it Mingo Falls, and to this day that name stands.

But the Cherokees already had a name for it in their own language. And they called it "The Big Bear Falls." They called it *"yon equo."* And that's what we always know. When they mention that name in the Cherokee language, we know where it is.

—Jerry Wolfe

Mingo Falls cascades two hundred feet nearly straight down past granite boulders and rhododendron—one of the most beautiful waterfalls of the mountains. But to see it you must hike up its 161 rough-hewn steps built along the rushing creek that descends from the falls. At the top of the stairway a short path leads to a bridge at the base of the falls, a safe place to stand and take in the sight. Cherokee people who live on the Qualla Boundary consider this waterfall one of the most beautiful places to visit on tribal land.

As you travel up Big Cove Road to Mingo Falls, you enter a part of the Qualla Boundary that is geographically remote, where people speak the Cherokee language a little differently, and where many of the old traditions are practiced. Kalvnyi, the Raven Place, as Big Cove is known in Cherokee, is a large watershed around Raven's Fork and its tributaries. Big Cove's remote woods and creeks have been home to some of the Eastern Band's most respected tradition bearers, who have kept alive and passed on to suc-

The Little People of Stoney Mountain

South of Big Cove, we call the lower end of Big Cove "Stoney Moun-
tain." Stoney Mountain was known for the little people—the Cherokee
dwarfs. They had been seen by many different people passing, walking
by. They would spot one of those, or a group of them.

And my dad said one time he and his friend had come down to
Stoney. They spotted two little people in the rhododendron thicket over
across the river from where they were standing. And one of them said,
"Look over there." And they saw those colorful two little dwarfs basking
in the sun on some rhododendron bushes.

And they said, "My, my." They were amazed at seeing these colorful
little people. And then they took their eyes off of them just for a second
maybe to look at each other in amazement, and when they looked back
over they were gone. They were there just long enough for them to see
them.

Someone else had been passing there, and they looked up on a big
rock cliff above the road. There's a big crack in that rock—a horizon-
tal crack—and it looks like there might be a room up there, maybe an
opening. And they saw a group of those climbing that big rock cliff.
They were crawling up like little bugs, or little creatures, going up that
rock, and they went in at that big crack in the rock and disappeared.

A lot of times we walked a lot when we were young growing up. And
we'd always hear all kinds of noises as we walked in that area. It was a
real hair-raising experience.

There were seven clans of the little people, my dad used to say. One
clan lives in the rhododendron thicket. And one of the clans lives in the
rock cliffs. And one clan lives in the bottoms—in the meadows. And one
clan lives along the rivers. And then one clan lives on the ridges of the
mountains. Not all the ridges of the mountains, just in certain areas.
And one clan lives in the valleys. And I believe there might be a tribe
that lives just around the cemeteries, just roams around in that area.

Jerry Wolfe

Mingo Falls, known to Cherokees as yon equo, *or Big Bear Falls.*
(Photograph by Cedric N. Chatterley)

In the 1880s, Swimmer, or Ayuini, became a primary source of information about Cherokee culture for ethnologist James Mooney. (National Anthropological Archives, Smithsonian Institution)

ceeding generations the myths, songs, dances, and medicine formulae of the Cherokee. In the 1880s Swimmer, Ayuini, provided most of the information for James Mooney's *Myths of the Cherokee* and *Sacred Formulas of the Cherokee.* In the next generation, Will West Long kept the ceremonial dances and songs alive and provided information for Speck and Broom's *Cherokee Dance and Drama.* In the late twentieth century, Walker Calhoun, Long's nephew, continued the sacred stomp dances, songs, and Cherokee language, and he continues to pass them on to a younger generation today.

CAUTION: Pregnant women, or anyone with back problems, a heart condition, or any other health problems should use careful judgment about climbing the stairs that lead to the falls. *No one* should attempt to climb up alongside the waterfall itself—the moist atmosphere creates slippery and dangerous conditions.

CONTACT: Eastern Band of Cherokee Indians, P.O. Box 455, Cherokee, NC 28719, 828-497-2771

LOCATION: From US 441 in downtown Cherokee, turn onto Acquoni Road, which runs beside the Oconaluftee River. Proceed to Saunooke Village shopping center, then turn right onto Big Cove Road. About 7 miles from downtown Cherokee on this two-lane paved road, signs appear

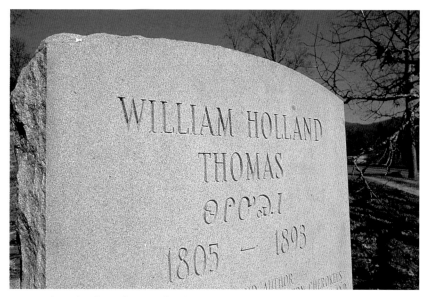

Memorial marker for William Holland Thomas near Cherokee.
(Photograph by Cedric N. Chatterley)

for Mingo Falls campground. The waterfall is adjacent to the campground. Parking for the waterfall accommodates a half-dozen cars or more. Watch for the Mingo Falls Campground sign and a smaller Mingo Falls sign.

■ William Holland Thomas Marker at Campground Cemetery

A white child whose father died before he was born, William Holland Thomas became the adopted son of Yonaguska and helped the Cherokees remain together as a tribe on their land in western North Carolina through removal, the Civil War, and after. He was known as Will Usdi, or Little Will because of his short stature, but his efforts played a large part in enabling the Eastern Band to continue to live in the mountains of western North Carolina as they do today. At Campground Cemetery, near the original location of Quallatown, a large granite marker commemorates this "friend and benefactor of the Cherokee people."

Located at the corner of the cemetery, this marker symbolizes Thomas's importance to the Cherokee, although his actual remains lie in the Hazelwood Cemetery in Haywood County. Many of Thomas's papers and diaries, along with his portrait and his traveling trunk, now belong to the Museum of the Cherokee Indian.

William H. Thomas was born on Pigeon River in Haywood County in 1805 and began clerking in stores at the age of thirteen. Thus he became acquainted with Cherokee people who brought in hides and ginseng to trade for tools, china, cloth, and other goods. Although his mother was still living, the fatherless boy was adopted by Yonaguska (Drowning Bear), head of the Oconaluftee Cherokees who came to the Scotts Creek store where Thomas worked for Felix Walker. A quick learner, Thomas absorbed the Cherokee language and also taught himself to read law when his employer, unable to pay him in cash, gave him a set of law books.

As a lawyer, he campaigned for the Oconaluftee Citizen Indians' right to remain in North Carolina. During the turmoil of removal, he supplied food and goods to the army, for distribution to the Cherokees, throughout North Carolina and Tennessee. When Tsali and his family became fugitives, Thomas was authorized by General Scott to negotiate with them. He was present at Tsali's execution near Big Bear's reserve on the Tuckaseegee.

Throughout the 1840s Thomas traveled frequently to Washington, D.C., working to ensure that the Oconaluftee Cherokees could remain on their homeland, that they would receive funds due to them from the Treaty of New Echota, and that they would receive spoliation claims for their property lost during removal. He finally obtained payments for the Cherokees through an act of Congress in 1848.

Through the 1850s Thomas served in the North Carolina senate, bringing roads and railroads to western North Carolina, allowing business enterprises there to prosper. He married in 1857 and had three children, whose descendants are still living. When the Civil War began, Thomas organized the Thomas Legion of Cherokees and mountaineers who served mainly as guards for the mountain passes. Including the grandsons of Yonaguska and Junaluska, they fought in Virginia and Tennessee and were among the last Confederate units to surrender when they laid down arms in Waynesville in May 1865.

After the Civil War, Thomas, like many other southern businessmen, was devastated, and his affairs ended up in court. For years, he had bought land for Cherokee people with their money and held it in his name because their legal status was doubtful. This land that Thomas held finally became the Qualla Boundary, following a court case and arbitration in 1874. North Carolina granted the Cherokee legal status as a corporation in 1889, only four years before Thomas's death in 1893 at the age of eighty-eight.

CONTACT: Eastern Band of Cherokee Indians, P.O. Box 455, Cherokee, NC 28719, 828-497-2771
LOCATION: Campground Cemetery, west of US 441, 2.7 miles south of the

Yonaguska and the Gospel of Matthew

The New Echota Press in Georgia published the Gospel of Matthew in 1829, translated into Cherokee language and syllabary by Reverend Samuel Worcester and Elias Boundinot. A copy of the gospel made its way to the "Kituhwa Cherokee" on the Oconaluftee.

Yonaguska, as peace chief, insisted that this be read to him before it was circulated among the people. His comment still circulates in oral tradition today: "It seems to be a good book. Strange that the white people are not better, after having had it so long."

junction of US 441 and US 19 in Cherokee, 2 miles north of the junction of US 74 and US 441

■ Cherokee United Methodist Church and Keener Cabin

The Keener Cabin, originally built as a parsonage in the 1840s, has become the oldest piece of architecture remaining on a Cherokee site in North Carolina. A two-story log building, it stands on the site of the Echota Mission, established in 1830 as the first mission to the "Kituhwa Cherokee" by Methodist Minister Reverend Horace Ulrich Keener. Over the years it has served as residence and craft shop.

On the site of the original mission stands a stone church that serves one of the largest congregations on the Qualla Boundary, where hymns are sometimes sung in both English and Cherokee. The public is invited to attend services. The church also coordinates projects for service groups who visit Cherokee.

The Keener Cabin and United Methodist Church stand on US 19. This two-lane paved road becomes a scenic winding road leading to Soco Gap and an intersection with the Blue Ridge Parkway. Continuing on US 19 leads to Maggie Valley.

CONTACT: Cherokee United Methodist Church, P.O. Box 367, Cherokee, NC 28719, 828-497-2948 or -7274

HOURS: The church office is open Monday through Friday from 9:00 A.M. until 3:00 P.M. Because staff schedules are subject to change, call ahead to make an appointment for a guided tour.

LOCATION: US 19 east of Cherokee, exactly 1.7 miles from intersection of

Keener Cabin, built ca. 1847, was moved from a nearby site to the grounds of the United Methodist Church in Cherokee. (Photograph by Cedric N. Chatterley)

Business US 441 and US 19. Cars can park in the pull-off area by the road, buses in the church parking lot.

SIDE TRIPS

■ Kituhwa Mound and Deep Creek

KITUHWA MOUND

Over a century and a half ago, my great-grandmother and great-grandfather left these mountains never to return. Carrying with them only the memories of places and things, they were force marched on an uncompromising road of sorrow and death to a place they didn't know a thousand miles away.

Along that road they buried centuries of past wisdom and the tiny hopeful souls of their future in four thousand unmarked graves. And they still continued on. When they reached their destination, they began carving wooden eating utensils, for they had nothing to eat with. And they also began to carve a new nation. But this was shortly to be taken away, and once again their home was wrenched away from their grasp. This time they were left as exiles in their own land. And still they continued on. For they carried with them yet the memories of places and things.

As a child I began to hear of these places and things, listening at my father's knee.

Listening to the old men as they would tell stories of how things used to be, and speaking names of places they had never been. I learned then that we called ourselves *Ani-Kituhwa,* the people of Kituhwa. By then the name Kituhwa was more a term of reference and reverence than an actual place in our collective memory. I heard them lament the possibility of future generations losing this memory.

But I remembered. Upon entering adulthood, I found many others who also remembered. And in that land so far away, we talked and we sang of what it means to be Kituhwa. This is the strength and the deep meaning of Kituhwa. It has survived our trials and our times. My grandmother and my father, even though they spoke of this place, were never able to see it with their eyes. I now stand and see it with my eyes for them. . . .

We are truly one people, one family. We are only separated by a short distance and a little time.

—Tom Belt, Cherokee Nation, at the dedication of the Kituhwa Mound
on its return to the possession of the Cherokee, 1997

Kituhwa was the first Cherokee village, and the Kituhwa Mound was its center, according to Cherokee legend and according to the beliefs of Cherokee people today. Bordered by the Tuckaseegee River and the low hills of the Smokies that rise all around it before giving way to the slopes of Thomas Ridge and Clingman's Dome, the Kituhwa Village held the sacred fire. From this the Cherokee people took their name: Ani-Kituhwa-gi was what they called themselves. While they also called themselves Ani-Yvwiya, the real people or principal people, and their neighbors used the word Chalaque, meaning those of foreign speech, the name of this particular place distinguished them as a people from all others.

In 1730, Kituhwa (pronounced Gi-DOO-wah) was known as one of the Cherokee "mother towns." Its mound, surmounted by a town house, stood in a large river bottom where people have lived for at least nine thousand years. Today the mound gently rises only six feet or so—greatly reduced in height because it was plowed down and farmed during the years when it passed out of Cherokee possession—from 1820 to 1996. The tribe asks that visitors do not walk on the mound itself.

Many Cherokee people consider this a sacred site. Originally, the mound was fifteen to twenty feet tall, one of the places of the "eternal flame." For religious reasons, the Cherokee priests kept a fire burning constantly in the temples atop the old mound, symbolizing the presence of the Creator and the life of the town. Once a year, all fires in the village were extinguished and then ceremonially rekindled from this sacred fire. During the Civil War soldiers reportedly saw smoke still rising from the Kituhwa Mound.

The Kituhwa Mound and three hundred acres surrounding it were bought back by the Eastern Band in 1996, their first major land purchase in

Aerial view of the Kituhwa town site.
(Courtesy of the Eastern Band of Cherokee Indians)

more than a century. All Cherokees—the Eastern Band, the Cherokee Nation in Oklahoma, and the United Ketoowah Band, look to this as the place
where they originated as a people. It means a great deal to them that this
land is now in the possession of the Cherokees and they can visit it again.

This site also played a significant role throughout the turbulent period
of removal. It was the home of Yonaguska (Drowning Bear), leader of the
Oconaluftee Cherokees, and a North Carolina historical marker commemorates him. Tsali was executed just down the river near Big Bear's property—
a sacrificial act that enabled both the Oconaluftee Cherokees and those
hiding in the mountains to remain here in their homeland.

CONTACT: Cultural Resources Office of the Eastern Band of Cherokee
Indians, P.O. Box 455, Cherokee, NC 28719, 828-497-2771
LOCATION: US 19 about 7 miles west of Cherokee, near Bryson City

DEEP CREEK

The cold clear waters of Deep Creek rush over rocks and gather in pools for miles, running downward between two high ridges covered with hardwood forests and many varieties of wildflowers. The creek gets its name from being deep down between the two ridges, but its waters are not deep except in a few "holes." A wide trail follows beside the creek, crossing back and forth on bridges as one rapidly ascends the lower slopes of Clingman's Dome (Kuwahi). Here one experiences the mountains intimately—ferns brush against bare legs, delicate wildflowers catch the eye, rumbling water makes background music as it freshens the air with spray.

The original Tuckaleechee town stood on the location of present-day Bryson City, with Cherokee fields and homesteads scattered along what is now the boundary of the Great Smoky Mountains National Park. This town was destroyed by Grant's expedition in 1761 and again by Rutherford's expedition in 1776. Part of tribal lands until the Treaty of 1819, this area was then claimed in numerous individual tracts by Cherokee people who lived here until removal.

Legends tell that in the fall of 1838 Tsali and his sons stayed in a cave on Indian Creek, a tributary of Deep Creek, while hiding from the U.S. Army. Following the capture of Tsali and his sons, some Cherokee people were able to remain on their land in this area. They may have been included by Will Thomas as one of his original seven townships: "Pretty Woman's Town," associated with the Long Hair clan. (Women warriors were known as "pretty women" who with age might become "beloved women," and men who were renowned warriors became "beloved men," beloved because they had risked their lives for the people.)

In 1850, thirty Cherokee people were living on Deep Creek. Jesse Siler, a white man from Macon County, may have been holding land for them in his name here as he did for the Sand Town community at Cartoogechaye. The Cherokee community on Deep Creek continued through the Civil War.

Now part of the Great Smoky Mountains National Park's half-million acres in North Carolina and Tennessee, Deep Creek can be accessed through Bryson City, which is about 7 miles from the town of Cherokee. Miles of trails extend into the park from here, used by hikers, horseback riders, mountain bikers, fishermen, and in the summer, "tubers" who carry large, inflated inner tubes a mile up the creek and then float back down in the refreshingly icy waters. An outfitter can provide horseback tours. Campsites for tents and RVs are available here, as are restrooms and a large picnic shelter for group events. Primitive campsites can be found farther up the trails.

CONTACT: Great Smoky Mountains National Park, 107 Park Headquarters Rd., Gatlinburg, TN 37738, 865-436-1200; Deep Creek Campground, 1912 East Deep Creek Rd., Bryson City, NC 28713, 828-488-3184

HOURS: Deep Creek Campground is open April 15 through October 31, for primitive camping. Cold running water, bathrooms, and tent pads are provided, and RVs are permitted. Camping is on a first-come first-served basis, except for group reservations, which can be made online at <reservations.nps.gov>.

LOCATION: About 2 miles outside Bryson City on East Deep Creek Road

■ Mountain Farm Museum and Clingman's Dome

OCONALUFTEE VISITOR CENTER/MOUNTAIN FARM MUSEUM

The Mountain Farm Museum depicts rural agricultural life in the Appalachians, and serves as the center for the National Park Service as you enter the Great Smoky Mountains National Park from the Cherokee side. Although presented as an Appalachian farm, it also represents Cherokee farms during the same period, 1820–1920. During the summer, living history demonstrations of farm life include some Cherokee people from the Qualla Boundary. A walking trail along the Oconaluftee River connects the Mountain Farm Museum and the Qualla Boundary and provides interpretation, on wayside signs, about the cultural and spiritual significance of mountains for the Cherokees.

Situated in an open field below high hills, the farmstead includes a two-story log house from 1900. The house is furnished, down to the leather britches (dried beans) hanging by the fireplace. Historic structures include a large barn, pig pens, corn cribs, split-rail fence, drovers' barn, and outbuildings. Inside the visitor center, a new hands-on Discovery Center allows visitors to explore the diversity of the mountain ecosystem.

CONTACT: Mountain Farm Museum, Great Smoky Mountains National Park, 150 US 441 North, Cherokee, NC 28719, 828-497-1940, <www.nps.gov/grsm>

HOURS: Open daily, year-round, from 8:00 A.M. until 4:30 P.M.

LOCATION: US 441 a few miles north of the town of Cherokee

CLINGMAN'S DOME

The bears are transformed Cherokee of the old clan of the Ani-Tsaguhi. Their chief is the
White Bear, who lives at Kuwahi, Mulberry Place, one of the high peaks of the Great Smoky
Mountains, near to the enchanted lake of *Atagahi,* to which the wounded bears go to be
cured of their hurts. Under *Kuwahi* and each of three other peaks in the same mountain
region, the bears have townhouses, where they congregate and hold dances every fall
before retiring to their dens for the winter. Being really human, they can talk if they
only would, and once a mother bear was heard singing to her cub in words which
the hunter understood.

— Swimmer, Ayuini, and others

Known as Kuwahi or Mulberry Place to the Cherokees, this high peak
was one of four mountain peaks under which the bears had their townhouses, where they would gather to dance before going to their dens to
sleep for the winter. According to Cherokee mythology the Magic Lake was
also located here—where sick and wounded bears would go for healing.
To human eyes, however, the magic lake just looked like clouds filling the
valleys from the vista of the mountaintop. When forced removal threatened
the Cherokees, these slopes became a refuge for those who hid in their
rugged terrain. More important, however, this mountain was held sacred
by the Cherokees.

Kuwahi became Clingman's Dome, named for Thomas Clingman, senator from North Carolina, who in the mid-nineteenth century disputed with
Elisha Mitchell the most accurate way to measure the height of mountains.
Although the senator argued that another peak in the Black Mountains was
highest, Clingman's Dome, at 6,643 feet, is the highest peak in the Smokies,
while Mt. Mitchell, in the Black Mountain range east of Asheville, is the
highest peak east of the Mississippi.

From the parking lot, a short but steep trail leads to the very summit,
where an observation tower provides a dizzying 360-degree view of the
Great Smoky Mountains. Those with health problems should use caution
when ascending.

CONTACT: Great Smoky Mountains National Park, 107 Park Headquarters
Rd., Gatlinburg, TN 37738, 865-436-1200
LOCATION: From the town of Cherokee, follow US 441 North for
approximately 18 miles. Turn left onto Clingman's Dome Road. Follow
for 7 miles to Clingman's Dome parking lot. Clingman's Dome Road is
closed to vehicular traffic from December 1 to March 31. Occasionally,
Newfound Gap Road (US 441) will be closed due to weather.

Observation tower at Clingman's Dome. In Cherokee mythology, the bears held their councils underneath this mountain, and the magic lake appeared to bears and other animals here. During the Trail of Tears, the rugged mountain slopes provided refuge for Tsali and other Cherokees hiding from the U.S. Army. (Photograph by Murray Lee)

■ Cullowhee and Jackson County Sites

JUDACULLA ROCK

According to Cherokee legend, the giant Judaculla jumped from his farm high on Tanasi to the creek below, landing on a rock. The scratches made by his landing can be seen today on "Judaculla Rock," located on Caney Fork. The spirals, circles, squiggles, and figures carved into this large soapstone rock suggest maps, messages, and the iconography of legends, but they have not been interpreted. The rock itself may have served as a source of soapstone for making bowls during the Archaic period, about five thousand years ago. The carvers who removed the bowl forms created the hollowed-out surface of the rock that now exists. Designs carved into the surface of the rock include crosses in circles, hands, spear throwers, and sun symbols that may come from the Missisippian period of Cherokee culture (ca. A.D. 900–A.D. 1500).

The rock itself lies among meadows and low hills on an ancient trail, with a spring nearby. Above Judaculla Rock, in the watershed drained by Caney Fork, several legendary sites associated with Judaculla mark the rough high country that separates the watersheds of the Tuckaseegee River and the Pigeon River. His farm was Judaculla Old Fields, about a hundred acres on the slope of Tennessee Bald that can be viewed from the Blue Ridge Parkway. Judaculla's Dance Hall became known as Devil's Courthouse. Beyond them, Looking Glass Rock and Pilot Knob are also associated with Judaculla in Cherokee stories.

Truly it would take a giant to negotiate this terrain: high steep peaks one after another, with intersecting ranges cut by rushing creeks. On these high peaks, many balds can be found: Grass Bald, Snaggy Bald, Lone Bald, and Rough Butt Bald—the latter, above Caney Fork Creek, indicating the nature of this territory.

The Cherokee town closest to Judaculla Rock, Tanasi (or Tennessee) Old Town, lay about 3 miles away, where the west fork of the Tuckaseegee joins the main body of the river. Excavations by archaeologists from the University of North Carolina at Chapel Hill indicate that people lived here during the Archaic period (10,000–3,000 years ago), during the subsequent Woodland period, and in Cherokee settlements during the historic era. The Cherokees considered Tanasi Old Town one of their "Out Towns" because it was out beyond the Middle Towns of the Little Tennessee River and its tributaries. The nearby Tennessee Bald and Tennessee Creek all refer to the town of this name located here.

Some scholars have misidentified this site near Judaculla Rock as Tuckaseegee town, but the actual Tuckaseegee town was located near the Tucka-seegee River at present-day Webster, farther west of Judaculla Rock and a few miles east of US 441. This is the Tuckaseegee town destroyed by John Sevier's Revolutionary War raiders in 1781. The word *Tuckaseegee* means "Place of the box turtle," based on the Cherokee word for the Eastern wood-land terrapin, *dakasi.* Adding the suffix "yi makes it a place name: *Da ka si-yi.* (The mud turtle or snapping turtle was known as *saligugi.*)

The Tanasi Old Town site is on private property but can be viewed from the road. From Western Carolina University, proceed 6.5 miles southeast on NC 107. From the turn off to Judaculla Rock, proceed 3.5 miles farther on NC 107. At the bridge where NC 107 crosses the Tuckaseegee, near NC 281, you can see the old location of the town, opposite the West Fork of the river.

CONTACT: Jackson County Administration Office, 401 Grindstaff Cove Rd., Sylva, NC 28779, 828-586-7580 (Judaculla Rock is owned and preserved by Jackson County)

LOCATION: To get to Judaculla Rock from Western Carolina University in Cullowhee, proceed 3 miles south on NC 107. Turn left on County Road 1737, marked by a sign for Judaculla Rock. Proceed 2.5 miles, and turn left onto a gravel road at another sign for the rock. Proceed approximately 0.5 miles to another sign, park on the right-hand side of the road and walk down a short path to the rock. There is parking for cars only.

MOUNTAIN HERITAGE CENTER

The Mountain Heritage Center of Western Carolina University sits on an old Cherokee town site on Cullowhee Creek, which drains into the Tuckaseegee. The village mound was located between the Mountain Heri-tage Center and the Continuing Education Building near Cullowhee Creek, which runs through campus.

At the Mountain Heritage Center, displays and exhibits feature Chero-kee artifacts. The center's permanent exhibit provides information on the origins of white Appalachian culture, "The Scots-Irish Migration." The an-nual festival, Mountain Heritage Day, attracts forty thousand people and regularly features some Cherokee craft demonstrators and performers. For more information on this event, see the end of this chapter. Western Caro-lina University offers a minor in Cherokee studies and maintains a satellite office on the Qualla Boundary.

CONTACT: Tyler Blethen, Director, Mountain Heritage Center, Western
Carolina University, Cullowhee, NC 28723, 828-227-7129,
<www.wcu.edu/mhc/>

HOURS: The Mountain Heritage Center is open to the public free of
charge. Visiting hours are Monday through Friday from 8:00 A.M. until
5:00 P.M. The Center is also open on Sundays from 2:00 P.M. until
5:00 P.M., from June through October. Because the Center observes a
university holiday schedule, please call for information.

LOCATION: On the first floor of the H. F. Robinson Building at the main
entrance from NC 107 onto the Western Carolina University (WCU)
campus.

To reach WCU from the east, take Exit 85 off of US 23/74. At the
second traffic light, turn left onto NC 107 traveling south. In
approximately 7 miles, the campus of WCU will be on the left in
Cullowhee.

To reach WCU from the west or south, take US 441 North toward
Dillsboro. Approximately 3 miles south of Dillsboro (just past Greens
Creek), turn right onto NC 116 and follow to Webster. Just east of
Webster, turn right onto NC 107. Proceed south on NC 107 for several
miles to Cullowhee and WCU will be on your left.

■ Cataloochee Valley

Some men were working over in what we call Cataloochee now. A big storm came up—
lightning, thunder, rain, a big windstorm. And they saw it coming. It was coming fast, and
they were looking for shelter. So they lay down behind a mound of dirt, a pile of earth that
had been piled up. They lay down flat, and the wind passed over them. The earth saved
them. So that's what we call it "Earth, it saved them," or "It shielded them." *Gadu ha lu gi.*
And that got translated, or passed on in English as Cataloochee.

—Jerry Wolfe in a workshop for the Great Smoky Mountains
National Park interpretive staff, May 24, 2001

This high valley was used for hunting by the Cherokees and their ancestors and was home to them and to white Appalachian settlers before
becoming part of the Great Smoky Mountains National Park in 1934. Today,
visitors can marvel at old-growth trees on Boogerman Trail, can sight abundant wildlife, including newly released elk, and can find still-standing Victorian houses and old country churches.

Peaks more than 5,000 feet high encircle this ten-thousand-acre valley:
Cataloochee Divide, Balsam Mountains, Chiltoes Mountain, Spruce Mountain, and Mount Sterling. The streams of Caldwell Fork and Rough Fork

drain into Cataloochee Creek at about 3,000 feet elevation at the lowest point of the valley. People lived here in small settlements as long as five thousand years ago, and also stayed in hunting camps. White settlers lived here from 1830 to 1934, and some of their descendants still hold homecomings at the church in Cataloochee Valley.

Almost all of the Great Smoky Mountains were logged in the early twentieth century, but some pockets of old-growth trees remain, such as the stand located up Boogerman Fork Trail. Today, under the management of the Great Smoky Mountains National Park, Cataloochee Valley offers miles of trails for hiking and horseback riding, trout fishing, camping, and picnicking. It is a favorite area for local horseback riders. The only difficulty in visiting Cataloochee Valley is its rough access road—a one-lane gravel road with switchbacks ascending Cataloochee Divide from the east. Roads within the park are both paved and gravel. On the way from Maggie Valley to Cataloochee Valley, the privately owned Cataloochee Ranch offers accommodations, dining, horseback riding, outdoor recreation, and during the summer, evening sessions of Cherokee storytelling and dance.

CONTACT: Great Smoky Mountains National Park, 107 Park Headquarters Rd., Gatlinburg, TN 37738, 865-436-1200, <www.smokymountainsnc.com/cataloochee_valley.htm>; Cataloochee Ranch, 119 Ranch Dr., Maggie Valley, NC 28751, 828-926-1401, <info@cataloochee-ranch.com>, <www.cataloochee-ranch.com>

HOURS: Cataloochee is open year-round.

LOCATION: In the Great Smoky Mountains National Park between Cherokee and Waynesville. From Waynesville, take US 276 north for approximately 8 miles. Continue on US 276 through Dellwood and Jonathan to Cove Creek. Just before reaching the intersection with I 40, turn left onto Cove Creek Road (Old NC 284), which begins as a gravel road. Follow this winding gravel road until it becomes paved again. Then follow the paved road to Cataloochee Valley.

SCENIC DRIVE

■ Blue Ridge Parkway from Cherokee to Spruce Pine

I keep going back to Franklin Delano Roosevelt's statement up on top of Clingman's Dome area—it was actually Newfound Gap—but he looked out over the terrain and he said, "The savages have had this land for so long," and he pointed out to the beautiful mountains and he said, "They've done nothing. And look what we have done in only a few years." And he pointed down to this big gap that they'd cut into the mountainside.

And I tend to look back up there today and look at all the dead trees and the mountains sliding off and beginning to look like the Rockies, and I tend to say, "Look what we have done in only a few years." And it would be better that the savages have the land to keep it and to care for it.

— Freeman Owle

The southern end of the Blue Ridge Parkway is in Cherokee. From here, you can "ride the ridges," seeing the vistas of Cherokee territory from the Qualla Boundary to Mount Mitchell. But the Parkway offers more than vistas. Visit the home of the first man and woman in Cherokee mythology, Kanati and Selu, at Shining Rock Wilderness, south of Cold Mountain. Stop at the Folk Art Center near Asheville to shop for Cherokee baskets and contemporary crafts. Climb Mount Mitchell, highest peak east of the Mississippi, called "Black Mountain" by the Cherokee.

Don't plan to rush. Created by engineers and landscape architects for the "recreational motorist," the Parkway has a speed limit of 45 miles per hour. Its contours and surrounding landscapes were designed to create a scenic tour.

As you travel the Parkway anywhere from Cherokee north to middle Virginia, you can look out at the vistas and know that everything in sight was once Cherokee territory. The Cherokee trails followed the mountain ridges, in some cases near Parkway routes. The old Indian trails and buffalo migration trails also became the Appalachian Trail in some places. Cherokees typically lived in villages along rivers and creeks at lower elevations than the Blue Ridge Parkway, but during the winter, Cherokee men made hunting camps on the higher elevations, much like people during the Paleo-Indian period eleven thousand years ago.

Today, the Eastern Cherokees feel a special connection with the Parkway. Its closeness to Cherokee land, the effects of its construction, and its ongoing use are all part of the tribe's traditions. Many of the elders remember the coming of the Parkway. "I was born on the center line of the Parkway," Jerry Wolfe tells people, pausing while listeners conjure up images of a backseat birth or an auto mishap before adding, "of course it wasn't the Parkway then."

The coming of the Parkway was hotly debated in tribal council in the 1930s, but was ultimately approved. Its proponents understood the value of tourism for economic survival for the tribe. The efforts of Mollie Blankenship were significant in helping to bring the Parkway near tribal lands, and Mollie Gap is named for her.

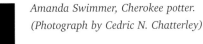

Amanda Swimmer, Cherokee potter.
(Photograph by Cedric N. Chatterley)

Many Cherokee people worked on building the Parkway through the mountains of western North Carolina, and some lost their lives in the effort. The Parkway brought another kind of loss too—Amanda Swimmer's special source for pottery clay was covered up by the road. Springs were covered up.

When the Parkway was officially opened, President Franklin Roosevelt extolled the efforts of the federal government and deplored the inactivity of the Cherokee people who "had this land for centuries and did nothing with it." Their careful stewardship was not as obvious as the tunnels and cuts dynamited through the hills.

Today, the Parkway has become part of Cherokee life, and people use it, especially where it runs through the Qualla Boundary, in special ways. Generations have traveled it to pick huckleberries and blueberries at Graveyard Fields. From the town of Cherokee, people go to the Overlook of Thomas Divide to watch mysterious lights rise from the divide and travel up the mountains in late summer evenings. Families gather at Waterrock Knob in the summertime to picnic and to watch the sun set over the mountains stretching away into the distance.

Not every overlook and feature on the Blue Ridge Parkway is listed here; only those with special significance in Cherokee history and culture are

Cherokee Names in Big Cove

In Cherokee, we call Big Cove "The Place of the Raven." Ka la nv is a raven. Ka la nv-yi makes the place of the raven, or the name of a place. And also we have a name for Bunches Creek, the name of the Beaver, da yu nah. And Indian Creek branches off from Bunches Creek; we call it "Where the Community Had Sat." They called it ga du a na na ti. Then we have Straight Fork. It's on the right-hand prong coming out of Big Cove, and it's called ste sh kv, and it's kind of a sallet that grew in that area. And I don't know the English name—but I know the Cherokee name. The plant itself is called, u ste sh kv. The Cherokee people gathered that, and they fixed it like you would greens from the garden, maybe turnip greens.

So back on the left-hand side of Big Cove is called Ka lu nv yi—"The Place of the Raven." And the raven to the Cherokee people is known as a witchery-bird—I suppose you could put it that way. The Cherokee imitated the old raven by becoming a flying raven at night. They went through a ritual and became a witch, and they would always imitate the raven—the call of the raven and so on.

In the Sherrill Cove area where I was born and raised—in the Cherokee language it's called ga du de ga ni ha a ma and that's "where the water is on top" or next to the top, or maybe there's a lot of water nearby—maybe a spring head or something. All through these mountains there's water in every little valley.

Back to Big Cove again, on the left-hand side of Bunches Creek—you take a left-hand shot and you go into a place called Heintooga. Now in the Cherokee language it's called un too ga. Now that means a group of people taking a drink. There may be a spring there. Someone said they were soldiers, and they had ran into a still up there and they all got drunk from drinking that whisky that someone had made.

Jerry Wolfe

included. They are listed as Parkway sites even when they are located in other counties, because they are most easily accessed from the Parkway itself. Sites beyond Gillespie Gap were eliminated to make a one-day drive possible from Cherokee and back. Beyond this area, many other sites were known and used by the Cherokees, including Yonalohssee Trail, built as a stagecoach road over an old Indian trail, which leads to Grandfather Mountain.

Enter the Blue Ridge Parkway as you travel north on US 441 from Cherokee, turning right at the clearly marked sign. Remember that sections may be closed during winter months. Parkway rangers do patrol the roads and overlooks, if assistance is needed. Driving time from Qualla Boundary to the Folk Art Center on the Parkway is four to eight hours, depending on how often you stop; however, you can return from Asheville to Cherokee in about an hour, traveling on four-lane highways. Several return routes are possible. From Asheville, take I 40 west to Clyde. Take Exit 27 onto US 74 west to Waynesville. For a scenic mountain route, follow US 19 through Maggie Valley to Cherokee. For a route along the Tuckaseegee River, proceed to Dillsboro on US 74 West, and then take US 441 north to Cherokee.

CONTACT: Blue Ridge Parkway, 199 Hemphill Knob Rd., Asheville, NC 28802, 828-271-4779, <www.nps.gov/blri>

RAVEN FORK VIEW (MILEPOST 467.9, ELEVATION 2,400 FEET)

This overlook provides a view of the Raven Fork river, referred to on the sign as Raven's Ford. Here the Parkway crosses the ridge overlooking the Big Cove area of the Qualla Boundary, the watershed of the Raven Fork River and its tributaries.

Called *kalanv* in Cherokee language, the raven is a glossy black bird about two feet long, larger than a crow, with distinctive pointed feathers at its neck. Playing a major role in Cherokee mythology, and known around the world, this bird has become rare and is now seen mostly in remote areas and at higher elevations. Ravens tend to roost together on rock cliffs, and place names throughout the Appalachians mark their presence. When flying, they sometimes fold one wing and somersault through the air.

VIEW OF THOMAS DIVIDE (MILEPOST 464.5, ELEVATION 3,735 FEET)

From the parking area, Thomas Divide appears as a high ridge ahead and to your left. It runs northwest to join the spine of the Great Smoky Mountains along the North Carolina–Tennessee border. The Thomas Divide Trail runs along the top of Thomas Ridge leading toward Tennessee. During the

The Raven Rock Dancers

Walker Calhoun, leader of the Raven Rock Dancers, also plays old-time banjo. (Photograph by Barbara Duncan)

The Raven Rock Dancers include some of the children and grandchildren of Walker Calhoun, who leads the group with his singing and drumming. Walker Calhoun has maintained Cherokee dance traditions for his generation from his home near the Raven Rock cliffs. Awarded the National Heritage Fellowship from the National Endowment for the Arts in 1993 for his role in maintaining and passing on traditions, Calhoun says that dances are a form of prayer, a way of honoring the animals and honoring the Creator. He says that the dances are what makes Cherokee religion different from Christian religion.

Civil War, the Thomas Legion of Cherokees and mountaineers guarded the Qualla Boundary by keeping lookouts on top of this ridge.

Today, this overlook is also known for a strange phenomenon much like the better-known Brown Mountain lights, which can be viewed from the Parkway near Asheville. During the late summer months, particularly, strange lights can be seen forming in the valley and moving up the cove toward the top of Thomas Divide. Local residents come about sunset to park, watch, and wonder.

Also at this overlook, many Carolina silverbell saplings grow throughout the woods. This beautiful and rare native tree (*Halesia caroliniana*) is found throughout the southern Appalachians.

BIG WITCH GAP (MILEPOST 461.6, ELEVATION 4,150 FEET)

Big Witch Gap and Big Witch Tunnel are named for a Cherokee man, Tskil-e-gwa. Today, the Cherokee community here is still known as the Big Witch community. Big Witch, who remembered the Creek War of 1812–14, died in 1897, at that time the oldest man of the tribe. He was reputed to be a skilled medicine man and herbalist as well as someone who knew the rituals for killing an eagle so that its feathers could be used for sacred ceremonies.

LICKSTONE RIDGE OVERLOOK
(MILEPOST 458.9, ELEVATION 5,150 FEET)

Lickstone Ridge is a broad, flat-topped mountain running roughly southwest. This overlook provides a panoramic view of most of the Qualla Boundary. Lickstone Ridge and Lickstone Tunnel get their name from the practice of putting salt out on a stone for animals to lick. Lickstones (and licklogs) attract both wild and domestic animals. Prior to the 1930s, people ranged cattle and hogs throughout the mountains where they fattened on chestnuts and other forage. When the livestock were full grown and fattened, they were rounded up and driven to market or butchered for family use. The lickstone provided minerals that the animals needed, and also made them easier to find, since they returned there often.

The practice of ranging animals through the mountains ended in the 1930s for several reasons. The chestnut trees were all killed by the chestnut blight, dramatically reducing the amount of food available for domestic and wild animals and reducing populations of wild animals for the rest of the century. Timbering also reduced the amount of woodland habitat. Millions of acres became part of federal lands, where grazing was restricted. Finally, legislation was passed ending this practice that had enabled both white and Cherokee families to survive using common land.

SOCO GAP (MILEPOST 455.7, ELEVATION 4,340 FEET)

A gap is a place where mountain ridges dip down or intersect, creating a way for travelers to cross over the mountain. Many gaps are at high elevations, and while some can be seen as part of the skyline, others can be perceived only by passing through them.

Soco Gap has been recognized for centuries by the Cherokees as one of the gateways into their country. Its names reflect this: "ambush place"

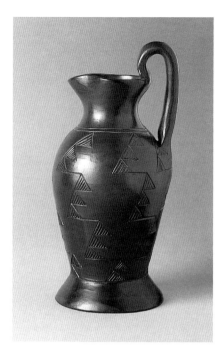

The Road to Soco pattern as depicted on pottery by Louise Maney. (Photograph by Julie Stovall)

or Ahalunvyi, referring to an encounter with the Shawnees. Another name applied to a place nearby is "Where the Spaniard is thrown in the water" or Askwan digugv yi, referring to a place on Soco Creek near present-day Rocky Branch church. Soco Gap was also the location of the legendary encounter between Tecumseh and Junaluska, about 1811, when Junaluska refused Tecumseh's request that the Cherokees unite with them to fight the whites.

Today the Cherokees use "Soco" to refer to the road over the mountain, the gap itself, and the creek. A waterfall, Soco Falls, can be glimpsed from US 19 on the Qualla Boundary, and is more visible in the winter. Soco also refers to the community of people who live on the Qualla Boundary near the foot of this mountain, in Wolftown. A weaving and quilting pattern invented by Cherokee women in the 1930s looks like trails and mountains and was named "Road to Soco."

This point on the Parkway accesses US 19, which goes to Cherokee, 8 miles west, or to Waynesville, 13 miles east. Traveling east, US 19 passes through the resort area of Maggie Valley. A North Carolina historical marker describing the Junaluska-Tecumseh encounter can be found on US 19 just off the Parkway.

VIEW OF HORNBUCKLE VALLEY
(MILEPOST 453.4, ELEVATION 5,105 FEET)

The creek is named for my father, James Hornbuckle. He died in 1896 at about sixty. He served in the Union Army, enlisted in Knoxville, Tennessee, Company D, 3rd regiment under Major W. W. Rollins of Asheville.

My father was in a skirmish at the close of the war. The federals came across the Smokies, down through Soco Gap to the Cherokee land. An Indian sergeant held a parlay with some of the outpost Cherokee who were in Confederate uniform. He wanted them to come over to the Union side. They wouldn't. After a skirmish, the Union men retreated back through the gap.

—Israel Hornbuckle, Cherokee, North Carolina, 1954 *Blue Ridge Parkway Guide*

The headwaters of Hornbuckle Creek begin near the Parkway, and the creek has created a cove leading down into Soco Creek, which in turn runs into the Oconoluftee River. At this point the Plott Balsam mountain range extends like giant wings on both sides of the Parkway.

WATERROCK KNOB (MILEPOST 451.2, ELEVATION 5,718 FEET)

Here at the junction of two mountain ranges, the Plott Balsams and the Great Balsams, you have a 360-degree view of the southern Appalachians. The elevation of Waterrock Knob is 6,292 feet, and the peak can be reached by a steep, half-mile hiking trail. The spring that gives this peak its name is located off the trail.

The new Parkway visitor center here includes several displays. One describes the black bear and its habitat. Another, with a life-sized tree, describes the insects, diseases, and conditions that are killing trees in the Great Smoky Mountains National Park. A map describes the Snowbird Mountains as viewed in the distance. Publications on sale here include numerous selections on the Cherokee. The new visitor center is open from 9:00 A.M. until 5:00 P.M. seven days a week from May through October, and restrooms are available. The parking lot has room for cars and buses.

This popular spot on the Parkway attracts approximately 200,000 visitors in season. Its panoramic view has made this a favorite gathering place of Cherokee people and others for picnicking and watching the sunsets through long summer evenings.

RABB KNOB OVERLOOK
(MILEPOST 441.9, ELEVATION 3,370 FEET)

This overlook provides a view of Balsam Gap. Although gaps may provide the lowest point to cross a mountain range, they can still be quite high

View from Waterrock Knob. (Photograph by Mike Booher)

themselves, as Balsam Gap illustrates, with an elevation that exceeds some mountains in the Blue Ridge Range.

When you drive NC 23/74, the four-lane road between Waynesville and Sylva, you are driving through Balsam Gap. This route was used by Native Americans for centuries, perhaps thousands of years, as a natural gateway from the watershed of the Pigeon River west into the watersheds of the Tuckaseegee and Little Tennessee Rivers.

This overlook's interpretive sign refers to a view of "Rutherford's war trace." During the Revolutionary War, an expedition led by General Griffith Rutherford marched from the east through Balsam Gap, destroying Cherokee villages along the Tuckaseegee in retaliation for the Cherokees' alliance with the British. In the summer of 1776, Cherokee warriors had attacked American frontier settlements in upper South Carolina, east Tennessee, southwestern Virginia, and western North Carolina. In many of these raids, the Cherokees were accompanied by Tories who dressed as Indians. The British had been allies in the French and Indian War, and the Cherokees, like other tribes, were convinced that their best interests lay with the British because of King George's Proclamation of 1763 declaring that no lands west of the Blue Ridge could be settled by Americans.

In retaliation for Cherokee military actions, Rutherford entered Cherokee territory and destroyed thirty-six villages, killing as many men, women, and children as possible, along the Oconaluftee, the Tuckaseegee, the Little Tennessee, and the Hiwassee below its junction with the Valley River—all the Cherokee towns on these rivers. At the same time, the South Carolina army led by Colonel Andrew Williamson destroyed the Cherokee Lower Towns. American armies from Georgia and Virginia also destroyed Cherokee towns in their vicinity. Cherokee people fled into the mountains and lived off the land, returning later to rebuild their towns.

COWEE MOUNTAINS OVERLOOK
(MILEPOST 430.7, ELEVATION 5,960 FEET)

At this overlook, a wayside exhibit shows the outline of the mountain ridges and their names. It shows where the Little Tennessee River cuts through the mountains, on the far side of the Cowee range, running north from its headwaters in present-day Rabun County, Georgia. Wave upon wave of mountain vistas look much the same as they have for thousands of years.

The Little Tennessee River Valley, from the river's headwaters north to the Nantahala River, was the location of no fewer than fifteen Cherokee towns at the beginning of the eighteenth century. On the river and its tributaries were the towns of Stecoe, Old Estatoe, Tessuntee, Nunnunyi, Echoe, Tunanutte, Cartoogechaye, Erachy, Ellijay, Nikwasi, Watauga, Iotla, Cowee, Coweche, and Nunlahala. At some of these sites, Cherokee towns date back to A.D. 1000, and people may have occupied these locations for much longer. Today, modern towns and communities stand on several of these places, and highways follow the old trails in some locations.

These heights give an overview of these village sites, but a journey to Franklin takes visitors to the banks of the Little Tennessee River, at the former Cherokee town of Nikwasi. For more information on these "Middle Towns," see Chapter 3.

VIEW OF TANASSEE BALD/JUDACULLA OLD FIELDS (MILEPOST 423.7)

Tanassee Bald lies on the south side of this mountain, facing away from the Parkway. Its English name comes from Tanassee Creek, which flows down from it into the Tuckaseegee. In the Cherokee language, it is called Tsu ne gun yi or "There where it is white." Because this was believed to be the farm of the mythical slant-eyed giant, it is also known as Tsunegun yi tsul kalu or Judaculla Old Fields. From here the giant was said to jump down onto Judaculla Rock, making the petroglyphs we can see there today. Judaculla Rock is located on Caney Fork Creek, about 12 miles west of the bald and two thousand feet lower.

(Some say that Judaculla Old Fields were located at Richland Balsam, just above the headwaters of Caney Fork Creek, near milepost 431 on the Parkway.)

The Cherokees respected the balds found throughout the mountains and believed that the Nunnehi, the mythical spirit people, kept them cleared so that the eagles could hunt rabbits there. Scientists have not been able to explain their existence.

DEVIL'S COURTHOUSE (MILEPOST 422.4, ELEVATION 5,462 FEET)

"The Devil's Courthouse" rises ominously above the Blue Ridge Parkway. This bare rock summit is best viewed traveling from the west toward Asheville. (Coming from Asheville, one approaches through the Devil's Courthouse Tunnel.) The rugged granite formation towers over the parking lot to its final height of 5,720 feet. A trail leads gradually up to the rock summit, where a rocky platform provides a 360-degree view of the French Broad, Tuckaseegee, and Pigeon River watersheds.

A cave deep inside the rock was described by the Cherokee as Judaculla's dancing chambers and by the white settlers as "The Devil's Courthouse." According to Eddie Bushyhead, Cherokee musician and language expert, this place was used to administer justice in the old days. Cherokees who were to be killed were taken here, their hands and feet tied, and thrown off the top of the rock to their certain death. "It was known as a place of execution," he said.

The Appalachian name for this formation seems to have combined this administration of justice with the idea of the Devil. Throughout the eastern United States, places considered sacred by Native Americans have had their names translated by those of European descent as "place of the Devil" rather than "place of spirits," as they were referred to originally. The Cherokee word *asgina* originally referred to spirit, but when the Bible was translated into Cherokee, this word was used to mean "Devil"; today Cherokee language speakers use *asgina* for both meanings. In any case, Judaculla's townhouse, at a size appropriate for a giant of his stature, has become known as the Devil's Courthouse.

SHINING ROCK MOUNTAIN/GRAVEYARD FIELDS OVERLOOK (MILEPOST 418.8, ELEVATION 5,115 FEET)

A spur road to Shining Rock Wilderness can be found at milepost 420.2 on the Blue Ridge Parkway. Cherokee people still recognize Shining Rock as the home of the first Cherokee man and woman, Kanati and Selu. Their origin myth is included at the end of this guidebook. Cherokee families travel to Graveyard Fields in the summer to pick blueberries. Pilot Knob, referred to in the story of Kanati and Selu, is located 2 miles directly south, across the Parkway.

Shining Rock literally refers to a white quartz outcropping, the Shining Rock Ledge formation located on the headwaters of the Pigeon River, south of Cold Mountain, in Shining Rock Wilderness Area. Here, five mountain peaks tower at 6,000 feet elevation. The Shining Rock Wilderness area encompasses 18,500 rugged acres, accessible only by foot trails, within the Pisgah National Forest. Rules for wilderness areas apply here: groups must be no larger than ten people; no fires are permitted, and no wheels are permitted. One horse trail exists in this wilderness area.

Graveyard Fields and Graveyard Ridge, elevation 5,600 feet, which lie between the Parkway and Shining Rock, did not get their names because of burials here. Hundreds of years ago, a severe windstorm blew down much of the spruce forest covering this ridge. As the uprooted trees and stumps began decaying and were covered with new growth, they created unusual looking mounds, which to the first white settlers resembled a graveyard, and so they named it. In 1925 "The Big Fire," started by a spark from a locomotive, burned twenty-five thousand acres of timber, including the Graveyard Fields area. The natural stages of hardwood forest succession at this altitude have now created a blueberry bog resembling those of the Great Lakes region. Rhododendron, mountain laurel, red maple, mountain ash, and serviceberry, along with the highbush blueberry, thrive here.

On U.S. Forest Service land at the trailhead, a short distance from the Parkway, one can find parking, restrooms, and a kiosk with a map of the area. For Shining Rock Wilderness Area, contact the U.S. Forest Service, Pisgah Ranger District, 1001 Pisgah Highway, Pisgah Forest, NC 28768, 828-877-3265.

Graveyard Fields. (Photograph by Mike Booher)

LOOKING GLASS ROCK (MILEPOST 417.1, ELEVATION 4,493 FEET)

This granite dome rises four hundred feet above the valley floor, created by mountain streams eroding the softer gneiss around it. Its appearance is made even more striking by the way light reflects off of its Whiteside granite, particularly when the rock is wet. The Parkway overlook is about five hundred feet above the top of Looking Glass Rock, whose elevation is 3,969 feet.

The Cherokee associated this rock with Judaculla (Tsulkalu), whose Old Fields, Dancing Chambers, and footprints are all located in this region. Looking Glass Rock can be seen for several miles along the Parkway.

THE FOLK ART CENTER (MILEPOST 382)

The Folk Art Center, headquarters of the Southern Highland Craft Guild, showcases regional arts and crafts, including those of the Cherokees, in its gift shop, exhibits, and special programs. The Folk Art Center often features

Cherokees associate Looking Glass Rock with legends about Judaculla.
(Photograph by Murray Lee)

Work by Cherokee woodcarver Amanda Crowe is included in the Southern Highland Craft Guild's permanent collection at the Folk Art Center in Asheville, N.C. (Photograph by Roger Haile)

exhibits, craft demonstrations, and festivals in its contemporary building constructed of native wood and stone.

Beginning in 1930, the Southern Highland Craft Guild exhibited and marketed the crafts of mountain people, including some Cherokee baskets, blowguns, and carvings. When Qualla Arts and Crafts Mutual was formed in 1949, it joined the guild, and individual Cherokee crafts people have been members as well.

CONTACT: Folk Art Center/Southern Highland Craft Guild, P.O. Box 9545, Asheville, NC 28815, 828-298-7928, <shcg@buncombe.main.nc.us>, <www.southernhighlandguild.org>.

HOURS: Open daily from 9:00 A.M. until 5:00 P.M., January through March 31, with extended seasonal hours of 9:00 A.M. until 6:00 P.M., April through December. Closed Thanksgiving, Christmas, and New Year's Day. Admission to the Folk Art Center is free. Admission fees may be required for special events and workshops.

LOCATION: The Folk Art Center is located approximately 5 miles east of

Asheville on the Blue Ridge Parkway, milepost 382. From I 40, take Exit 55 to US 70 West to the Parkway traveling north.

VIEW OF ASHEVILLE (MILEPOST 380)

This overlook provides a view of the city of Asheville, known to contemporary Cherokee as "Ashes place" or Kasdu-yi, a translation into Cherokee of its English name. Its older Cherokee name was Untakiyasti-yi, meaning "Where they race," the name of the old Cherokee town on the French Broad River. People have lived for at least two thousand years at this location where the Swannanoa River joins the French Broad. Farther east on the Swannanoa River, archaeologists have been studying an even older site on the property of Warren Wilson College, where people have lived for seven thousand years.

White settlers began living here after the Revolutionary War, although the land was not officially taken until the Treaty of the Holston in 1791, which included present-day Knoxville, Tennessee, and Greenville, South Carolina.

The city of Asheville sponsors the Giduwah Festival in late September, bringing together crafts people, dancers, storytellers, and elders from all Native American tribes. Check with the Chamber of Commerce for dates. One can also find Native American food in Asheville at the Spirits on the River restaurant. Today, some Cherokee families live and work in Asheville, which is about 50 miles from the Qualla Boundary.

MOUNT MITCHELL (MILEPOST 355.4)

Mount Mitchell, at 6,684 feet, is the highest peak east of the Mississippi, higher by forty-one feet than Clingman's Dome. It is named for Dr. Elisha Mitchell, who died surveying its slopes in 1857. The museum here tells the story of his rivalry with Thomas Clingman, who claimed that his peak was higher. Interpretive panels also tell the story of Big Tom "Bearkiller" Wilson, who had hunted this region all his life and who not only guided Mitchell to the top of the mountain, but also recovered his body by tracking a ten-day-old trail. Just as Wilson knew the mountain before Mitchell's arrival, generations of Cherokees knew the mountain before the arrival of the Scots-Irish settlers. The Cherokees called this "Black Mountain." It is the setting for the story of the terrapin's race, which appears in the section of stories in this guidebook.

At the state park at the summit, you can visit the museum for more information about the mountain and its fauna and flora. Hiking trails loop through the spruce forest, and a short, steep walk takes you to a four-story observation tower on the very top of the mountain. Picnicking and camping

Visitors can find information on the soapstone used by Cherokee stonecarvers at the Museum of North Carolina Minerals. (Photograph by Cedric N. Chatterley)

are allowed in the thirty-two-thousand-acre Mt. Mitchell cooperative management area, administered by the Pisgah National Forest and the North Carolina Wildlife Commission. Be prepared for cooler temperatures and stronger breezes on the mountain.

CONTACT: Mount Mitchell State Park, Rt. 5 Box 700, Burnsville, NC 28714, 828-675-4611, <mount.mitchell@ncmail.net>

HOURS: The park is closed on Christmas Day and open all other days of the year, weather permitting.

LOCATION: Mount Mitchell can be reached via the Blue Ridge Parkway at milepost 355.

GILLESPIE GAP AND THE MUSEUM OF NORTH CAROLINA MINERALS (MILEPOST 330.9)

The Cherokees and their ancestors—as far back as ten thousand years ago—used a quarry near the present-day Museum of North Carolina Minerals to get soapstone, or steatite. This type of rock was carved into sinkers for fishing nets, weights for atlatls, and "cooking stones"—small slabs with holes in them that were heated and then dropped into containers to cook the soups and stews. This ancient technique cooked food quickly, although indirectly, because the containers, made of hides, wood, gourds, and baskets, could not be placed into the fire without burning them. Beginning about five thousand years ago people began carving soapstone bowls, which could be placed directly on coals to cook food, and these became valued trade items.

Exhibits at the Museum of North Carolina Minerals provide information on all of the minerals native to the state, and the museum itself is located in an area known for its deposits of soapstone, feldspar, mica, emeralds, rubies, garnets, amethysts, quartz crystal, and other semiprecious stones. Mica was also valued by the Cherokees and was traded from this region as far north as present-day Ohio, especially in the later Mississippian period.

The gap in the mountains here was called Etchoe Pass, part of an ancient trail used by the Cherokee to travel to their Lower Towns in present-day South Carolina. In 1780, an Irishman named Henry Gillespie was living here when John Sevier, Isaac Shelby, and the "Overmountain Men" passed through on their way to turn the tide of the Revolutionary War at the Battle of King's Mountain in South Carolina. The gap was named for Henry Gillespie. Many white settlers already occupied this land when it was taken from the Cherokees by the Treaty of the Holston in 1791.

CONTACT: Museum of North Carolina Minerals, 214 Parkway Maintenance Road, Spruce Pine, NC 28777, 828-765-2761
HOURS: Open Monday through Saturday from 10:00 A.M. until 4:00 P.M., May 1 through October 31.
LOCATION: Off the Blue Ridge Parkway at milepost 330.9

EVENTS

■ Cherokee Spring Ramp Festival

In the spring, a Cherokee community festival heralds the return of the ramps (*Allium tricoccum*). Imagine garlic combined with onions and made ten times stronger than usual, and you will have some idea of what ramps are. This extremely pungent member of the onion and garlic family grows only at elevations of 3,000 feet or higher, in remote mountain coves. Every spring, as they have for generations, Cherokee families harvest ramps and enjoy them both raw and cooked. This Cherokee tradition was adopted by early Appalachian settlers, and today many surrounding communities also have ramp festivals.

The Cherokee method of harvesting ramps differs from that of other mountain communities. Cherokees continue to practice their traditional

Greens

This is Jellico, mom would say.
Look at its leaves and see how it grows.
Taste it, put it in your mouth.
It's good when it's cooked right.
We need to come and pick a mess.
It's tender right now.

This is Sochan, mom would say.
Look at its leaves and see how it grows.
Taste it, put it in your mouth.
It's good when it's cooked right.
We need to come and pick a mess.
It's tender right now.
It would be good with beanbread and fatback.

These are creases, mom would say.
Look at its leaves and see how it grows.
Taste it, put it in your mouth.
It's good when it's cooked right.
We need to come and pick a mess.
It's tender right now.
I might can some of these, they'll be good this winter.

This is life, mom would say.
Look at its leaves and see how it grows.
Taste it, put it in your mouth.
It's good when it's done right.
We need to come and pick a mess.
It won't be here for long we must enjoy it while we can.

Jody Adams, community member,
Shifting Winds: A Literary and Arts Publication
of Cherokee High School, *1998*

Iva Reed cooking ramps at the Cherokee Ramp Festival. (Photograph by Roger Haile)

method of harvesting, which allows the ramp to grow back from its roots. Rather than pull up the entire plant, they loosen the soil around it, then reach down into the soil with a knife and cut off a quarter-inch or so of the bulb just above the roots, leaving the roots in the soil to grow a new plant. Thus ramps continue to flourish. When pulled up by the roots like onions from the garden, whole stands of ramps disappear.

The ramp festival mainly entails eating ramps prepared in a variety of ways: raw, steamed, and fried. They are usually accompanied by fried potatoes, fried trout, or fried chicken. Many people enjoy them with scrambled eggs. Warning: if you consume ramps, you will smell like them for several days. People on extended car trips take note.

The Ceremonial Grounds are located on US 441 between the Veterans Memorial and the Museum of the Cherokee Indian. In addition to the Cherokee Fall Fair the first week in October and the Ramp Festival in mid-April, the Ceremonial Grounds are used to host events throughout the year, including powwows, Honor the Elders celebrations, and concerts. Prior to removal, every village had ceremonial grounds that were used for dance, ball play, and ceremonies. This site along the Oconaluftee River was tradi-

A scene from Unto These Hills. *(Courtesy of the Cherokee Historical Association)*

tionally used for these activities and is now the official ceremonial grounds for the tribe.

CONTACT: Eastern Band of Cherokee Indians, P.O. Box 455, Cherokee, NC 28719, 828-497-2771

LOCATION: The Ceremonial Grounds, where the Ramp Festival is held in April, are located on US 441 between downtown Cherokee and Drama Road.

■ *Unto These Hills* Outdoor Drama

This moving outdoor drama tells the story of the Eastern Band, their removal from Cherokee country on the Trail of Tears, and how the heroic sacrifice of Tsali enabled them to stay in these mountains. Set in an outdoor amphitheater, the Mountainside Theater, the drama runs from June through August. Directed by Bill Hardy, this production uses local Cherokee people as well as students from UNC–Chapel Hill's drama department. Each year's production adds new elements.

The evening performances before the show feature dance, music, and drama amid the chirping of crickets and the fading light of mountain sunsets. For more than fifty years, this play has captivated audiences. Although some historians disagree with the details of the Tsali story as presented here, the drama remains a powerful retelling of legend, representing the heartbreak of removal and the ideal of putting the good of the many ahead of the good of the individual.

A version of this play was presented as early as the 1930s at the Cherokee Fall Fair. Development of the outdoor theater and the drama in its present form was made possible by the investment of a consortium of business people from nine surrounding mountain counties, which became the Cherokee Historical Association, a nonprofit organization, in 1949. Kermit Hunter, from UNC–Chapel Hill, and John Parris, from the *Asheville Citizen,* collaborated on the first version of the drama.

The Eternal Flame burns at the entrance to the Mountainside Theater. The Cherokees believe that as long as the fire burns, they will survive as a people. This flame, which was originally kept in the old villages of the Cherokee homeland—Kituwha, Tugaloo, and Echota—was carried to Oklahoma on the Trail of Tears, and was brought back here from Oklahoma in 1951. It is still burning.

CONTACT: Margie Douthitt, Marketing Director, Cherokee Historical
Association, P.O. Box 398, Cherokee, NC 28719, 828-497-2111
HOURS: Performed nightly, except Sunday, from mid-June through late
August. Admission, restrooms, concessions, souvenirs.
LOCATION: Tickets can be purchased at the Cherokee Historical
Association Office at US 441 and Drama Road, Cherokee. The
Mountainside Theater is located on Drama Road, off US 441.

■ Cherokee Voices Festival at the Museum of the Cherokee Indian

Many Cherokee elders participate in this festival close to home. Open to the public free of charge, the one-day festival highlights the community's elders and their families as well as younger generations of tradition bearers. Many of the elders have received recognition far beyond the community, like Richard "Geet" Crowe, Cherokee cultural ambassador to the world, and Walker Calhoun, National Endowment for the Arts Heritage Fellowship Award recipient. Several community members have been honored with the North Carolina Folk Heritage Award, like Amanda Swimmer, who demonstrates pottery making with her granddaughters, and Emma Taylor, who demonstrates basket making with her daughter Louise and with her grandson Ed, who tells stories and makes arrowheads. Bud Smith demonstrates woodcarving; he learned from Amanda Crowe, another internation-

The Cherokee Auxiliary Women's Choir, a volunteer group, performs gospel songs and hymns. (© 2000 Steve Wall)

ally recognized Cherokee artist, and considers it his mission to pass on this tradition to another generation—his students at Cherokee High School.

Throughout the day, storytellers old and young entertain with Cherokee tales. Musicians play the traditional flute and others sing Cherokee dance songs. The blending of European and Cherokee traditions can be heard in gospel quartet renditions of old shape note hymns, and in the guitar and banjo music that has become part of Cherokee life. Dancers perform the Beaver Dance, the Bear Dance, and other dances unique to Cherokee tradition, always ending with the Friendship Dance. At noon, "Indian dinners" are available for sale.

CONTACT: Museum of the Cherokee Indian, 589 Tsali Blvd., P.O. Box 1599, Cherokee, NC 28719, 828-497-3481, <www.cherokeemuseum.org>
LOCATION: Intersection of US 441 and Drama Road in the town of Cherokee

■ Mountain Heritage Day

Held the last Saturday in September for more than thirty years, Mountain Heritage Day presents to the public free of charge hundreds of performers and vendors representing Appalachian traditions. Cherokee tradi-

Health and the Land

Downtown Cherokee on a rainy night. (© 2000 Steve Wall)

In the past, I've seen the land put out so much food. And now I look around, we still have this beautiful land, and we're not using it like we did whenever I was growing up. And sometimes I wonder, what is the Creator thinking about us now.

Now we're getting hit by diabetes—our health is going down. If we were still growing our food, what it would be like today? I don't think we would have the problems like we have with diabetes, because whenever we made our gardens, we were active, we worked, we were closer to the land than we are now. And when you get close to the land, when you're working it, you start to think, and your respect for it starts building up because just all of sudden you realize what it's doing for you.

And then we come along and pave the land. Pave it until we can't pave it anymore in some areas, to the point that the grass can't even grow anymore because it's covered up, and the trees are taken out. I think that has a lot to do with changes. And then we wonder, why are the floods coming? The water has no place to go, when the land is paved, and it just goes crazy. So we do it to ourselves when we mistreat the land.

Marie Junaluska

tions have been represented with both crafts demonstrators and performers in the traditional stage area near the Mountain Heritage Center.

CONTACT: Mountain Heritage Center, Western Carolina University, Cullowhee, NC 28723, 828-227-7129
LOCATION: On NC 107, east of Sylva

■ Cherokee Fall Fair at Cherokee Ceremonial Grounds

The Cherokee Fall Fair celebrates Cherokee culture every year during the first full week in October, and has delighted visitors and hometown folks alike since 1914. You can view Cherokee arts and crafts on display, and also purchase handmade items at booths. A parade, music, dance, and stickball games take place throughout the week.

Like other country fairs, this one includes prize-winning pumpkins and the fruits of the summer's labors, but the uniqueness of Cherokee gardens can be seen in heirloom varieties of eleven-kernel Cherokee corn and October beans. Beautifully arranged baskets of hickory nuts, walnuts, and chestnuts collected from the woods evoke the Cherokees' ongoing connection with the natural abundance of the southern Appalachians. Every evening includes music and dancing. Food booths provide Cherokee bean bread and greens as well as fry bread and "Indian tacos."

The fair features several stickball games, played in traditional roughhouse fashion by the men and boys of the community. These are "called" by an announcer like any sports event, and provide a rare opportunity to witness this ancient sport. In 2000, the first women's stickball game since 1870 was played by rough and tumble, skilled women on teams from Big Cove and Wolftown.

Every year's program varies slightly, so call tribal offices for a detailed schedule, usually available in mid-September.

CONTACT: Eastern Band of Cherokee Indians, P.O. Box 455, Cherokee, NC 28719, 828-497-2771
LOCATION: The Ceremonial Grounds are located on US 441 between downtown Cherokee and Drama Road.

The Cherokee Fall Fair highlights distinctive Cherokee traditions.

Cherokee men's stickball game. (Photograph by Roger Haile)

Preparation of traditional chestnut bread. (Photograph by Roger Haile)

Cherokee women's stickball game. (Photograph by Roger Haile)

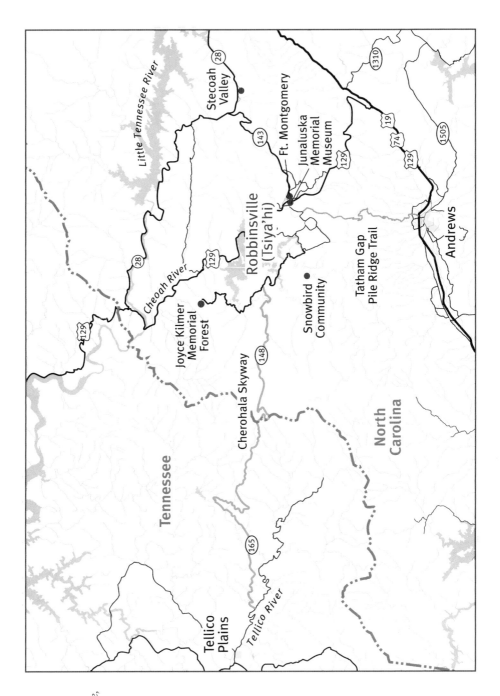

MAP 6
*Cherokee
Heritage
Trails,
Robbinsville,
N.C.*

Fontana

I hear ancient voices rise about the water,
Speaking from a watery grave.
Long forgotten, long gone
And I wonder how many of my ancestors walked these valleys and
*   mountains*
Before they were covered in this great green water.
What lies forgotten and lost forever?
Were there villages, were there babies?
Were there songs, were there towns?
And though the ancient voices speak,
I do not understand.
It is too great.
It is too long forgotten.

Jody Adams, community contributor,
Shifting Winds: A Literary and Arts
Publication of Cherokee High School, *1998*

continues here, as does the ancient mound-building ceremony. Cherokee gospel groups sing songs in nineteenth-century shape-note harmonies in English and Cherokee language. Many people here grow up speaking Cherokee, in a dialect more like the Overhill dialect spoken now in Oklahoma than the Kituhwa dialect spoken among the rest of the Eastern Band.

Within the Eastern Band, the Snowbird community is known for the close-knit ties of its people. The community supports its members, with organizations clustered about 9 miles southwest of Robbinsville, nestled in the lower slopes of the Snowird Mountains. Organizations include four churches, the Snowbird Rescue Squad, Snowbird Health Clinic, Snowbird Volunteer Fire Department, Snowbird Funeral Association, Trail of Tears Singing Organization, Snowbird Library, Snowbird Community Store, a scholarship fund, and the Snowbird Community Development Club, a modern form of the *gadugi,* or work group.

Cherokee villages originally clustered around Sweetwater Creek, now the location of Robbinsville, and around Tallulah Creek, east of Robbinsville. Buffalo Town, located at the mouth of Buffalo Creek, now lies under Santeetlah Lake. Cheoah Town (meaning "Otter" town) stood just down

Robbinsville is surrounded by the Snowbird and Cheoah Mountains.
(Photograph by Roger Haile)

the street from the present-day Junaluska Memorial, near Long Branch Creek, which was formerly known as the Cheoah River. Several towns were located east of present-day Robbinsville on Tallulah Creek. All of these fertile river bottoms lie at an elevation of about 2,000 feet, while around them the Cheoah Mountains, the Snowbird Mountains, the Unicoi Mountains, and the Yellow Creek Mountains rise to more than 5,000 feet. An ancient trading path, the "Twenty-Four Mountains Trail," crossed through this area, from the Overhill Towns at Tallassee to the Valley Towns at Konahete. Between Cheoah and Chilhowee it ascended and descended twenty-four mountains. At the time of removal, about three hundred Cherokee people from here were taken prisoner, kept at Fort Montgomery, and then moved

Jim Bowman and Iva Rattler have led the development of the Junaluska Museum.
(Photograph by Roger Haile)

Gospel singers at the Fading Voices Festival include Iva Rattler, Maybelle Welch,
Alfred Welch, and Mark Brown. (© 2000 Steve Wall)

The Snowbird community emphasizes traditions in an exhibit at the Cherokee Fall Fair. (Photograph by Roger Haile)

across the Tatham Gap Trail to Fort Butler in Murphy before being sent west on the Trail of Tears. Some families hid in the rugged mountains and were able to escape removal. Junaluska, one of the tribe's most prominent citizens, went to Oklahoma on the Trail of Tears and then walked back to Snowbird.

Near Robbinsville, the Tatham Gap Trail can still be walked or driven. A side trip to Joyce Kilmer Memorial Forest shows old growth as it may have looked a thousand years ago. A trip to the Nantahala Gorge reveals another natural wonder, now famous for whitewater recreation. The recently completed Cherohala Skyway, Snowbird community's most scenic drive, links North Carolina and Tennessee along ridge tops with panoramic views.

Cherokee arts and crafts made by members of the Snowbird community are for sale at the Junaluska Museum and at the Fading Voices Festival on Memorial Day weekend, where Cherokee food includes bean bread, hominy, wild greens, herb tea, and other delicacies. Recently Shirley Oswalt and Diamond Brown began operating crafts shops near their homes in Snowbird; information on visiting them can be found through the Junaluska Museum or on the website, <www.cherokeeheritagetrails.org>.

In addition to Cherokee places and events, Graham County offers many thousands of acres for hiking, camping, fishing, horseback riding, mountain biking, and enjoying the outdoors. While the natural surroundings have been obviously altered by humans over the past hundred years, with dams, roads, and timbering, still the unbroken vistas, wilderness streams, and pockets of old-growth forest remain to give one a sense of how this place

Shirley Oswalt selling her crafts.
(Photograph by Murray Lee)

looked during the Cherokees' earlier days here. At Joyce Kilmer Memorial Forest, short loop trails from a parking lot lead through huge poplars and delicate ferns and wildflowers. The Slickrock Wilderness Area includes trout streams and primitive camping. The Great Smoky Mountains National Park covers the northern part of the county. Trails at Tsali Campground have become a mecca for mountain bikers from all over the United States. Lake Fontana and Lake Santeetlah, created by TVA dams, offer boating and bass fishing, while mountain trout streams flow throughout the area. The Appalachian Trail follows mountain crests along the Great Smokies.

Routes into and out of Graham County offer scenic opportunities in every direction. From the direction of Cherokee, traveling first on US 129 and then on NC 143, the road passes through Stecoah Valley, once a Cherokee community, then crosses the Cheoah Mountains through Stecoah Gap at 3,156 feet, where wave after wave of mountains recede into the distance. The Cherohala Skyway, a scenic two-lane road along mountain crests and high meadows, links Robbinsville with Tellico Plains, Tennessee. US 129 has become a favorite route of motorcyclists, as it winds along the Cheoah River into Tennessee. And the Tatham Gap Road, a gravel road maintained by the U.S. Forest Service, traces the route taken during the Trail of Tears emigration directly up and over the Snowbird Mountains into the Valley River valley.

*A Cherokee stickball game
at the Fading Voices Festival.
(Photograph by Murray Lee)*

Several events provide opportunities for the public to interact with the Snowbird community. First the Fading Voices Festival on Memorial Day weekend invites visitors to join community members along the banks of Little Snowbird Creek for singing, storytelling, a stickball game, and demonstrations of carving, basket making, bead work, and other traditions. Later in the summer, "singings" provide gospel music in English and Cherokee in an informal atmosphere. In November of each year, a wreath-laying ceremony takes place at the Junaluska Memorial.

SITES IN ROBBINSVILLE

■ Junaluska Memorial and Museum

The Junaluska Memorial and Museum honor this Cherokee leader who was held in high esteem by both Cherokees and whites. Seven large granite markers erected around his grave tell the story of his life, 1776–1858, which was shaped by the events of the turbulent period leading up to and following removal. The Junaluska Museum, located just downhill from the memorial, provides further information about his life. On exhibit there are

Seven granite markers tell the story of Junaluska at the Junaluska Memorial. (© 2000 Steve Wall)

artifacts from the Cheoah Valley that date back more than six thousand years. Community members, especially Iva Rattler and Jim Bowman, who helped to create the museum and who often volunteer here, can provide additional information on Junaluska and the Snowbird Cherokees. Baskets, beadwork, silversmithing, and other crafts made by Cherokee people are sold here. Recently, the museum created a "Medicine Plants" walking trail that loops around the hill below the gravesite, and the Friends of Junaluska are planning to expand their programming.

Born in 1776 in the village of Echoe, near present-day Dillard, Georgia, Junaluska and his family kept moving as the borders of the Cherokee territory kept shrinking—first to land on the Cullasaja River and then near the Valley Towns. In 1811, Cherokee oral tradition records that he met with Tecumseh at Soco Gap and declined, for the Cherokees, Tecumseh's offer to join him in uniting with other tribes to defeat the whites.

In 1812 Junaluska and hundreds of other Cherokees fought with the Americans against the Creeks, playing a decisive role in winning the Battle of Horseshoe Bend for Andrew Jackson. During the battle, Junaluska saved Andrew Jackson's life by killing a Creek warrior who was attacking Jackson. Later, when Jackson advocated the removal of the Cherokees and was elected president, Junaluska traveled to Washington, D.C., to see him and

The Medicine Trail at the Junaluska Museum features plants used in traditional Cherokee healing practices. (Photographs by Roger Haile)

to present the Cherokee position on removal, but Jackson would not see him.

In 1838, Junaluska lived near Andrews and was captured during a trip to Calhoun. He went to Indian Territory on the Trail of Tears. He and his brother Wachacha led a party attempting to escape on the trail, and Wachacha successfully got away with about twenty-five Cherokees. Junaluska went on to Oklahoma, but shortly thereafter he came back to his home in the Cheoah Valley. Cherokee oral tradition maintains that Junaluska said: "If I had known what Andrew Jackson would do to the Cherokees, I would have killed him myself that day at Horseshoe Bend."

In 1846, with the Eastern Cherokees in legal limbo, the North Carolina legislature voted to give Junaluska 337 acres and $100 cash in recognition of his status as war hero. Throughout the mountains, many places and organizations are named for him, like Lake Junaluska, a Methodist retreat, and Junaluskee Masonic Lodge of Franklin, formed in 1851 and named for the war hero when Junaluska was still alive.

Junaluska's grave and that of his wife, Nicie, lie on a hillside just one-half mile from downtown Robbinsville. A monument was placed there by the Winston-Salem chapter of the Daughters of the American Revolution and dedicated in 1910. Beginning in the 1980s, the Friends of Junaluska organized in order to preserve the site. They created new monuments and added landscaping before they rededicated the site in 1990.

Junaluska

Junaluska's contemporaries described him as tall and dignified, and say that he was a good speaker. His name comes from the Cherokee language tsunalahvski, "He tried and failed," because he boasted that he would go and kill all the Creeks, and when he returned, having obviously failed, this was the name he took. A courageous warrior and natural leader, Junaluska had three wives, having been widowed twice, and his descendants still live among the Eastern Band today.

A monument was erected at his gravesite by the Daughters of the American Revolution. Their dedication program on November 5, 1910, included music by the Murphy Brass Band, prayers, and remarks by the pastor of the Robbinsville Church, by the "Patriotic Orders of Juniors and Odd Fellows," by the superintendent of education for Graham County, and by those who had known Junaluska personally: Reverend Armstrong Cornsilk, Reverend Joseph Wiggins, Captain N. G. Phillips, and Dow Hooper. The Cherokee people present sang "Blessed Home" in the Cherokee language. After further remarks by J. N. Moody and by C. B. Walker, two Cherokee girls—Maggie Axe and Ellie Jackson—unveiled the monument. Prayers, thanks, and music closed the ceremony.

The remarks of Reverend Armstrong Cornsilk were delivered in Cherokee language and translated into English by Lewis Smith. They were taken down by one of those present:

> Ladies and gentlemen, friends: We have met here at Junaluska's grave. We have met as friends and brothers and sisters. We are refreshing our memories over Juno's burial.
>
> We appreciate his going to war, and gaining the big victory for Jackson. The Cherokees and whites were fighting the Creeks at that time. And we Cherokees feel that it was through him we have the privilege of being here today.
>
> I knew Juno at that time. I knew him well. I recollect how he looked. He wore the hair cut off the back of his head, and he would plait the hair on top of his head so as to make it stick up like horns.
>
> He was a good man. He was a good friend. He was a good friend in his home and everywhere. He would ask the hungry man to eat. He would ask the cold one to warm by his fire. He would ask the tired one to rest, and he would give a good place to sleep. Juno's home was a good home for others.

Junaluska gravesite dedication ceremony. (Courtesy of the Junaluska Museum)

He was a smart man. He made his mind think good. He was very brave. He was not afraid.

Juno at this time has been dead about fifty years. I am glad he is up above [pointing upward]. I am glad we have this beautiful monument. It shows Junaluska did good, and it shows we all appreciate him together—having a pleasant time together.

I hope we shall all meet Junaluska in heaven [pointing upward] and all be happy there together.

CONTACT: Junaluska Memorial and Museum, P.O. Box 1547, Robbinsville, NC 28771, 828-479-4727, <cheoah@junaluska.com>, <www.junaluska.com>

HOURS: Open Monday through Saturday from 9:00 A.M. until 4:00 P.M.

LOCATION: One-half mile from the courthouse on Main Street of Robbinsville. Located on the left as you are leaving town going north on Main Street heading toward US 129 north. On the street, a pullout provides room for several cars. For visitors who cannot climb the hill, cars and vans can carefully wind their way to the gravesite and park there. Parking for several cars is available at the museum, partway up the hill. Buses can park fifty yards or so down the street in the church parking lot.

SITES NEAR ROBBINSVILLE

■ Tatham Gap Trail

On June 21, 1838, North Carolina troops escorted three hundred Cherokee prisoners from Fort Montgomery (now Robbinsville) across the Snowbird Mountains on the first leg of their thousand-mile trek to Oklahoma. They crossed the Snowbirds on the military road built on the long-familiar Cherokee trail between the Cheoah community and the Valley Towns (from present-day Robbinsville to Andrews). One can walk or drive along this route, today, finding in some places the wagon ruts made by the U.S. Army as they began the forced removal of the Cherokees on the Trail of Tears.

The Tatham Gap/Rockpile Trail was significant in Cherokee history even before the events of removal, and it figures in legends and oral history. Like other ancient trails made by game and by early people, it could be thousands of years old. It takes a direct route from the watershed of the Valley River (in Cherokee, Gunahita, meaning "long") into the valley and watershed of the Cheoah River. Both of these river valleys stand at about 2,000 feet elevation, but the surrounding peaks rise above 5,000 feet. The trail makes its way through the 3,500-foot-high gap, a relatively easy way between the two valleys, and one that avoids traveling through the Nantahala Gorge. (On the northern side of the valley, Stecoah Gap, on NC 143, provides similar access into the Cheoah River valley.)

The trail can be retraced along the modern Tatham Gap Road. In some places the present-day road parallels the older road, where wagon ruts from the time of the Trail of Tears can be seen. The entire 10 miles between Robbinsville and Andrews can be driven in a car (four wheel drive is not required), but 7.5 miles of this is a one-lane gravel road with turnouts for cars to pass each other. Much of this road (US 423) passes through the Nantahala National Forest and is maintained by the U.S. Forest Service. At the gap, a side road leads to a lookout tower.

The trail gets its original Cherokee name, Rockpile Trail, from a number of stone cairns on the southern side of the ridge. The piles are leveled now, but thirty years ago the stones were still heaped up into pyramids, to which every Cherokee who passed added a stone. According to oral history collected by James Mooney in the 1880s, these "piles marked the graves of a number of Cherokee women and children of the tribe who were sur-

Removal of the Cheoah Cherokees, June 1838

When Colonel James Gray Bynum and three companies of North Carolina volunteers took their post at Fort Montgomery (on Fort Hill in present-day Robbinsville) on June 1, 1838, they found the fort unfinished and the recently constructed military road so rough that it hampered procurement of rations and equipment. While making preparations for the forced removal, Bynum acquainted himself with his future prisoners and became sympathetic with their plight. The commander was impressed by the Cherokees' Christianity, orderliness, and pacific attitude: "A more religious people than inhabits this [Cheoah] valley cannot be found anywhere. No civilized community with which I am acquainted is as observant of religious service and ceremonies. Their religious meetings are characterized by the greatest decorum and propriety of conduct and apparently from religious feelings. Their preachers speak of the prospect of their speedy removal and the subject never fails to throw the congregation into tears."

Bynum requested special exemptions to allow the Cherokees to remain in the Cheoah Valley, but this request was denied, and the North Carolina militia began arresting the Cherokees of Cheoah, Tallula, Connichiloe, Buffalo Town, and Stecoa on June 12, 1838. Bynum and his troops attempted to conduct the removal as humanely as possible, and requested a delay in order to allow an epidemic of whooping cough to abate before moving the Cherokee prisoners:

> Those whom I have enrolled seem well contented & those whom I have let out as runners, I have seen since they come & reported themselves according to promise. A great deal of sickness is prevailing among the children of the Indians. I permit the females to remain at home with their sick children & the Indians physicians to attend them. . . .
>
> I am very desirous that you would allow me until Wednesday or Thursday next to start my prisoners from this post. I have to inform you also that almost every child & many grown persons in this valley are sick with the whooping cough & that a large number of deaths having taken place since they run to the mountains amongst those families who have returned. There are many now taken who cannot be removed without very great danger—without almost certain death.

> *The request for delay was granted, and Bynum waited another week*
> *before moving his prisoners to division headquarters at Fort Butler*
> *(Murphy, N.C.), where they were to stay in stockades for three months*
> *until their removal in September 1838.*

prised and killed on the spot by a raiding party of the Iroquois shortly be-fore the final peace between the two nations (ca. 1767). As soon as the news was brought to the settlements on Hiwassee and Cheoah, a party was made under Taletanigiski, 'Hemp-carrier,' to follow and take vengeance on the enemy. Among others of the party was the father of the noted chief Tsunulahunski, Junaluska." The stone piles or cairns to which this tradi-tional story refers were located on Pile Ridge between Pile Creek and Brit-ton Creek, an area traversed by the Tatham Gap Road and an ancient trail that ascends the crest of Pile Ridge, runs along the crest of the Snowbird Mountains, then descends the Long Creek Valley to Robbinsville.

CONTACT: U.S. Forest Service, Cheoah Ranger District, 1133 Massey
   Branch Rd., Robbinsville, NC 28771, 828-479-6431
LOCATION: From the Graham County Courthouse in downtown
   Robbinsville, drive south on Main Street, past the Junaluska Memorial
   and Museum (the street becomes SR 1110). Go past Milltown, and turn
   left onto Long Creek Road, which proceeds up the Long Creek Valley.
   At the U.S. Forest Service boundary, the road becomes USFS Road 423
   and continues to Tatham Gap.
      From Main Street in Andrews, turn onto Robbinsville Road, opposite
   Valleytown Motel. Drive 0.6 mile to Stewart Road. Turn right onto
   Stewart, and then turn left onto NC 423. Drive 0.4 mile, turn right onto
   Tatham Gap Road, a gravel road marked by a sign. After about 7.5
   miles, Tatham Gap Road becomes Long Creek Road, a paved road that
   continues on 2.5 miles into Robbinsville.
      The old military road extends from the foot of Pile Ridge,
   immediately north of Andrews, across the Snowbird Mountains to
   Robbinsville. The trace is paralleled and intersected by the Tatham Gap
   Road (USFS Road 423), which can be accessed from US 19/74 via
   SR 1391 north of Andrews.
      Gravel pullouts on Tatham Gap Road at Tatham Gap will
   accommodate three to four vehicles. Tour buses and motor homes

We're Still Here

I have so much to be thankful for today. My husband and I have two beautiful girls. And now we have two beautiful grandsons. And my mother, she's the reason I know my culture. And my dad, they just taught me things that I know today, and I'm using today.

So I have really a lot to be thankful for. Also for this tribe, the Cherokee tribe. I'm a member of that, and we have overcome a lot. We were a bigger nation at one time. The Removal took a lot of us out, but we still survived. Our history survived. Our culture survived. Our language survived. We're still here. And I want to see it all be here two hundred years down the road.

And getting back to the land: I want this land to be here for our children that are coming up now. And I want it to be a clean land. I want that water to be there, too, I want it to be clean. So that's why we need to be careful how we treat it today, to respect it more.

Marie Junaluska

should *not* attempt to travel Tatham Gap Road, because a full-sized bus cannot negotiate some of the turns.

SIDE TRIPS

■ Joyce Kilmer Memorial Forest

The giant, old trees here in Joyce Kilmer Memorial Forest stand more than a hundred feet high and twenty feet around—testaments to the loveliness of trees as they once existed in the old-growth forests. Giant tulip poplars and hemlocks create cathedrals of shade in which understory trees and wildflowers thrive. A two-mile loop trail extends from the parking lot for an easy hike through this grove. This special memorial park bears the name of British poet, soldier, and journalist Joyce Kilmer (1886–1918) in tribute to his poem "Trees." Although he never visited the southern Appalachians, his lines could have been penned about these giants: "I think that I shall never see / A poem lovely as a tree." Pockets of old growth in the southern Appalachians remain rare because virtually all of these moun-

Old-growth poplars dwarf a visitor to Joyce Kilmer Memorial Forest.
(Photograph by Roger Haile)

tains were logged—in many places clear-cut—from the 1880s through the 1930s. While this industry created fortunes for lumber companies and employment for local men, it left a landscape that looked as bleak as the surface of the moon. Photographs from the 1930s show Civilian Conservation Corps workers planting tree seedlings in a desolate, barren, wasteland that stretches over ridge after ridge as far as the eye can see. Only a few isolated stands of timber escaped.

Although their stewardship was not apparent to those of European descent, the Cherokees had managed forests throughout their territory for centuries with a variety of practices. In autumn they burned off fallen

leaves to eliminate underbrush and insects, and to aid in gathering chestnuts; this also minimized the effect of forest fires. Cherokee house construction required young saplings and cooking fires required firewood, leading
to the clearing out of young growth around village areas; this along with
the setting of intentional fires created forest with open understory in many
places. Around villages the people created stands of desirable trees at the
forest edge, such as hickory, walnut, and persimmon. In harvesting woodland plants and trees for food, medicine, and crafts, Cherokee people ob-
served traditions rooted in a sense of the sacredness of life and respect for
all life—traditions that encouraged regeneration and sustainability. These
included, for example, taking only the fourth plant of the species being collected, taking bark only from one side of a tree (in a prescribed direction),
and cutting ramps above their roots rather than pulling the whole plant.

While we may never know for certain how forests looked five hundred
years ago, the remaining pockets of old growth, such as the groves at Joyce
Kilmer Memorial Forest, may provide the closest resemblance. Accounts
from the eighteenth century describe forests with large trees in open park-
like woodland, with spaces large enough to drive wagons through. This
thirty-eight-hundred-acre tract of virgin hardwood forest was set aside as
the Joyce Kilmer–Slickrock Wilderness in 1936, and it adjoins the Citico
Creek Wilderness Area in Tennessee.

Trails take visitors deep into the Joyce Kilmer–Slickrock Wilderness Area
for hiking, primitive camping, and fishing. Be aware that wilderness areas
such as this have no trail signs, no restrooms, no water spigots, and no
campgrounds.

CONTACT: U.S. Forest Service, Cheoah Ranger District, 1133 Massey
   Branch Rd., Robbinsville, NC 28771, 828-479-6431
LOCATION: Joyce Kilmer Memorial Forest is located about 15 miles from
   Robbinsville in the western part of Graham County. From Robbinsville,
   take US 129 North for 1.5 miles to its junction with NC 143 West (Massey
   Branch Road). Turn left and proceed west on NC 143 for approximately
   5 miles to a stop sign. Turn right onto Kilmer Road. You will drive for
   about 7.3 miles and arrive at the top of Santeetlah Gap and the
   junction with the Cherohala Skyway. Bear to your right and continue
   on for another 2.5 miles to the entrance of the Joyce Kilmer Memorial
   Forest. Turn left into the entrance and it is about 0.5 mile to the
   parking area. There are picnic tables and restrooms available.

■ Stecoah Valley Center

The Stecoah Valley Arts, Crafts, and Educational Center is located in the small town of Stecoah on the northern side of Graham County. If you are traveling to Robbinsville from Cherokee and Bryson City, Stecoah is on NC 129 shortly after turning right off of the main four-lane road.

Located along Stecoah Creek, below Meetinghouse Mountain and Deep Gap Mountain, this old Cherokee town site is separated from Robbinsville and the Snowbird valley by the Cheoah Mountain Range, which the road crosses at Stecoah Gap. The name "Stecoah" (Usti-go-hi, or "little place") identifies several Cherokee villages in the original homeland.

In a refurbished rock school constructed by the Civilian Conservation Corps in the 1930s, the Stecoah Valley Center primarily focuses on white Appalachian culture: bluegrass and old-time music, weaving, bee-keeping, and other crafts. Because of its location near the home site of Tsali and the old village of Stecoah, however, it also includes interpretive information about Tsali, the Trail of Tears, and the Cherokee presence in this valley.

CONTACT: Lynn Shields, Executive Director, Stecoah Valley Arts, Crafts, and Educational Center, Inc., 121 Schoolhouse Rd., Robbinsville, NC 28771, 828-479-3364, <www.visitSVCenter.com>, <info@visitSVCenter.com>
HOURS: Open Monday through Friday from 9:30 A.M. until 5:30 P.M. For special events, call or visit the website for updated information.
LOCATION: On NC 28 North between Bryson City and Fontana Village

■ Nantahala Gorge

This narrow gorge, with steep sides and violently rushing waters, is known as the haunt of monsters in Cherokee lore: Spearfinger, the giant inchworm, and the Uk'tena. An old stone wall high on the slope of the gorge was said to be the form of the monster snake, Uk'tena, after it had been turned to stone. Spearfinger, Utlvta, the liver-eating ogress who had powers over stone, was said to frequent this place. The Uwtsvta, or giant bouncing snake, lived here. It moved like an inchworm with only part of its body on the ground at a time, and was so large that when it stretched across the gorge it blocked out the sun. All of these legendary terrors are cited as the reason Cherokee people avoided the narrow part of the gorge.

But Cherokee people did live at Briartown, Kanugayv-yi, and also, just prior to removal, at Chinleanahtli, the village of Tsali and his former neigh-

Whitewater on the Nantahala River. (Photograph by Roger Haile)

bor and final pursuer, Euchella. Both had moved from Cowee when it was taken in the Treaties of 1817 and 1819.

The old Cherokee village of Chinleanahtli was located a few miles down the railroad tracks from the present-day Nantahala Outdoor Center (toward Almond). According to Jerry Wolfe, the word Nantahala comes from the Cherokee *nvda ayeli,* meaning "sun in the center." Though "Nantahala" is often translated as "Land of the Noonday Sun," Wolfe says the name actually refers to the fact that in the Nantahala Gorge, the sun appears to rise and set in the same place year-round—not moving north and south with the seasons. During removal, hundreds of Cherokees hid in the rhododendron thickets lining the gorge, frustrating soldiers who struggled through the rhododendron to the location of rising smoke, only to find that the Indians had eluded them by slipping through the entangled growth and rugged terrain.

Today the Nantahala Gorge is known internationally for its whitewater rafting and recreation. The Great Smoky Mountains Railway line runs through the gorge.

CONTACT: Nantahala Gorge is managed by the U.S. Forest Service.
Contact the U.S. Forest Service, Wayah Ranger District, 90 Sloane Rd., Franklin, NC 28734, 828-524-6441.

LOCATION: The gorge is located along US 19/74 between Bryson City and Andrews.

SCENIC DRIVE

■ Cherohala Skyway

In 1965, a wagon train made up of horseback riders and wagons pulled by horses and by mules traveled across part of this route to dramatize the need for a connecting road between Andrews, North Carolina, and east Tennessee. This scenic highway, completed after thirty years at a cost of more than $100 million, now connects Robbinsville, North Carolina, with Tellico Plains, Tennessee.

Beginning outside of Robbinsville, near the Snowbird community, the 40-mile-long, two-lane road immediately ascends to the mountain ridges and follows them along its whole route, providing miles of panoramic vistas. It passes high mountain meadows covered with rhododendron as it winds gently across the crest of the Great Smoky Mountains. Its highest overlook, Santeetlah, sits at more than a mile high (5,390 feet). Following an ancient trading route in places, the Cherohala Skyway passes rivers, creeks, a lake, and a waterfall as well as a black bear preserve. Many of the overlooks include picnic tables, restrooms, and short hiking trails. Its name does not come from Cherokee language, but rather a combination of "Cherokee" and "Nantahala"—the two national forest areas through which the road passes. Allow one-and-a-half to two hours driving time and, if traveling in winter, be aware that weather may be more severe at these elevations.

At the entrance of the highway from Graham County, a bulletin board at Santeetlah Gap (elevation 2,660 feet) provides information about the route. The Skyway proceeds to climb, with overlooks at Hooper Cove, Shute Cove, Obadiah, Wright Cove, Spirit Ridge, and Huckleberry. At the Hooper Bald Trailhead, one finds an information board, picnic tables, restrooms, and a quarter-mile hike leading to Hooper Bald itself. From there, overlooks at Santeetlah, Big Junction, Haw Knob Slopes, Whigg Cove, and the Mud Gap Trailhead lead on to Stratton Ridge. Here again are restrooms, picnic tables, and a bulletin board. Not far from here lie Stratton Meadows, which was used as a campground more than six thousand years ago. A rock with mysterious carvings may indicate that one of the early Spanish expeditions passed nearby as well. The Unicoi Crest provides picnic tables and

Emmeline Cucumber and Lucy Riley participated in the dedication of the Cherohala Skyway, singing hymns in the Cherokee language. (© 2000 Steve Wall)

photo opportunities just before the highway crosses the state line at Beech Gap (elevation 4,490 feet).

Once in Tennessee, the Skyway enters the watershed of the Tellico River, famous for its trout fishing. Overlooks include East Rattlesnake Rock, West Rattlesnake Rock Trailhead, Brushy Ridge, Grassy Gap Trailhead, Eagle Gap Trailhead, and Lake View, where Tellico Lake can be seen in the distance. At Turkey Creek, the overlook provides restrooms and picnic tables with a view of Tellico Plains. The next stop on the Skyway is Indian Boundary Campground, on USFS Road 345, with a hundred campsites available April through September. The campground also can be used by visitors for picnicking, hiking, fishing, biking, and swimming.

Back on the Skyway and past Caney Branch Overlook, USFS Road 210 leads to a view of Bald River Falls. The Oosterneck Creek Overlook includes a boat takeout on the Tellico River, used by canoeists and kayakers. Two stops on the Tellico River lead to the Information Station at the Tennessee terminus of the Skyway.

Every summer since 1965, the wagon train has traveled gravel roads and two-lane highways, camped in meadows, and concluded its trip by joining with the Fourth of July parade in one of the mountain towns—Andrews, Murphy, or Franklin. Although they are still traveling back roads, their highway now reaches the sky.

View from the Cherohala Skyway.
(Courtesy of the Tennessee Overhill Heritage Association)

CONTACT: In North Carolina, contact Nantahala National Forest, Cheoah
  Ranger District, 1133 Massey Branch Rd., Robbinsville, NC 28771, 828-
  479-6431; or the Sheriff's Department, Graham County, NC,
  828-479-3352.

  In Tennessee, contact Cherokee National Forest, Ranger Station, 250
  Tellico Ranger Station Rd., Tellico Plains, TN 37385, 423-253-2520; or
  the Sheriff's Department, Monroe County, TN, 423-442-3911.
LOCATION: From Robbinsville take US 129 North for 1 mile. Turn left onto
  NC 143 West and follow signs for 10 miles. Proceed onto the Skyway.

■ Fading Voices Festival

Once a year, on the Saturday of Memorial Day weekend, the Chero-kee people of the Snowbird community invite the public to join with them in a mound-building ceremony, demonstrations of arts and crafts, perfor-mances of music and storytelling, and Cherokee food. This festival presents the authentic traditions of Cherokee people in a beautiful natural setting and noncommercial atmosphere. Instead of the crowds, dances, and hub-bub of a powwow, one finds a warm welcome from Snowbird commu-nity members along the banks of Little Snowbird Creek, whose mists cool the air.

Begun in 1986, the Fading Voices "Annual Demonstration Day" continues to be a celebration of Cherokee culture both for the Snowbird community and for visitors. In the spring of 2000, its program featured the mound building ceremony, Cherokee hymn singing, storytelling, blowgun demon-stration, fish game, stickball game, and traditional dancing. Crafts demon-strations were set up in the shade along the length of Little Snowbird Creek, and these included shingle making, coffin building, wood carving, basket making, beadwork, Cherokee language, soap making, quilting, bean bread making, hominy making (from heirloom variety Cherokee corn cooked with wood ashes in a black iron pot on an open fire), corn pounding, but-ter churning, fry bread making, and bean bread preparation. Handmade crafts, festival t-shirts, Cherokee music tapes, and traditional Cherokee meals were available for sale. Following the festival, the Snowbird Volun-teer Fire Department held a fish-fry (with trout from Snowbird Creek) to raise money for their operation.

CONTACT: Junaluska Museum, P.O. Box 1547, Robbinsville, NC 28771, 828-479-4727, <www.junaluska.com>, <cheoah@junaluska.com>; U.S. Forest Service, Cheoah Ranger District, 1133 Massey Branch Rd., Robbinsville, NC 28771, 828-479-6431

LOCATION: From the traffic light in Robbinsville, proceed north on US 129 for approximately 1 mile. Turn left onto NC 143 going west, following the signs to the Cherohala Skyway. Just before the Cherohala Skyway begins, turn left onto Snowbird Road and follow straight for several miles to the Little Snowbird Baptist Church (on the left) and the festival grounds will be on the right.

The Mound-Building Ceremony

The mound-building ceremony opens the Fading Voices Festival in the Snowbird community each year. In 2000, the crowd sat under a large poplar tree, facing east toward Jim Bowman and the fire, with Little Snowbird Creek on their left. About ten Cherokee people—men, women, and children—stood in a circle around the fire, each carrying a turtle shell filled with dirt. Some were wearing traditional ribbon shirts and tear dresses, and others were in jeans or shorts.

> *I want to welcome you to the Fading Voices Demonstration Day. We are going to demonstrate the mound-building ceremony for you. In the old days, when Cherokee people gathered to discuss a problem or come to a decision, they did this ceremony. It signified a gathering place. Every person brought dirt from their home to add to the mound, and that meant they were coming together as a people. They would circle the fire, and at a certain time, would add their earth.*
>
> *The fire is built with seven kinds of wood, and you can see that we have laid four sticks around it, for the sacred four directions.*
>
> *When we begin, we will begin with tribal members, members of the Eastern Band. They will circle the fire seven times, and then we will invite all of you who wish to, to join with us. We will begin with prayer.*

An elder prayed in Cherokee language, and then Alfred Welch began singing in Cherokee, accompanying himself with a rattle, and circling

■ Trail of Tears Singing, Brush Arbor Singing

During the month of July, Cherokee gospel groups in the Snowbird community host a series of "singings" at which the public is welcome. The Trail of Tears Singing lasts for three days, bringing together Cherokee and white gospel groups from Oklahoma and the Southeast. These informal but heartfelt events are usually held outdoors. Participants stay in local motels or camp nearby.

The Cherokee tradition of gospel singing dates back two hundred years, when Moravian missionaries found that Cherokee children easily learned hymn tunes and showed considerable musical ability. Some of the first pub-

The mound-building ceremony opens the annual Fading Voices Festival in the Snowbird Community near Robbinsville. (Photograph by Murray Lee)

the fire counterclockwise as his wife Maybelle and the others followed him. The wind began to blow.

As they circled the fire, they added earth from their turtle shells while Alfred sang quietly, in a minor key: "Sti ske li ski, Sti ske li ski, Sti ske li ski, Sti ske li." People moved slowly and respectfully. After they circled seven times, Bowman invited others to join, and people from the crowd joined the circle, some of them also carrying turtle shells with earth.

lications of the New Echota Press were hymnbooks in the Sequoyah syllabary, about 1829. Over the centuries, Cherokee gospel singing has evolved into a tradition of its own, influenced by the shape-note traditions of the nineteenth century as well as country music and bluegrass traditions in the twentieth century.

Today, Cherokee quartets perform old hymns in four-part harmony, usually accompanied by guitar and bass. Some quartets like the Snowbird Boys feature all-male voices, while others like the Alfred Welch Family combine men's and women's voices. Often songs are sung in Cherokee language and in English. Some of these hymns are unique in Cherokee tradition, like the "Trail of Tears song," a translation of "Guide Me Thou O Great Jehovah"

Mound-building ceremony. (Photograph by Murray Lee)

Emma Garrett and her baskets delight a visitor. (Photograph by Murray Lee)

Blowgun demonstration. (Photograph by Murray Lee)

sung to a tune in a minor key. Others are gospel favorites common in the southern tradition.

The Trail of Tears Singing, the Brush Arbor Singing, and the Smoker Singing take place in July and August in the Snowbird community. For more information on exact dates and locations, check the Cherokee Heritage Trails website at <www.cherokeeheritagetrails.org>.

CONTACT: Junaluska Museum, P.O. Box 1547, Robbinsville NC 28771,
828-479-4727, <www.junaluska.com>, <cheoah@junaluska.com>
LOCATION: From the traffic light in Robbinsville, proceed north on US 129 for approximately 1 mile. Turn left onto NC 143 going west, following the signs to the Cherohala Skyway. Just before the Skyway begins, turn left onto Snowbird Road and follow straight for several miles to the Snowbird community.

■ Annual Wreath Laying at Junaluska Memorial

Commemorating the life of Junaluska, this ceremony takes place at the gravesite every November. Contact the Junaluska Museum or check on the Cherokee Heritage Trails website for the exact date every year. The public is welcome.

CONTACT: Junaluska Memorial and Museum, P.O. Box 1547, Robbinsville, NC 28771, 828-479-4727, <cheoah@junaluska.com>, <www.junaluska.com>

LOCATION: In downtown Robbinsville on NC 143 Business (Junaluska Dr.), approximately one hundred yards from the Graham County Courthouse

The Middle Towns
Franklin, North Carolina

3

My family has always grown corn, ever since I was little. They used corn for skinned corn—hominy, for cornmeal, bean bread, popcorn for wintertime by the fire. We'd listen to the stories and pop some corn. It's just an important staple to the tribe, and to my family when I was growing up. It was always there. It was always grown.

There was a special kind of corn for making hominy—Mama called it the traditional kind, or the native kind, "the corn that's always been there." She'll plant the garden or the cornfield, and then she'll save so many for seed for the next year. She's done that for as long as I can remember. Whenever you start cooking that corn, it's small, but as it cooks it gets bigger. That's the hominy. They call it "flour corn," or in Cherokee, *selu-ya*.

Then there's *sanahi,* flint corn. They use it mainly for feed for the animals. Then of course there's the Silver Queen that you can buy at the hardware store, the hybrid corn. Then there's the Indian corn with multicolored kernels, but my family didn't grow that. As far as I know the Cherokees have never eaten that—it's just for decoration.

We also have traditional beans—the butter beans that our people have had handed down the years. They're huge, flat, multi-colored: purplish black, dark red, black, speckled with white. They're beautiful beans, and they're used also to mix in with our bean bread. They're called *tuyanegwa,* big beans.

—Marie Junaluska

The Cherokee Middle Towns stretched along the Little Tennessee River (Tanasi) and its tributaries from its headwaters to its passage through the Smokies—towns every few miles, surrounded by fields and connected by trails and by the river. Today one can explore the world of the Middle Towns by driving scenic highways, or by using some of the same means of travel used by the Cherokees a thousand years ago—walking the banks of the Little Tennessee River or canoeing on it. The interpretive hub for the area of the original Cherokee Middle Towns can be found at the Scottish Tartans Museum on Main Street in Franklin. The Scottish Tartans Museum

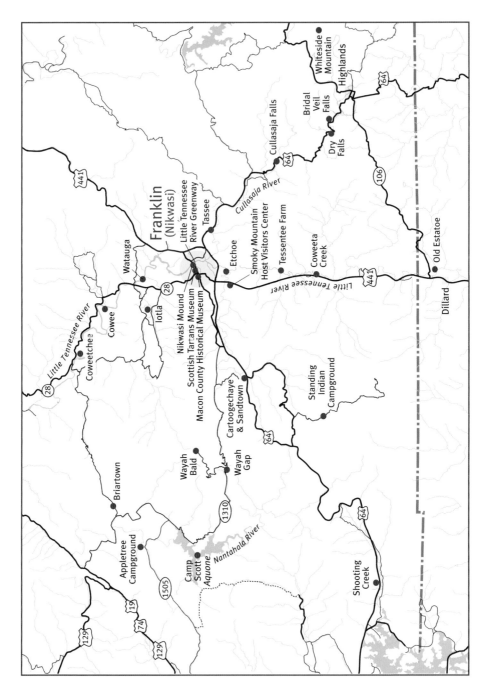

MAP 7
Cherokee
Heritage
Trails,
Franklin,
N.C.

Marie Junaluska.
(Courtesy of Marie Junaluska)

also tells the story of the relationship between the Cherokees and early Scots traders and Scots-Irish settlers.

The spiritual center for this area lies at the Nikwasi Mound, near the Little Tennessee River, now downtown Franklin. This mound still stands at something near its original height, unlike most other mounds in Cherokee country. This mound once supported a townhouse in which the sacred fire burned constantly. It stood at the center of the "mother town" of Nikwasi, which was also a "white" town (meaning a peace town).

For centuries, perhaps millennia, Cherokee towns and people flourished along the Little Tennessee River and its tributaries here where fertile bottomlands spread out into valleys more spacious than anywhere else in the mountains this side of the Blue Ridge. Even today, Cherokee people call Franklin gadu:niha, "Where they have the soil for growing things," or literally translated, "Bread Town." Mountains reaching more than 5,000 feet encircle this fertile valley like the petals of a blue granite rose: the Nantahalas to the west, the Cowee Mountains to the north, and the Blue Ridge to the east.

Here rubies, sapphires, quartz, and mica also enrich the soil. People traded mica from here as far north as the Ohio River as early as A.D. 250. People lived in present-day Macon County as early as eleven thousand years ago, leaving fluted Clovis spear points near springs on Wayah Bald

Little Tennessee River Valley from Winding Stairs Gap. (Photograph by Barbara Duncan)

and camping ten thousand years ago at what is now Appletree Campground. The Little Tennessee River still holds all the aquatic species that were present a thousand years ago—like a library for rivers, still stocked with all its original volumes. In a few places, old sites of settlements on the river's banks may be eight thousand years old. Today about a hundred

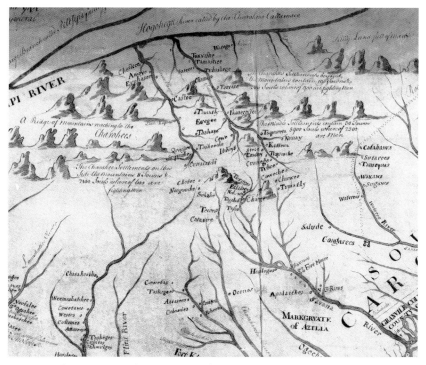

A portion of "A New Map of His Majesty's Flourishing Province in South Carolina,"
by George Herbert, 1725, illustrating the Cherokee country. (Courtesy of the Hargrett
Rare Book and Manuscript Library, University of Georgia)

Cherokee people live and work in Macon County, although there is no tribal
land here.

Along the Tanasi, the feeder creeks and rivers still bear their Cherokee
names—Cartoogechaye, Watauga, Ellijay, Cullasaja, Coweeta, Iotla, Tessentee, Cowee. In 1720, fifteen Cherokee towns stood along the Little Tennessee from its headwaters (now Dillard, Georgia) to its confluence with the
Nantahala and Tuckaseegee Rivers, a distance of about 60 miles. Most were
on the west bank, often where a creek entered the river.

These villages, the "Middle Towns," were spaced several miles apart. Surrounded by hundreds of acres of fields and orchards, each town had a central townhouse, dance grounds, ball fields, and family dwellings consisting
of a winter house, a summer house, a hot house (*asi*), and a food storage house on stilts. Women owned the houses and the fields where they
grew corn, squash, and beans—the "Three Sisters"—as well as sunflowers,
gourds, and pumpkins. Women were primarily in charge of farming, but
they also collected wild greens, fruits, berries, and nuts. Men, women, and

Mounds

Some say that the mounds were built by another people. Others say they were built by the ancestors of the old Ani-Kituhwa-gi (the Kituwah people) for townhouse foundations, so that the townhouses would be safe when freshets came. The townhouse was always built on the level bottom lands by the river in order that the people might have smooth ground for their dances and ball plays and might be able to go down to water during the dance.

When they were ready to build the mound, they began by laying a circle of stones on the surface of the ground. Next they made a fire in the center of the circle and put near it the body of some prominent chief or priest who had lately died—some say seven chief men from the different clans—together with an Ulunsuti stone, an uktena scale or horn, a feather from the right wing of an eagle or great tlanuwa which lived in those days, and beads of seven colors, red, white, black, blue, purple, yellow, and gray-blue. The priest then conjured all these with disease, so that, if ever an enemy invaded the country, even though he should burn and destroy the town and the townhouse, he would never live to return home.

The mound was then built up with earth, which the women brought in baskets, and as they piled it above the stones, the bodies of their great men, and the sacred things, they left an open place at the fire in the center and let down a hollow cedar trunk, with the bark on, which fitted around the fire and protected it from the earth. This cedar log was cut long enough to reach nearly to the surface inside the townhouse when it was done. The earth was piled up around it, and the whole mound was finished off smoothly, and then the townhouse was built upon it. One man, called the fire keeper, stayed always in the townhouse to feed and tend the fire. . . .

children fished with nets and with spears, sometimes all joining to drive fish into a weir, catching them in large baskets. Men hunted for bear, deer, and small game, with deer providing most of the meat for food. Cherokee people traveled easily among towns by dugout canoe and on trails along the river with crossings at fords.

Mounds became part of Cherokee villages more than a thousand years ago. Located in the center of villages, mounds supported the council house

> *Just before the Green Corn Dance, in the old times, every fire in the settlement was extinguished, and all the people came and got new fire from the townhouse. This was called* Atsila galvkwtiyu, *the honored or sacred fire. . . . Some say this everlasting fire was only in the larger mounds at Nikwasi, Kituhwa, and a few other towns, and that when the new fire was thus drawn up for the Green Corn Dance, it was distributed from them to the other settlements. The fire burns yet at the bottom of these great mounds, and when the Cherokee soldiers were camped near Kituhwa during the Civil War, they saw smoke still rising from the mound.*
>
> *Swimmer (Ayuini), in James Mooney,* Myths of the Cherokee

where the sacred fire burned, and where everyone gathered to hear news, make decisions, and participate in ceremonies. Many of the Middle Towns had mounds, as did villages throughout all the original Cherokee territory. The townhouse at Coweeta Creek village was about thirty-six feet to a side, while the townhouse at Cowee village was much larger, holding as many as five hundred people.

Unlike some mounds in northern Europe, these did not serve as burial places. Most of the dead were buried in the village area or even in the floors of their houses if they died in winter, and these graves could occur over twenty acres or more of a village site. At the Coweeta Creek village, archaeologists found that burials near the townhouse area tended to be men, and burials near dwelling areas tended to be women. The few burials in Cherokee mounds appear to be people with some special significance. Like mounds in Celtic mythology, however, some of the Cherokee mounds were regarded as gateways to other worlds. Stories of the Nikwasi Mound preserve this tradition.

Of the hundreds of mounds found throughout the mountains, only a few remain at anything near their original size. They have been excavated by archaeologists and their contents removed to museums. They have been plowed down by farmers and their contents looted and sold. They have been bulldozed to make way for shopping malls. One can drive past the original site of the Peachtree Mound, excavated in the 1930s by the Smithsonian Institution, which still holds its artifacts. In the 1960s, mounds at Garden Creek on the Pigeon River were excavated by UNC–Chapel Hill, which has their collections. The mound at Cullowhee, on the campus of

Western Carolina University, was plundered and destroyed as the area was developed; and some of its contents are held by the Mountain Heritage Center.

On Cherokee Heritage Trails, one can visit the Nikwasi Mound in Franklin, the Kituhwa Mound near Cherokee, the Spikebuck Village Mound near Hayesville, and the Nacoochee Mound in north Georgia. In north Georgia, three of the original Etowah Mounds remain intact, towering more than thirty feet high, their perfect pyramidal forms raising speculation about connections with Mayan culture. Beginning about A.D. 600, many southeastern tribes began raising mounds, and a large city of mounds was built at Cahokia on the Mississippi River. Although people of this time are sometimes called the "Moundbuilders," they were members of tribes we know today—the Creek, the Chickasaw, the Shawnee, and the Cherokee.

For more than a thousand years Cherokees lived in these large towns connected by the Little Tennessee River and its tributaries. Although stories tell of raids here by Creeks and by the Shawano, the Middle Towns were protected somewhat by their location deep within the mountains. They nevertheless suffered in 1761, when Colonel James Grant's forces destroyed fifteen towns and burned their crops. Although Cherokee people returned and rebuilt many of these towns, they were devastated again in 1776 by General Griffith Rutherford of the Continental Army, who destroyed thirty-six Cherokee towns on the Little Tennessee, Oconaluftee, Tuckaseegee, and Hiwassee Rivers.

Despite this devastation, defeat in the Revolutionary War, and smallpox epidemics, the Cherokees still had large settlements at Cowee and Nikwasi when this area was taken in the Treaty of 1819. Some Cherokees moved to the remaining tribal land just west of the crest of the Nantahala Mountains, over Wayah Gap, resettling in the Valley Towns or the Hanging Dog area. But others took reservations in their own names throughout this area, so as to be able to remain in or near their homes. The Sandtown community of Cherokees remained on lands in their own names and on land bought for them by a white neighbor, Albert Siler. A dispute over property near the Cowee community led to the case of *Euchella v. Welch* in 1824, in which the North Carolina courts upheld the rights of Cherokees to hold this land in their own name, a decision that helped Cherokees stay in North Carolina.

In the town of Franklin, the Nikwasi Mound lies near the Little Tennessee River, where the Little Tennessee Greenway provides a walking path along the west bank of the river. Several hundred yards from the mound, the Scottish Tartans Museum tells the story of the Cherokees' relationship with the Scots and the Scots-Irish, as part of their main subject, the history of the tartan. Down the block, on the courthouse square, a large bronze

The Bible in the Cherokee language. (Photograph by Roger Haile)

panel and map give details on the Battles of Etchoe. A few doors away on Main Street, the Macon County Historical Museum displays some Cherokee artifacts, from stone points to a Cherokee Bible.

Side trips from Franklin lead to high mountains, waterfalls, and places of legend. West of town, Wayah Bald and Standing Indian areas provide camping, hiking, and recreation on lands now owned by the U.S. Forest Service. Traveling southeast from Franklin, along the Cullasaja River on NC 28, through the Cullasaja Gorge, waterfalls lead to Whiteside Mountain, home of the legendary Spearfinger.

Scenic drives open up the world of the Middle Towns. In much of western North Carolina, towns and roads cover Cherokee towns and trails, because Cherokees had already found the best sites for living and the easiest ways of traveling. Traveling from Franklin south to Dillard on US 441, the highway passes several town sites as well as battle sites. Traveling from Franklin north through Cowee, NC 28 takes you through the historic Cowee district with its once prosperous Cherokee town and more ancient fish weir still visible in the river.

Extensive U.S. Forest Service lands have trails for hiking, mountain biking, and horseback riding along with campsites available for a range of accommodations from RV's to primitive backcountry camping. The Appa-

Yellow-blazed Bartram Trail after a snowstorm. (Photograph by Burt Kornegay)

lachian Trail and the Bartram Trail have extensive miles through this region. Canoeing the Little Tennessee River north (downstream) from Otto through Franklin takes one through the sites of several of the old original Middle Towns, through miles of natural scenery. Boat put-ins are located at Otto, and the river is navigable through Franklin to the dam on Lake Emory. Below the dam, the river can be canoed from Franklin through Needmore, although dry weather sometimes prohibits this.

Other interpretive hubs on the Cherokee Heritage Trails can be accessed from Franklin in several ways. To go on to Murphy (see Chapter 4), take US 64 west past the former town of Cartoogechaye, past the road to Standing Indian, and continue on to Chunky Gal and Shooting Creek, thus to Hayesville and Murphy. To connect to Cherokee, take US 441 north across Cowee Mountain and then follow the Tuckaseegee. To connect to the "Out Towns" of Jackson County, the side trip through the Cullasaja Gorge can bring you via scenic mountain two-lane blacktops to Cashiers and Cullowhee. To connect to Snowbird, a beautiful drive from the Cowee area takes you along the Little Tennessee River through Needmore on a gravel road. Or, the Wayah Road, which traces part of Rutherford's route, takes you over the mountaintop and into the Nantahala Gorge, where you can connect with Robbinsville or Murphy.

Near Franklin, the Smoky Mountain Host Visitor Center provides information on Cherokee Heritage Trails as well as accommodations, dining, and other activities. It is located on US 441 south of Franklin, about 12 miles north of the Georgia state line. The visitor center is open Monday through Thursday from 9:00 A.M. until 5:00 P.M. and Friday through Sunday from 9:00 A.M. until 6:00 P.M. The phone number is 828-369-9606.

SITES IN FRANKLIN

■ Nikwasi Mound

The Cherokees have made up many, many stories as they've lived in these valleys. . . . One of the ones they tell is about Nikwasi.

Nikwasi was down on the valley of the Tennessee, and all of a sudden the Creeks began to come up and attack and threaten to destroy the village of Nikwasi. The Cherokee people rallied, they came to protect the village, but over and over again the Creeks came in greater numbers, and eventually the Cherokees were losing, very badly.

And they'd almost given up, when all of a sudden the mound of Nikwasi opened up, and little soldiers began to march out of this mound by the thousands. And so they go out

Nikwasi Mound. (Photograph by Roger Haile)

and they defeat the Creeks, and like in biblical times they kill all of the Creeks except for one. And he goes back and tells the other Creek brothers and sisters, "Never ever mess with the village of Nikwasi, because they have spirit people who protect it."

And never again was this village attacked by the Creeks.

—Freeman Owle, in *Living Stories of the Cherokee*

Once the center of a thriving Cherokee village, the Nikwasi Mound now stands at the center of the town of Franklin. Not only has it escaped destruction by excavation, farming, and development, Nikwasi Mound remains something like its original size. Its stature can not be appreciated driving by on the street, because the level around the mound has been filled for modern construction. Only when one stands at its base can one appreciate the sheer bulk and graceful lines of this earthen construction. Originally crowned with a large townhouse, this mound held the ever-burning sacred fire and was the dwelling place of the immortal spirit-beings, the Nunnehi. The Eastern Band of Cherokee Indians asks that visitors not climb the mound or walk on its top, in order to help preserve it.

When the Nikwasi Mound was threatened by development in 1946, the schoolchildren of Macon County saved their pennies and purchased the mound through the Macon County Historical Society. This nonprofit organization, formed for this purpose, then deeded the mound to the town of Franklin with the restriction that it always be preserved. Today this mound is significant because it is one of very few mounds that remain intact, and its survival is important to the Cherokees.

Because the mound has not been excavated, no one knows its age, but its location among the Middle Towns makes it typical of sites from perhaps a thousand years ago or more. One of more than a dozen such villages strung along the banks of the Little Tennessee, Nikwasi was home to generations of Cherokee people, whose fields and orchards filled the bottomland around it.

In 1730 Alexander Cuming, a Scots adventurer, called for a council at Nikwasi in a grand scheme to name a Cherokee emperor. Thousands of Cherokees attended. Following this council, seven Cherokee men (including Madohi, or Moytoy, the chosen emperor) went with Cuming to England, where they met with the king and renewed the treaty. Their presents to the king included a feather crown, five eagle tails, and four scalps. In return, they received presents of guns, ammunition, and red paint.

In 1761 the British, former allies of the Cherokee, destroyed the houses and fields of Nikwasi, and troops used its townhouse as a field hospital. Cherokee women and children hid securely in the woods while the town was occupied, then returned, rebuilt Nikwasi, and continued to live there. In 1776 American troops under Rutherford again razed Nikwasi; again women and children hid in the woods while houses and crops were destroyed, and Cherokee men fought several battles—one on the trail up to Wayah Gap. Again the Cherokees rebuilt and lived at Nikwasi. Finally, in the treaties of 1817 and 1819, this land was taken and the state of North Carolina granted white settlers four thousand acres to create the town of Franklin.

Junaluska's sister, Rebecca Morris (married to Gideon Morris) tried to claim the Nikwasi Mound and the land around it as her personal reserve under treaty terms. In 1826 her case reached the North Carolina courts. Although they upheld her right to hold land under the treaty (as they had already established in *Euchella v. Welch* in 1824), the courts ordered a cash settlement for her rather than the land, because by that time white settlers had already built their own village, Franklin, on the site of Nikwasi.

From the Nikwasi Mound, visitors can cross the street to the Little Tennessee Greenway, a walking path along the river. From the mound, a short walk up Town Hill leads to the Scottish Tartans Museum, Courthouse Square, and Macon County Historical Museum.

Occupation of Nikwasi

In 1761, Lt. Col. James Grant's expedition pushed through Cherokee forces on the Little Tennessee River, succeeding where the previous year's expedition had failed. These entries from the journal of one of the Royal Highlanders describes part of their progress northward, past Echoy (now Otto), Tasse (near the confluence of the Cullasaja with the Little Tennessee), and Noucassih (or Nikwasi, now Franklin).

Wednesday 10th June
About three the Army march'd again toward Echoy, keeping the mountains as the Road led to another Pass. About nine we reach'd it after passing the River again. It stands in a large Plain commandid [sic] by Hills, this we tore to pieces & set Fire to. Here we halted for about two Hours, when the Light Infantry, Royal & Burton's march'd to surprise a small Town call'd Tasse, 2 miles. I had orders to put every soul to Death. I sent a plattoon to each house but found them Deserted.

We then march'd with Intentions to surprise Noucassih [Nikwasi] 2 miles but found it deserted also. In leaving Tasse which stands in a Plain you cross a deep branch of the River & then you must cross the main River near to Noucassih. The Fords are good and reach about the middle. It was about four when we reach'd this last place. We went into their Town House which is a large Dome, surrounded with resting places made of Kane & pretty enough. This we converted into an Hospital. We were 24 Hours on this March which was about 21 miles. We lay on our Arms till the arrival of the remainder of the Army which was on Thursday 11th June when we built our Wigwams of the materials of the houses. This morning Mr. Monroe dyed on the march & was buryed in the Evening in one of the Houses, which was afterward burn'd over him, that the Indians might not know where he was lay'd as they would take him up to scalp him.

Friday 12th June
Halted, which we wanted very much as the head of the Army had been 28 Hours under Arms, & most of the Time without eating. This Day all the Troops off Duty were sent with their Arms to destroy the Corn around about the Town which they did very effectualy. Papon & I burn'd two of their Houses & a Pow-wow House.

Capt. Christopher French, 22nd Royal Highlanders

The Nikwasi Mound as documented in a nineteenth-century photograph.
(Courtesy of the Macon County Historical Society)

CONTACT: Franklin Town Office, 188 West Main St., Franklin, NC 28734, 828-524-2516; or Macon County Historical Society, 36 West Main St., Franklin, NC 28734, 828-524-9758, <historical@smnet.net>

LOCATION: Between the one-way streets of East Main (US 441 Business) and North East Main. The mound will be on the driver's left. It is accessible from a short connector, Nikwasi Lane. A small graveled area provides parking for several cars.

■ Little Tennessee River Greenway

Within sight of the Nikwasi Mound, about twenty-five yards east, the Little Tennessee River Greenway follows the river, passing through the Nikwasi village site and passing near the Tasse village site upstream (south) about a mile. From the Nikwasi Mound, the greenway lies within easy walking distance, across the street and down North East Main Street. There, parking space, restrooms, and a covered picnic shelter are available; the greenway, however, is closed to vehicles. Hiking and bicycling are permitted.

When completed, the greenway will follow 6 miles of the Little Tennessee River, beginning at its confluence with Cartoogechaye Creek (Macon County Recreational Park), passing the entrance of the Cullasaja River (junction of Depot Street and Wells Grove Road), and the entrance of Watauga Creek (near Lake Emory), all tributaries with village sites. Bridges

The Little Tennessee River Greenway, when completed, will interpret Cherokee
village sites along a six-mile walkway that follows an old trading path
(Photograph by Roger Haile)

cross the river as the greenway switches from bank to bank, often following the old trading path. The Greenway follows the high power transmis-
sion line recently completed by Nantahala Power and Light Company, now
owned by Duke Power.

The river can be canoed from Otto (originally Etchoe Village) through
this area to the Lake Emory dam just above Franklin. From below the dam,
the river can be canoed on through the remaining village town sites, past
Iotla and Cowee. This route includes miles of natural scenery. Boat put-ins
can be found near Otto on Riverside Drive and US 441, and in Franklin at
Ulco Street off of Wells Grove Road.

CONTACT: Barbara MacRae, Nantahala Power and Light Co., 301 NP&L
    Loop, Franklin, NC 28734, 828-369-4500 X4525,
    <www.littletennessee.org>, <bamcrae@duke-energy.com>
LOCATION: Along the Little Tennessee River in downtown Franklin

■ Scottish Tartans Museum and Heritage Center

The Scottish Tartans Museum and Heritage Center stands on East Main
Street near where a Scots trader lived with the Cherokees in the early

1700s. Many Cherokee women married Scots and English traders in the early eighteenth century, and many Cherokee leaders, including Principal Chief John Ross, were of Scottish descent (John's father was Daniel Ross, and his grandfather was a MacDonald). Today, some members of the Eastern Band claim Scottish ancestry also.

The Scottish Tartans Museum, a nonprofit organization, serves as one of the interpretive hubs for the Cherokee Heritage Trails. Its main exhibit presents the history of the tartan over the past two thousand years. Exhibit panels tell the story of the Scots-Irish and early settlers in Macon County as well as the history of the Scots and the Cherokees. The earliest Scots in the area were traders among the Cherokees, and a display case with two full-size figures depicts this relationship.

Staff often help visitors research their family's tartan using computer software, and then show examples of the tartan itself. Associated with the Scottish Tartans Society and Museum in Scotland, this museum includes a gift shop well-stocked with tartans and gifts imported from Scotland. Events include lectures, programs, and festivals.

CONTACT: Scottish Tartans Museum, 86 East Main St., Franklin, NC 28734, 828-524-7472

HOURS: Open Monday through Saturday from 10:00 A.M. until 5:00 P.M., and Sunday from 1:00 P.M. until 5:00 P.M. There is a small admission fee for adults; children ten and under are free.

LOCATION: Main Street (US 441 Business) in downtown Franklin, on Town Hill several blocks west of Nikwasi Mound

■ Macon County Historical Society and Battle Marker

One block from the Scottish Tartans Museum, down Main Street in Franklin, on Courthouse Square, a large bronze plaque on a brick monument tells the story of the battle of Etchoe. Although the battle took place about 7 miles south of here, it is commemorated here as well as on North Carolina historical markers closer to the site. Franklin's town square also includes a marker noting William Bartram's passage through this area.

Just down the street, on the same block, the Macon County Historical Society, preserver of Nikwasi Mound, has a small museum. Mostly dedicated to the history of white Appalachian settlers, the museum also has a collection of stone points and tools as well as a Bible in the Cherokee language.

Streetscape in Franklin near the Macon County Historical Museum. (Photograph by Roger Haile)

CONTACT: Macon County Historical Society, 36 West Main St., Franklin, NC 28734, 828-524-9758, <historical@smnet.net>

HOURS: The Historical Society museum is open Tuesday through Friday from 10:00 A.M. until 4:00 P.M. and on Saturday from 1:00 P.M. until 5:00 P.M.

SIDE TRIPS

■ Wayah Bald and Wayah Gap

Wayah Bald, rising to an elevation of 5,342 feet, is named for the wolves, *wa ya,* that once lived on its slopes. Wayah Gap was called Atahita, "Where They Shouted." All of Wayah was known to the Cherokees: their trails crossed it, their stories refer to it, their hunters used it, and their Middle Towns stood within sight of its distinctive shape on the skyline to the west. More than eleven thousand years ago, hunters camped near the springs on its crest, leaving spear points behind.

Walker Calhoun said: "Wayah Gap. That must have been where the wolves was going over. They used to travel on the ridges. When I was a kid we used to set on the porch [in Big Cove]. Some nights we heard the

The Great Yellow-Jacket

A long time ago the people of the old town of Kanugalvyi ("Brier place" or Briertown) on Nantahala River, in the present Macon County, North Carolina, were much annoyed by a great insect called Ulagv, as large as a house, which used to come from some secret hiding place, and darting swiftly through the air, would snap up children from their play and carry them away. It was unlike any other insect ever known, and the people tried many times to track it to its home, but it was too swift to be followed.

They killed a squirrel and tied a white string to it, so that its course could be followed with the eye. The Ulagv came and carried off the squirrel with the string hanging to it, but darted away so swiftly that it was out of sight in a moment. They killed a turkey and put a longer white string to it, and the Ulagv came and took the turkey, but was gone again before they could see in what direction it flew. They took a deer ham and tied a white string to it, and again the Ulagv swooped down and bore it off so swiftly that it could not be followed. At last they killed a yearling dear and tied a very long white string to it. The Ulagv came again and seized the deer, but this time the load was so heavy that it had to fly slowly and so low down that the string could be plainly seen.

The hunters got together for the pursuit. They followed it along a ridge to the east until they came near where Franklin now is, when, on looking across the valley to the other side, they saw the nest of the Ulagv in a large cave in the rocks. On this they raised a great shout and made their way rapidly down the mountain and across to the cave. The nest had the entrance below with tiers of cells built up one above another to the roof of the cave. The great Ulagv was there, with thousands of smaller ones, that we now call yellow-jackets. The hunters built fires around the hole, so that the smoke filled the cave and smothered the great insect and multitudes of the smaller ones. But others which were outside the cave were not killed, and these escaped and increased until now the yellow-jackets, which before were unknown, are all over the world.

The people called the cave Tsagagv-yi, "Where the yellow jacket was," and the place from which they first saw the nest they called Atahita, "Where they shouted" [Wayah Gap], and these are their names today.

Swimmer (Ayuini) in James Mooney, Myths of the Cherokee

wolves like a bunch of dogs going through these mountains. We didn't hear them howling, just heard them running. They'd run to cross over and get on the other side of the ridge."

Wayah, like numerous other mountains in the southern Appalachians, had a bald near its crest. Such balds resemble the open spaces that the Cherokees kept cleared near their villages to attract game. Their legends say that the Nunnehi, the immortal spirit beings, kept these balds cleared on the high peaks so that the eagles could catch rabbits. Scientists have no explanation for the existence of southern Appalachian balds, but over the past two hundred years, since the Cherokee removal, and with the closing of open range and the suppression of fire, shrubs and other woody vegetation have begun to overtake the balds.

The trail up Wayah and Wayah Gap itself were the sites of Cherokee battles with the Continental Army in 1776. General Griffith Rutherford led twenty-four hundred men in the Army of North Carolina across the Swannanoa Gap and into the watershed of the Tuckaseegee. The purpose of this expedition was to punish Cherokee civilians because of the alliance of Cherokee warriors with the British. (No fighting was going on in this region, because this was entirely Cherokee territory. Most white settlers were east of the Blue Ridge, about 100 miles from this valley.) Rutherford's punitive expedition destroyed thirty-six Cherokee towns on the Oconaluftee, Tuckaseegee, Hiwassee (above the junction of the Valley River), and upper Little Tennessee.

From the area of present-day Whittier, Rutherford's forces followed Cowee Creek to its junction with the Little Tennessee and then proceeded west following Cartoogechaye Creek up Wayah. The Cherokees made a stand near Wayah Gap, where they killed nineteen Americans in a hard-fought battle before being driven back. As the main party of Cherokees was retreating, one of its members remained, continuing to fire from behind a tree, hindering the passage of Rutherford's men. Finally the Americans killed the warrior. When they looked at the body, they found that it was a woman, stripped for battle, painted, and armed with bow and arrows. Shot in the thigh, she had been unable to retreat with the other Cherokees but had continued to hold off the Americans until her death, thus taking her place among other legendary Cherokee women warriors such as Gatvlati ("Wild Hemp") and Nanyehi (Nancy Ward).

After the treaties of 1817 and 1819, the Nantahala Mountains formed the boundary of tribal lands, in this area, with the area to the west remaining as part of the Cherokee Nation. Many Cherokees in the Little Tennessee River Valley claimed land in their names in order to remain near their old homes. Others moved west onto tribal lands.

The old path up Wayah from Franklin was used during the Trail of Tears forced emigration in 1838, after it was expanded from a trail to a road with Cherokee labor. It was the route for the North Carolina militia traveling from their gathering place in Franklin to Fort Aquone, the stockade on the north side of Wayah, near the village of Aquone. The Wayah road became the military's supply route as well. And it was used to take Cherokee prisoners from what is now Macon County to Fort Scott at Aquone, where they were held during the first stage of the Trail of Tears. Part of the old road corresponds with the present-day road winding up Wayah and down to Aquone, where the site of the village and fort lie beneath Nantahala Lake. Another old road went from Laurel Creek to Cartoogechaye Creek.

At Wayah Gap—a high point for the road, but a low point for the mountain—USFS Road 69 turns north to the top of the mountain. There, part of the bald can still be seen. A stone tower built in 1937 provides 360-degree panoramic views of the Nantahalas, the Tusquitees, the Little Tennessee River Valley, and—on a clear day—Clingman's Dome (Kuwahi). Parking, restrooms, and picnic tables are available. The Appalachian Trail crosses Wayah from south to north, as does part of the Bartram Trail.

CONTACT: U.S. Forest Service, Wayah Ranger District, 90 Sloane Rd., Franklin, NC 28734, 828-524-6441
LOCATION: From Franklin, take US 64 West for 3 miles. Turn right onto Old Murphy Road. Take a left at the 66 Station onto Wayah Road (State Road 1310). Follow Wayah Road through the valley and up the mountain for approximately 10 miles. At the top of the mountain, you will be in Wayah Gap. To go to Wayah Bald and the tower, turn right (north) onto USFS Road 69 (gravel), and proceed for approximately 6 more miles.

■ Standing Indian

Standing Indian encompasses the headwaters of the Nantahala River in a horseshoe-shaped basin, the two sides of which are formed by the 5,000-foot peaks of the Nantahala and Blue Ridge Mountains. Still rich in game such as bear, deer, and wild turkey, this area was known to and used by Cherokees of the Middle Towns, although they left few signs of their occupation. Cherokee people today come here to gather ramps in the spring, and some consider this a sacred site.

Its original Cherokee name, Yvwi tsulenv-yi, means "Where the man stood," which refers to a stone formation shaped like a man that once stood on the side of the mountain. At some point, this formation broke, leaving

The approach to Standing Indian. (Photograph by Roger Haile)

only the bottom of the form. It can be seen among other rock outcroppings by hiking up Kimsey Creek Trail and then taking the trail to the top of the ridge.

Most of the trees and plants that live in the southern Appalachians can be found here. Blooms in early May include mountain magnolia, dogwood, Carolina silverbell, flame azalea, trillium, violets, bluets, goat's rue, stone-crop, wild geranium, and wake robin. The rare lady's slippers follow these. In June mountain laurel and rhododendron fill the woods with flowers. In autumn the woods blaze with all the colors of oak, maple, beech, poplar, hickory, chinquapin, dogwood, and more, contrasted with the evergreen of hemlock, pine, and fir. Looking at the display of fall colors inspired the following comment from Freeman Owle: "At this time of year, you can tell the Creator loves differences, because all the leaves are different colors. He could have made them all the same, but look, they're all different."

The second largest yellow poplar in the United States grows at Stand-ing Indian and has been there for centuries. More than 8 feet in diameter and 25 feet in circumference, this giant reached 135 feet in height before its top was blown out by a storm. A nearby tree of this size was felled during the wholesale logging of the mountains in the early 1930s, but its weight created such a strain for the oxen hauling out the timber that this poplar was left standing. Named the John Wasilik Memorial Poplar for an early ranger in the Wayah District, it stands a short hike from a parking lot on

Fall color in the southern Appalachians. (Photograph by Murray Lee)

Sand Town Indians

On the way to Standing Indian from Franklin, traveling west on US 64, the road passes a former Cherokee village site, now in the Macon County Industrial Park. This site was occupied from about A.D. 250. Here people worked mica that was traded as far away as the Ohio River Valley. About four miles from the intersection of US 441 and US 64, the old Cartoogechaye School stands near the location of another village. Two miles farther west, Muskrat Creek marks the home of the Sand Town Indians, a Cherokee community that survived removal.

The Cherokees were able to remain near their old village site on Cartoogechaye Creek, about six miles west of Nikwasi, and they became known as the Sand Town Indians (Nohu-yi, "Sand Place") because of their location near the sandy banks of Muskrat Creek. About one hundred Cherokees lived here, initially because of the good will of William Siler, who had claimed this land. About 1850, Jim Woodpecker, Chutahsoti, bought two hundred acres of land from the Silers on both sides of Muskrat Creek. Alce, his daughter, who was married to Yona Gunahit, "Long Bear," purchased more than a hundred adjacent acres. At this time, the Sand Town Indians lived in log cabins with separate log kitchens and smokehouses; they farmed, hunted, and ranged hogs and cattle on the mountain. They had a townhouse where they gathered for preaching from an English Bible, hymn singing in Cherokee language, and traditional dances where women wore turtle shell rattles tied below the knee. The Siler families continued to be friends with the Cherokees for generations and some of the Silers learned to speak the Cherokee language.

When Chutasohti, Jim Woodpecker, and his wife Cunstaee died in 1879, they were buried in the churchyard of nearby St. John's Episcopal

USFS Road 67, a little more than a mile after turning off Old US 64 and just before the main Standing Indian campground.

Now owned and managed by the U.S. Forest Service, Standing Indian's thousands of acres adjoin the Nantahala Wilderness Area and the Coweeta Hydrological Station's research watershed of five thousand acres. While Wayah's rugged slopes dominate the landscape and challenge hikers, Standing Indian's more gentle terrain invites more leisurely exploration. Thirty-two miles of the Appalachian Trail cross Standing Indian and fol-

Gravestone for Sand Town community Cherokees. (© 2000 Steve Wall)

Church. Jim died first and his wife the next day. One of Albert Siler's daughters marked their graves with the two halves of a marble dresser top that she had broken in two for the purpose. Later their graves were marked with native granite inscribed with their names. Alee and Yona Gunahit were buried on Alee's property above the head of Muskrat Creek and below Siler Bald, known as Taliski Old Fields (now U.S. Forest Service property).

The Sand Town community persisted for more than a hundred years after removal, but by the 1950s, most of these families had moved to the Qualla Boundary. The graves of Chutasohti and Cunstaee still stand in St. John's Episcopal Churchyard, where they are tended and cherished by that congregation.

low its high ridges, and another 30 miles of hiking trails follow the Nantahala River, Kimsey Creek, Hurricane Creek, and Big Indian Creek. In some places these are old logging trails, in others just footpaths. One trail leads to the lookout tower atop Albert Mountain, giving another view of the Little Tennessee River Valley. Twenty miles of horse trails loop through rhododendron and hardwood forest, meandering through coves, up ridges, and across creeks.

The main Standing Indian campground, locally known as White Oak

Bottoms, is run as a private concession and accommodates RVs and tents for primitive camping; there are showers, restrooms, picnic tables, and water. Group camping is available at Kimsey Creek, and primitive horse camping is available at Hurricane Creek.

CONTACT: U.S. Forest Service, Wayah Ranger District, 90 Sloane Rd., Franklin, NC 28734, 828-524-6441
LOCATION: From Franklin go west on US 64 for 12 miles. Turn left on old US 64 and go east 2 miles. Turn right (south) on USFS Road 67, and go 2 miles to the campground and backcountry information bulletin board.

■ Waterfalls and Whiteside Mountain

In Cherokee language, *cullasaja* means sweet, or literally, "honey locust." That name may have described the taste of the water in the Cullasaja River, or the beauty of its waterfalls. The Cherokee settlement here was known as Sugar Town or Honey Locust place. From Franklin one can travel by automobile through the Cullasaja Gorge, with the option of stopping to walk behind waterfalls, before finally reaching Whiteside Mountain, legendary home of the Cherokee monster Spearfinger.

Between Franklin and Highlands, the road ascends along the Cullasaja River, passing Cullasaja Falls, Bridal Veil Falls, and Dry Falls. Cullasaja Falls drops spectacularly into the gorge, but care should be taken in stopping to look from the narrow road between the bluff and the drop-off. Farther up, Dry Falls can be viewed on foot: a trail with safety rails leads from a parking area down along the wall of the gorge and behind the falls itself, whose sound fills its ravine. Bridal Veil Falls drops like sheer lace from an outcropping that hangs out over a turnout from the road, creating a drive-through waterfall.

In Cherokee stories, waterfalls can be doorways to other worlds: the world of the Nunnehi (the immortals), or the world of the little people. And water itself is respected as the Long Man, with his head in the mountains and his feet in the sea. The sacred ritual of going to water provides physical and spiritual cleansing prior to ceremonies or ball games, as well as renewal for daily life. Cherokee traditions prohibited putting anything unclean in the water, including any human waste. Several years ago, local groups tried to prevent the town of Highlands from discharging sewage into the Cullasaja, but failed. Their protest signs still stand along the highway and river.

Cherokee towns existed in this more rugged landscape, near present-

Bridal Veil Falls. (Photograph by Barbara Duncan)

Spearfinger

Long long ago—hi la hi yu there dwelt in the mountains a terrible
ogress, a woman monster, whose food was human livers. She could take
on any shape or appearance to suit her purpose, but in her right form,
she looked very much like an old woman, excepting that her whole body
was covered with a skin as hard as a rock that no weapon could wound
or penetrate, and on her right hand she had a long, stony forefinger of
bone, like an awl or spearhead, with which she stabbed people. On ac-
count of this fact she was called U tlv ta, "Spear-finger," and on account
of her stony skin she was sometimes called Nv yunuwi, "Stone-dress."
There was another stone-clothed monster that killed people, but that is
a different story.

Spear-finger had such powers over stone that she could easily lift and
carry immense rocks, and could cement them together by merely strik-
ing one against another. To get over the rough country more easily she
undertook to build a great rock bridge through the air from Nv yu-tlu
gv yi the "Tree-Rock" on Hiwassee, over to Sanigilagi (Whiteside Moun-
tain) on the Blue Ridge, and had it well started from the top of the "Tree
Rock" when the lightning struck it and scattered the fragments along
the whole ridge, where the pieces can still be see by those who go there.
She used to range all over the mountains about the heads of the streams
and in the dark passes of Nantahala, always hungry and looking for
victims. Her favorite haunt on the Tennessee side was about the gap on
the trail where Chilowee mountain comes down to the river.

John Ax (Itaganuhi), about 1890,
in James Mooney, Myths of the Cherokee

day Sugar Fork and near the intersection of Ellijay Creek and the Cullasaja
River, about 7 miles up the gorge. Farther up the mountain, traces of ancient hunting camps have been found near the town of Highlands and other
settlements near Horse Cove.

Six miles from Highlands, Whiteside Mountain rises above a high broken landscape of granite domes capped with dark spruce and fir trees. Its
long white cliffs sparkle along its sides, making it a landmark on the eastern continental divide at an altitude of 4,930 feet. Geologists estimate this
rock to be more than four hundred million years old.

According to Cherokee legend, the monster Spearfinger made her home here and built a rock bridge that sheared off, leaving bare rock exposed. As the hiker walks up the broad trail sparkling with quartz toward the top of the mountain, the silence echoes with wind moving across the tops of domes and is punctuated by the drip of spring water from mossy rock faces—elemental sounds. This 2-mile loop trail—rated "more difficult" because it is steep—climbs above 750-foot cliffs where peregrine falcons nest. Views of mountains stretch into the distance to the east, south, and west.

CONTACT: U.S. Forest Service, Highlands Ranger District, 2010 Flat Mountain Rd., Highlands, NC 28741, 828-526-3765

LOCATION: Cullasaja Falls, Dry Falls, and Bridal Veil Falls are located along US 64/NC 28 between Franklin and Highlands. Traveling southeast on US 64/NC 28 toward Highlands, Cullasaja Falls and Dry Falls will be on the right, while Bridal Veil Falls will be on the left. To visit Whiteside Mountain, continue traveling east on US 64 through Highlands. Whiteside Mountain will be on the right in approximately 6 miles. Restrooms and parking are available. The trail is open for hiking only. Climbing on the rock cliffs is prohibited January 15 through August 15, when the peregrine falcons are nesting.

SCENIC DRIVES

■ Middle Towns—US 441 South to Dillard

The first of the scenic drives through the Middle Towns begins in Franklin, going south along the Little Tennessee River to Dillard, Georgia, where the southernmost of the Middle Towns was located. Beginning with Nikwasi, the route next passes the location of a former town at the confluence of the Cullasaja River with the Little Tennessee. The site of another settlement is at the confluence of Cartoogechaye Creek, and another is near Otto. There is one near Coweeta Creek and, finally, one near Dillard. This route also traces the route of the Grant and Montgomery expeditions and their battle sites. US 441 basically follows the old trail along the west side of the river. Vestigial stands of rivercane survive near these village sites and can be seen lining the banks of the Little Tennessee in pastures along US 441 South.

Cherokee settlements over the past thousand years often centered around mounds, but not always. Some towns moved up and down the riverbanks over time, moving as fields were left fallow and new fields developed.

Their locations have been determined by archaeological excavation, by the presence of surviving mounds, by surviving eighteenth-century written descriptions, by accident when bulldozers were preparing land for development, and by the finds of arrowhead hunters walking the plowed fields in spring.

From the Nikwasi Mound or downtown Franklin, turn south on Depot Street. At the intersection of Depot Street and Wells Grove Road, turn left and proceed on Wells Grove Road. The town of Tasse, according to the Grant expedition, lay somewhere near the confluence of the Little Tennessee River and the Cullasaja River, which Wells Grove Road crosses here. The actual location of the town may have been closer to the present location of Macon Middle School, a mile or so farther down Wells Grove Road, where many artifacts were found in the fields and where students tell stories of Indian ghosts in the school. Turn around on Wells Grove Road and proceed back toward town.

At the intersection of Wells Grove Road with US 441 Business at the Chamber of Commerce, proceed south (straight) on US 441 Business. An overpass provides a scenic view of the valley with Standing Indian and Wayah on the skyline to the west (to the right, heading south). As US 441 Business passes through some commercial development and downhill, the Macon County Community Facilities Building on the left marks the confluence of Cartoogechaye Creek with the Little Tennessee River. About 5 miles south of town is the Smoky Mountain Host Visitor Center, and about 1.5 miles south of the visitor center, Riverside Road turns left off of US 441. Within 100 yards, a small park provides parking and access to the Little Tennessee River.

To hike several miles of trails that access the Little Tennessee River, visit the Tessentee Farm Preserve, which is open to the public and has been preserved by the Land Trust for the Little Tennessee. From US 441, continue on Riverside Road a total of .4 miles, then turn right on Hickory Knoll Road and go 1.7 miles south. The entrance to the farm is marked as 2249 Hickory Knoll Road, and a grassy parking area is located just off the paved road.

Cherokee trails followed the river here, and old towns occupied riverbanks throughout this valley. In 1760 and 1761, the Battles of Etchoe were fought just south of the farm's location and possibly along the river on this property. In 1776 the South Carolina militia camped here on their way to attack Cowee as part of their Revolutionary War campaign against the Cherokees. Recently, the Land Trust for the Little Tennessee received a grant to establish new stands of rivercane here for use by contemporary Cherokee artists and basketmakers.

To continue south, from the farm turn right on Hickory Knoll Road and shortly thereafter turn right again onto Tessentee Road. This intersects US 441 after about one mile and brings you to the community of Otto, across from the post office. Both Otto and the vicinity of the Macon County Recreation Park are marked on old maps as the location of Etchoe.

To continue south on US 441, turn left from Tessentee Road. Two North Carolina historical markers proclaim Cherokee Victory and Cherokee Defeat, indicating the approximate locations of battle sites from the Montgomery campaign of 1760 and the Grant campaign of 1761. Here thousands of British forces fought with thousands of Cherokee warriors led by Oconostota. About a mile farther south, the Spring Ridge Creamery marks the site of the first shots fired in the Montgomery campaign. A bridge at the end of the creamery's parking lot leads to a field where the battle may have begun.

Between Otto and the Spring Ridge Creamery, the Coweeta Creek village was occupied until about 1650. A sign for Coweeta Hydrological Laboratory marks the entrance of Coweeta Creek into the Little Tennessee River; the village was a little farther up the creek.

US 441 crosses the Georgia line and proceeds south to the town of Dillard. Here stood the Cherokee town of Old Estatoe and its mound, near a waterfall. Today, these are on private property. Local oral tradition maintains that the Rabun Gap–Nacoochee School's fields, through which the highway passes, were once ball fields and dance grounds of the Cherokees.

Continuing south, US 441 takes the traveler to Clayton, Warwoman Dell, and Tallulah Falls (see Georgia scenic drives in Chapter 7).

CONTACT: Smoky Mountain Host Visitor Center, 4437 Georgia Hwy. (US 441), Franklin, NC 28734, 800-432-4678; or Scottish Tartans Museum and Heritage Center, 86 East Main St., Franklin, NC 28734, 828-524-7472 <www.scottishtartans.org>, <tartans@scottishtartans.org>

LOCATION: US 441 South from Franklin, North Carolina, to Dillard, Georgia

■ Middle Towns — NC 28 North

After riding near two miles through Indian plantations of Corn, which was well cultivated, being near eighteen inches in height, and the beans planted at the Corn-hills were above ground; we leave the fields on our right, turning towards the mountains and ascending through a delightful green vale or lawn, which conducted us in amongst the pyramidal hills and crossing a brisk flowing creek, meandering through the meads . . . besides a view of many other villages and settlements on the sides of the mountains, at various distances and elevations; the silver rivulets gliding by them and snow white cataracts glimmering on

View of the Iotla Village site at the Macon County airport.
(Photograph by Barbara Duncan)

the sides of the lofty hills; the bold promontories of the Jore Mountain stepping into the
Tanase River, whilst his foaming waters rushed between them.
— William Bartram, May 1776

This scenic drive from Franklin north on NC 28 follows the Little Tennessee River and passes some of the town sites associated with it: Nikwasi,
Watauga, Iotla, Burningtown, Cowee, and Coweetchee. The Cowee area has
been designated a National Historic District on the National Register of Historic Places and includes historic buildings and the West farm mill as well
as the original Cowee village area.

From the Nikwasi Mound in Franklin, proceed west on North East Main
Street to the second stoplight and turn right on Riverview Street. Follow
this winding street for a good view of the river, from its west bank, and
access to the northern terminus of the Little Tennessee Greenway. In just a
mile or so, this street joins NC 28 at a yield sign. Proceeding north (straight)
on NC 28, a North Carolina historical marker describes one of the battle
sites, which is actually located on US 441 South. The Macon County Airport,
located a few miles north of Franklin off of NC 28, stands on the site of the
old Iotla village. The Burningtown village was located several miles beyond
here, giving its name to the present-day communities of Upper Burningtown, Middle Burningtown, and Lower Burningtown.

Site of Cowee Village and Cowee Mound along the Little Tennessee River.
(Photograph by Burt Kornegay)

Back on NC 28, about 7 miles north of Franklin, near the junction of Cowee Creek with the Little Tennessee River, the traveler comes to the area of the old Cowee village. According to Cherokee elder Walker Calhoun, this was probably named for the people of the Deer Clan, the Ani-Kawi. This was a large and important village of the Middle Towns, whose townhouse held more than five hundred people. Today the mound and village site are on private property and have been protected by the owner.

Just past the old Cowee school, a North Carolina historical marker notes "Wedgewood Pottery Clay." Deposits of clay from the banks of Cowee Creek, near the Iotla community, were used by Cherokee potters. The high concentrations of kaolin found in these clay deposits led Josiah Wedge-wood's pottery in England to make its own treaty with the Cherokee in 1767 to obtain this special clay for use in making porcelain. Several craft stores now stand at the intersection of NC 28 and the creek, as does Rickman's Store, a general store dating to the turn of the century. The West farmstead also stands at this site, the heart of the newly designated national historic district.

Farther north on NC 28, another North Carolina historical marker notes the Cowee Mound, across the river on private property. The mound appears as a hill through the trees of the fence line. Preserved by its private owner, the Cowee Mound has not been reduced by farming like many other

Canoeists navigate through an ancient V shaped stone fish wier on the Little Tennessee River near the Cowee Village site. (Photograph by Burt Kornegay)

mounds, and its size is magnified by the natural landform that it was built upon. A few miles farther downstream, if you look in the river to the left, particularly in winter when trees are bare, you can see the stones of an ancient fish weir still in their V-shape. People fished in these rivers thousands of years ago using several methods: spearing fish, netting fish with woven nets anchored by carved stone weights, and using weirs to drive fish to the apex of the V of stones so that people standing there could scoop them out in baskets. North of Cowee, the village of Coweetchee stood several miles upriver, also on the west bank.

From here, the traveler proceeds across Wayah on NC 28, a winding and scenic road that leads to Almond, location of a Trail of Tears stockade. From this junction, proceed to Robbinsville through Stecoah, or to Andrews and Murphy through the Nantahala Gorge.

For an equally scenic trip on low ground, take NC 28 to Tellico Bridge (known locally as Lost Bridge) and turn left onto the Needmore Road. This follows the Little Tennessee through a beautiful, isolated stretch of the river, coming out near Almond. About 7 miles of this route consist of gravel road. Pullouts are available for parking along the river.

■ Wayah and Beyond — Appletree and Nantahala

This scenic drive begins at Nikwasi and passes old village sites to the west and then to the north over Wayah: Cartoogechaye, Neohee (Sandtown), Aquone, the Appletree Campground, and Briartown. Cherokee people and their ancestors frequented or lived at these sites from eleven thousand years ago until the present day.

Take us 441 Business to its intersection with us 64, then take us 64 West, a four-lane highway with pink dogwoods and euonymous shrubs planted in the median. Just a few miles from town, the Macon County Industrial Park, on the left, covers the site of a village dating to A.D. 250 where mica was mined and prepared for trade.

About 4 miles from Franklin, the old Cartoogechaye School on the left (traveling west) marks the site of the Cutagochi village. The fields of Kirkland Farms, the golf course of Parker Meadows, and the school grounds, all cover the general village site. Two miles farther, to the right-hand side of the road, Muskrat Creek winds through a little valley where a Cherokee community weathered removal and continued until the 1950s. Two of its leaders, Jim Woodpecker and his wife Cunstatee, were buried at St. John's Episcopal Church in 1879.

From this area, double back to access the road to Wayah. Return about 3 miles east toward Franklin, and take Old Murphy Road to the left (traveling east). (See also directions to Wayah, earlier in this chapter.) At Loafer's Glory, this becomes the Wayah Road, a two-lane blacktop following Wayah Creek, basically the route of Rutherford's expedition and also the Trail of Tears. Springs and balds on Wayah have been known and used for millennia. From Wayah Gap, a gravel road leads to the crest, bald, and stone observation tower.

Continuing on over Wayah, one finds the next Cherokee settlement, the former town of Aquone, now submerged under Nantahala Lake. This was also the location of Fort Scott, a North Carolina militia garrison during the Cherokee removal. Both were near the present intersection of Junaluska Road (State Road 1505) and this road.

At this intersection, Junaluska Road leads to Appletree Campground and Andrews (about 10 miles), or sr 1310 leads to the Nantahala community and Nantahala Gorge, location of the former Briartown (Kanugalv-yi). Down Junaluska Road just a few miles, the Appletree Campground welcomes groups for camping on U.S. Forest Service land. Here, in a small upland meadow near a good spring, people have camped more or less continuously for more than ten thousand years, according to recent archaeological research by Dr. Anne Rogers of Western Carolina University.

SR 1310 leads on to Nantahala Gorge, haunt of Cherokee monsters and refuge for Cherokee people hiding to escape the forced march on the Trail of Tears.

■ Chunky Gal and Shooting Creek

From Franklin, a scenic drive on US 64 connects to Hayesville and Murphy. The road passes former Cherokee village sites of Cartoogechaye, and Sandtown, and ascends Winding Stair Gap. At the top of the gap a parking lot connects with the Appalachian Trail, provides a scenic overlook, and offers drinking water running from a mountain spring. The road stays on high ground past Rainbow Springs (the entry road to Standing Indian) and on to Chunky Gal Gap before descending into the watershed of the Hiwassee River at Shooting Creek.

"Chunkey Girls Mountain" first appears on a map from 1838. The name refers not to a woman of ample proportions, but one who was named for the traditional Cherokee game, which required a smooth open area. Called *gatayusti* by the Cherokee, it was known to the whites by its Creek name, *chunkey.* Shooting Creek's name, Du stayalv-yi, refers not to a gun battle, but to "Where it made a noise like thunder or shooting," according to James Mooney.

A scenic overlook as the road descends into Shooting Creek provides views of Brasstown Bald and the valley of the Hiwassee. The traveler passes sites of former villages: Spikebuck, Peachtree (Hiwassee), Tlanusi-yi, and others.

Shooting Creek became refuge to new Cherokee settlers after the Lower Towns were destroyed in 1760 and 1761, and again when Georgia laws became oppressive in the 1820s. At the time of removal, about a hundred Cherokee families (more than five hundred people) lived in the Shooting Creek area.

4

The Leech Place and the Trail of Tears
Murphy, North Carolina

I heard a council member once say that the only difference between the Eastern Band and the Cherokee Nation in Oklahoma is a thousand miles and a hundred and sixty years. And it is a pretty good statement to me. When you come here and start traveling around, you start actually seeing the places that are mentioned in the stories you've heard all your lifetime from your grandmother, your father. And I am not talking about mythological stories, I am talking about the stories handed down about remembrances of certain places—more along the lines of geographical descriptions. The things you've heard about as a child actually exist. And this place, even though you have never been here, it just becomes a part of you. By some kind of psychological osmosis, you suddenly accept the fact that maybe you have always been here. Maybe the time hasn't been that long. Maybe the distance is not so far.

The feeling I got here was like coming back home. Coming home physically, emotionally, symbolically. All the things that happened are closer together and the split is not that great anymore. It's a very profound feeling to try to talk about very much because I am not really sure that people understand that. It really is like being home. I don't talk too much about it to anybody.

—Tom Belt, member of the Cherokee Nation of Oklahoma

In Murphy, known as the Leech Place (or Tlanusi-yi) in Cherokee lore, the Cherokee Heritage Trails interpretive hub is at the Cherokee County Historical Museum. Outside stands a large soapstone boulder—originally used as a source of soapstone for bowls—which came from the Nottely River area. Nodes on the boulder are preforms of stone bowls, carved more than 4,000 years ago, before the advent of pottery. Inside, displays and interpretation cover thousands of years of history that took place along the Hiwassee and Valley Rivers and their tributaries.

The story of the giant leech, Tlanusi, marks the junction of the Valley and Hiwassee Rivers, which along with their tributaries provided homes to people for thousands of years. In Brasstown Valley, recent archaeological research shows that people lived there for ten thousand years in a land-

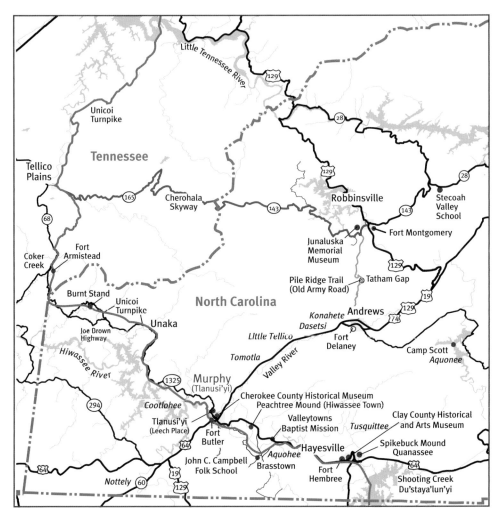

MAP 8. *Cherokee Heritage Trails, Murphy, N.C.*

scape that we would find familiar. People then fished for and ate trout, bass, and chub. They hunted and ate bear, deer, elk, and turkey. They gathered chestnuts and walnuts along with blackberries, raspberries, and huckleberries. For more than a thousand years, Cherokee people farmed corn, beans, and squash in fields along these river bottoms, where stands of rivercane continue to grow.

Cherokee people still live in this area today. About four hundred members of the Eastern Band of Cherokee Indians live on 5,575 acres scattered throughout Cherokee County, near the old Cherokee communities

The Leech Place

In the early years the Cherokee people lived in little villages. And their only means of travel was trails. And the trails normally followed the river. Along the river banks was always a trail. And from one little village to the next village maybe they had a runner that carried news. If something happened in one of the villages—like maybe a death or a sickness was taking place—they'd send a runner to tell the next village what was happening.

Now, along the Hiwassee River, as we know it today, was a trail. A deep hole of water was next to the trail. A family was passing. And from this deep hole of water something came and snatched up one of the little children of the family that was passing by. And there was a great concern over what had happened—of the kid disappearing into that great hole of water. It had been taken by some kind of a creature that lived in that hole of water. People were warned not to travel the trail anymore near that. Children were warned never to go around that area to play.

One morning upstream from that hole of water lived a family who had two sons. And they were teenagers. One was very young—maybe like twelve years old, and the other maybe fourteen—just young boys, we call them. One morning they had taken their father's canoe and they rowed across that river nearby the big hole of water. And they were looking up on the ledge. On the other side of the big hole of water was a big rock ledge—a big rock cliff. And they were saying that if they rode across and climbed that big rock, they thought they might be able to see what was in that hole of water. The higher you go and look down into the water the better you can see the bottom.

So they climbed that big cliff, looked down. They couldn't see anything. It was all dark. The water was so deep that they couldn't see anything but just dark water. So they started to leave, and as they started to leave the younger boy looked up above where they were and he said, "Look, look up there." And when his brother looked, he said, "See that big boulder?" He said, "We could roll that big boulder down and it would go right into that stream—right into that big hole of water." And he said, "It might get rid of what's living in that hole of water."

And when they went up and checked it, the older brother said, "No, let's don't roll it yet." He said, "Let's gather a lot of wood and we'll build a fire under it and make it white hot, and then we'll roll it." So they gathered the wood. But darkness caught them before they could get a fire started, so they returned home.

Their father met them at the door and he said, "Where you boys been?" And so they gave him a story. He said, "You didn't go near that hole of water down there, did you?" They said, "No," said, "we were out in the woods." So he kind of let them go at that. And he kind of had a feeling they might have been around that pool of water. Anyways he said, "I told you not to be around that hole of water." He said, "That's dangerous." Said, "That thing could come out and get you from any direction."

Anyway, the next morning they got up and they also had some fire starter, they call it. It's a dried mushroom they get out of a dried log, and once a spark hits it, it's kind of like a felt. That flame, that spark will hold—hold on and keep a coal alive. And they took a piece of that mushroom and they took two little flint rocks, and they struck those flints together. And a spark flew and caught and it started their fire under that big boulder. And they burned that wood all day that day under that big boulder.

Late that evening that big boulder was turning white, it was getting so hot. And the older boy says, "I believe it's ready to go." So they prised on that big boulder and sure enough—white hot—here it went. And it landed in that big hole of water. And the water boiled for a few minutes, it was so hot. And suddenly, up to the top of the water came a large monster. It was red, and it looked like a big lizard. A huge one. It was the length and the width of the river. And they didn't know what it was. And it was dead—it floated down where the water shoals were— where the water goes over. And they were looking at each other when it did that. And then suddenly here come another one, and it was smaller, and it floated down. Then they came off the rock cliff. They got in their daddy's canoe, and they rode back across the river to their home.

Again their daddy met them, and he was furious that time. He says, "You boys have been down there at that hole of water." And one of them, the youngest one answered. And he said, "Yeah." And he was getting ready just to give them a good thrashing. And he said, "Yeah, wait a minute now." He said, "Let us tell you something. We killed what's in that hole of water. They're gone." His daddy didn't hardly hear that— he continued right on till he was going to give them a good thrashing.

And they said, "Wait just a minute now. Listen to us. Listen." And he said, "You've killed what was in that pool of water?" "That's right." And they said, "If you don't believe us, come and we'll show you." So they convinced him into going and seeing. And he was kind of frightened. He was kind of afraid that whatever was in that hole of water was still in there and maybe they were just making up a story or maybe imagined a lot of things.

And when they came to the side of that hole of water, he was amazed. He saw those big bodies laying across that stream dead. And when he examined them, they were leeches—two of them. And one of those leeches is what snatched up one of the kids of the family that were passing nearby. And they call the leech tla nu si.

Now to this day when we speak to the older people that know the name of Murphy they call it "The Place of the Leech." They call it tla nu si-yi. And that's how it got its name—from those leeches that snatched up a little child then just a few days later they were killed by these two young boys. And my daddy used to say it was always young boys that did a man's job. [laughs] So that's how Murphy got the Cherokee name, "The Place of the Leech." But the English name is Murphy, North Carolina. The Cherokee name is tla nu si-yi.

Jerry Wolfe

and homesteads of Tomotla, Grape Creek, and Hanging Dog. One of the county commissioners elected here is a member of the Eastern Band; the Cherokee community also elects a representative to the tribal council.

This area, the Valley Towns (now Cherokee and Clay Counties), in the heartland of the original Cherokee country, remained part of tribal lands until the 1838 removal, while surrounding land was ceded in earlier treaties. Many displaced Cherokees from Georgia and North Carolina moved here in the early 1800s, living in hastily constructed log cabins and swelling the population of the communities of Shooting Creek and the Valley Towns. Census records, spoliation claims, U.S. Army surveys, and present-day archaeology combine to draw a detailed picture of Cherokee life here prior to removal.

By the 1830s, more than three thousand Cherokees lived in about six hundred households throughout this area, making it one of the most densely settled areas of the Cherokee Nation at the time. Army surveys document seven community townhouses, two ball fields, four stores, a

A Cherokee homestead, photographed by James Mooney around 1888.
(National Anthropological Archives, Smithsonian Institution)

gristmill, and numerous roads and trails. This Cherokee population included more full-bloods than other areas of the Cherokee Nation, but also
included thirty-seven African American slaves and twenty-two whites who
had married Cherokees. Although it was not the center of Cherokee literacy
and publication—found in New Echota at the time—even so, more than
five hundred of the Cherokee people in this area were literate in their own
language. Some were Christians, and some of the first Cherokee ministers
came from the Valley Towns.

A typical household of the 1830s included a log cabin or two, outbuildings, fields, and orchards. Most log cabins were one-story, made of logs
with the bark still on, a wood shake roof, packed dirt floors, and a fireplace made of wood and clay. Many households still used the old *asi* or hot
house, as well as a corncrib and stable. Large gardens along with cornfields
occupied five to ten acres or more for each household. Dozens of peach and
apple trees provided fruit.

Although still traditional in many ways—continuing to make baskets
and pottery, continuing the ball play and ceremonial dances—Cherokees
here also participated in trade and acquired the modern goods of the day.
Most households had some imported china—dishes, tea cups, and Delft
pitchers—along with traditional Cherokee pottery. Cherokee people used
tables and chairs, iron pots, silverware, looms, guns, plows, mattocks, shov-
els, spades, saws, axes, froes, wedges, and drawknives. They were raising

The Owle Family on the Trail of Tears

*I'll tell you the history of my father's side. My great-great grandfather's
name was Jennick HuHu, Jennick Owle. He lived in a little place called
Hanging Dog down around Murphy, North Carolina.*

*Early one morning he had a knock on the door. He and his wife and
a small baby named David were in the house. Opened the door and six
or eight bayonets were instantly stuck in his face. The Georgia Guard
had arrived. Told him to get out of the house and he asked them why.
They said that it belonged to them. It was Georgia property and they
were taking it.*

*So they marched him out of the house under force, burned down the
cabin, killed all of his livestock, and marched him into Murphy, to Fort
Butler. Put him in the stockade with his family. It was not very nice, at
least according to the history in the family I've heard passed down. It
was wet. It was cold and muddy inside those giant walls. They didn't
feed them very much, and many of them got sick.*

*They were very weak when they moved out one cold October morn-
ing. Marched them over the mountains headed towards the Mississippi
River. After days they finally reached the Mississippi. They found out
that Jennick could speak both English and Cherokee, so they told him to
count the Cherokees and sort of supervise them as they came along. So
he did.*

*He told his wife in Cherokee, "You stay on this side of the river. Hide
in the canebreaks, and I will tell them that everyone is here. And then
when they begin to march I will march a little distance with them and
I will run away and I will come back and join you." So she hid in the
canebreaks.*

*They crossed the Mississippi. Jennick told them they were all there,
and they started to march on. He goes a few steps, and he decides he
doesn't want to go too far, so he runs back and he jumps into the Mississippi, going underneath the water. They shot in the water several times
with their muskets, and gave him up for dead.*

*Jennick was breathing through a reed, and he stayed under for a
long period of time. After coming up he listened and heard no sounds,
so he climbed up to the top of the bank and looked and they were gone.
So he swims across the Mississippi River, looks in the canebreak for
Caroline. She wasn't there. She had headed back after hearing the
shots. She too had given him up for dead.*

Freeman Owle. (© 2000 Steve Wall)

He lingers on, back into North Carolina. Didn't see her anywhere along the way. So he figured maybe something had happened—it was a long journey back—that he'd lost her and the child. So he began to beg food.

Now make no mistake. There were good people in this area at the time of the Removal. The settlers, many of them in this area up through here and down around Bryson City, many of these people were sympathetic to the Cherokee condition. He begged food early in the morning and they fed him. He begged food for a year and they fed him.

Early one morning after a year he was begging food at this house. And he saw a silhouette up on the hillside, coming out of the pine thicket. And at first he couldn't make it out. But he looked and he watched cause he was afraid. He thought that someone was coming down upon him. And if they caught these settlers feeding him, they would put them all in jail and probably would have killed him. So he stood quietly.

The silhouette came closer and closer and he recognized it as being a woman carrying a baby. Soon he recognized it was his own wife and child. So they were reunited.

And moved to Cherokee, thanks to Will Thomas who bought the little *bit of land. They gave him the money after working at different farms and for settlers. They worked and secretly got the money together and bought it, and they live here today. We do. So that's how my family survived the Removal.*

So if you do any reading, look very carefully at the Removal itself. And there's many factions. It doesn't end here. It has never ended. The effects of Removal are still going on today.

Freeman Owle, in Living Stories of the Cherokee

cattle, hogs, and horses and driving some of them to market. Cherokee women were not only spinning and weaving cloth but also trading for prodigious amounts of calico, stroud cloth, and ribbons.

Removal intruded into this world as soldiers arrived and began constructing garrisons and stockades. Tlanusi-yi, at the junction of the Valley and Hiwassee Rivers, became the central location for removal activities. Soldiers constructed Fort Butler, a garrison for themselves, on the hill, and constructed stockades on the Hiwassee River bank. Other "forts" were constructed throughout western North Carolina: Camp Scott (now under Nantahala Lake), Fort Montgomery (now Fort Hill, Robbinsville), Fort Lindsay (now Almond), Fort Delaney (now Andrews), and Fort Hembree (now Hayesville). In May and June of 1838, the U.S. Army, aided by North Carolina militia, began taking Cherokees prisoner and incarcerating them in these forts. They all eventually came to Fort Butler, and thence west to a large internment camp in Charleston, Tennessee. From Fort Butler, more than three thousand Cherokees went on the Trail of Tears, crossing the Hiwassee by ferry near the Leech Place, where the ferry ruts are still visible below the stone cliff above the deep hole in the river.

In Murphy, you can learn more about the Trail of Tears at the Cherokee County Historical Museum on Peachtree Street. From this area, you can travel northwest on the route of the original Unicoi Turnpike, one of the routes of the Trail of Tears (now Joe Brown Highway).

In the nearby community of Brasstown, the John C. Campbell Folk School is constructing a "Rivercane Walk" along the creek. This walking trail provides interpretation of Cherokee history and culture and of the importance of rivercane. On the way to Brasstown, US 64 passes the site of the Peachtree Mound, once the center of the thriving town of Hiwassee, and continues on past the original Baptist mission to the Cherokees.

Bo Taylor sits near the Hunter's Ferry crossing site in Murphy, N.C.
(© 2000 Steve Wall)

Three side trips from Murphy take you to the locations of Cherokee towns and mountain trails. In Hayesville, the Clay County Historical and Arts Council Museum interprets archaeological finds at the nearby Spike-buck village, whose mound can be viewed from a walking trail. The museum stands near the site of Fort Hembree. North of Murphy, US 19 takes you through the area of the former Valley Towns. South of Murphy, US 19 leads to scenic Blood Mountain and the Walasi-Yi Center over rugged mountains in Georgia.

Authentic Cherokee arts and crafts are sold by tribal members in Young Harris, Georgia, a short trip south of Hayesville. The Native American Arts and Crafts Gallery there showcases work by Cherokee artists and crafts-people.

Bird by Virgil Ledford, Cherokee woodcarver. (Photograph by Cedric N. Chatterley)

■ Cherokee County Historical Museum

The Cherokee County Historical Museum is in downtown Murphy next to the Cherokee County courthouse. This nonprofit museum, housed in a historic brick Carnegie library building, holds extensive collections of prehistoric and historic era artifacts, as well as document collections important to the rich heritage of Cherokee County. Exhibits in the upstairs galleries include displays of seventeenth- and eighteenth-century Cherokee artifacts from Peachtree Mound and Village and other local sites. Displays of mid-nineteenth-century farm and homestead equipment illuminate the lives of early white settlers in the area, while interspersed photographs chronicle the development of Murphy and Andrews through the later nineteenth and early twentieth century. Photographic portraits of members of Murphy's early black community round out an image of Cherokee County's diverse heritage.

Also on display is an account book from A. R. S. Hunter's store, a mercantile that operated through the period of the 1838 Cherokee removal. Hunter's ledger details the daily transactions of local Cherokees and army troops stationed at Fort Butler, with purchases of everything from beads

Cherokee County Historical Museum in Murphy, N.C. (Photograph by Wayne Martin)

and calico to champagne and suspenders. A model of Fort Butler and a book of transcribed military communications from the removal era help visitors visualize the contribution of the military presence to the abrupt transformation of Cherokee country into Cherokee County, N.C.

The ground floor of the museum houses exhibits that provide overviews of prehistoric-era native culture and technology in the region. This part of the museum is being developed as a local center for the Trail of Tears National Historic Trail and the Unicoi Turnpike National Millennium Trail; planned exhibits focus on presentation and interpretation of the Cherokee Trail of Tears and nineteenth-century Cherokee life in the upper Hiwassee River Valley. These exhibits will include a reconstruction of a Cherokee cabin interior from the 1830s, interpretations and maps of the Cherokee cultural landscape circa 1837–38, and a treatment of local resistance against the military removal and the development of post-removal Cherokee communities in the local area.

CONTACT: Cherokee County Historical Museum, 87 Peachtree St., Murphy, NC 28906, 828-837-6792, <cchm@webworkz.com>

HOURS: Open Monday through Friday from 9:00 A.M. until 5:00 P.M. (closed on federal holidays). Admission by voluntary contribution.

LOCATION: Downtown Murphy, next to the Cherokee County Courthouse. At the junction of US 64 and US 19/74, turn west onto Peachtree Street and proceed three blocks to the museum on the right (north) side of the street.

■ Fort Butler

We arrived at Fort Butler on the 7th [June 7, 1838], but did not establish camp till today, which is on the north side of Valley River just above its entrance into Hiwassee, and about one mile from the Fort. We are said to be in the thickest settled portion of the Cherokee Country. There are about six thousand in our neighborhood—their houses are quite thick about us, and they all remain quietly at home at work on their little farms, as though no evil was intended them. They sell us very cheap anything they have to spare, and look upon the regular troops as their friends. . . . These are innocent and simple people into whose homes we are to obtrude ourselves, and take off by force. They have no idea of fighting, but submit quietly to be tied and led away.

—Captain L. B. Webster, an officer of the 4th Artillery
  detailed to the Cherokee removal operations, 1838

Fort Butler, once located on a hilltop overlooking present-day Murphy, was headquarters for the Eastern Division of the U.S. Army of the Cherokee Nation during the forced removal of 1838. From mid-June through mid-July of that year, more than three thousand Cherokee prisoners from southwestern North Carolina and adjacent parts of Georgia passed through Fort Butler at the outset of the Trail of Tears. Although some Cherokee prisoners were incarcerated for as much as two weeks in the internment areas surrounding Fort Butler, most stayed at the fort only a few days before marching west along the Unicoi Turnpike toward the Cherokee Agency and "emigration depot" at Fort Cass, now Charleston, Tennessee.

Fort Butler was established in July 1836 by General Ellis Wool and a contingent of Tennessee Volunteer troops, forces dispatched to the Valley River region to keep order among Cherokees and whites after ratification of the New Echota Treaty. Originally named Camp Huntington, the fort was situated on a knoll that commanded the strategic Christie Ford over the Hiwassee River, where the Unicoi Turnpike and the old state road through the Valley River intersect. Wool's troops abandoned the camp after a month, but the army reoccupied the post in 1837 and christened it Fort Butler in honor of Benjamin Butler, then secretary of war. Later in 1837, troops from Fort Butler built Fort Hembree (now Hayesville, North Carolina), Fort Delaney (now Andrews, North Carolina), and Fort Lindsay (now Almond, North Carolina) in anticipation of a forced military removal of Cherokees from southwestern North Carolina. Other posts were established at Fort Montgomery (now Robbinsville, North Carolina) and Camp Scott (now Aquone, North Carolina) in 1838.

By January 1838, it was clear that the majority of Cherokee people would never voluntarily emigrate across the Mississippi as specified by the fraudulent New Echota Treaty. The U.S. Army began serious preparations to carry out the deportation of the Cherokee Nation when the treaty deadline of May 23, 1838, expired. During the spring of 1838, the army added barracks, officers' quarters, offices, shops, ovens, and other buildings to Fort Butler, and may have enclosed the fort or nearby areas with stockades. General Abraham Eustis took command of Fort Butler in late May 1838; companies of the 1st, 2nd, and 4th Artillery regiments, fresh from the Seminole War in Florida, were stationed at and around the fort.

The military removal of the Cherokees began in Georgia in late May 1838. Georgia militia abused their Cherokee prisoners to such a degree that General Winfield Scott, commander of the regular troops, suspended further military action until June 12, 1838. Because the army viewed southwestern North Carolina as the most likely flash point for Cherokee resistance, Scott himself directed the beginning of the military roundup from Fort Butler on June 12.

Within a week, state and federal troops collected almost two-thirds of the region's Cherokee inhabitants; by July 4, more than twenty-five hundred Cherokee prisoners had encamped around Fort Butler before being transferred in smaller parties to Fort Cass, Tennessee. Among the prisoners were John Wickliff and Peter Oganaya, Cherokee Baptist preachers who erected an arbor at Fort Butler and held nightly prayer meetings and revival services. During their traumatic incarceration at Fort Butler, many Cherokees sought solace in the new religion that promised justice for the oppressed. Wickliff and Oganaya led the converts to baptism in the Hiwassee River under the watchful guard of armed U.S. troops.

The site of the fort, along Hitchcock Street near Lakeside Street in Murphy, North Carolina, is in a private residential neighborhood. It is hard now to visualize the manicured lawns and neat homes as a focal point for the tragedy of Cherokee removal, an emblem of national injustice and human suffering. Immediately downslope from the fort site, Cherokee Street follows the old Unicoi Turnpike alignment west toward the internment camps of Tennessee and the new home of the Cherokee Nation in Oklahoma.

CONTACT: Cherokee County Historical Museum, 87 Peachtree St., Murphy, NC 28906, 828-837-6792

LOCATION: The former fort site is located along Hitchcock Street, immediately west of Lakeside Street, Murphy, North Carolina. From the Cherokee County Historical Museum, go northwest one block on

The Trail of Tears Basket

Eva Wolfe, master basket weaver, making a rivercane basket. (Photograph by Rob Amberg)

I don't like to talk about the Trail of Tears, it's really sad. And sometimes it gets to me, and I can feel it. Especially when I got a basket that I carry that's over 150 years old, and it's still good and sturdy, a white oak basket that went on the Trail of Tears. This was given to me in Oklahoma.

No telling how many people have died in front of this basket. If this basket could talk to you, there's no telling what all it would tell you that happened along the Trail of Tears: how many people was killed, and many people got hurt and had to be buried beside the road when they couldn't walk.

And no telling what all I could tell from what I listened when I was a little girl.

Edna Chekelelee, *in* Living Stories of the Cherokee

Peachtree Street, then turn left (southwest) onto US 19 Business. Cross the bridge over the Hiwassee River, then take the first street on the right (Lakeside Street). Turn left almost immediately onto Hunter Street, then right onto Cherokee Street, then left onto Fifth Street. At the top of the hill, turn left onto Hitchcock Street. The fort site is mid-block on this short residential street.

SITES NEAR MURPHY

■ Rivercane Walk at the John C. Campbell Folk School

The John C. Campbell Folk School at Brasstown, North Carolina, is located near the mouth of Little Brasstown Creek, in the heart of the old Cherokee community of Aquohee ("Big Place"). The school, founded by Olive Dame Campbell in 1925, offers a wide variety of programs in folk arts and traditional music and dance aimed to foster appreciation for the traditional cultures of Appalachia while promoting personal development.

As part of its campus enhancement, the school is developing a 1.5-mile walkway on its property along Little Brasstown Creek. The Rivercane Walk will feature trailside exhibits that relate the natural and cultural history of the lower Brasstown Creek Valley and the surrounding area. The local river cane growing along the creek's margin provides inspiration for one of the trail's major themes. Cane (*Arundinaria gigantea*) figured prominently in traditional Cherokee architecture and is still used for traditional crafts such as basketry and blowgun manufacture. Its presence signifies the health of streamside environments in the southern mountains, and the folk school's efforts to restore and rejuvenate Little Brasstown Creek are symbolized by the return and spread of the natural "canebrakes."

Exhibit panels along the Rivercane Walk will discuss the Aquohee community and the lifeways of its Cherokee inhabitants on the eve of the 1838 military removal. Featured topics include the Aquohee District, a Cherokee administrative area centered at a local townhouse; Situwakee, the Aquohee District judge and removal-era leader who lived nearby on Settawig Road; and the Unicoi Turnpike, which ran along Settawig Road and crossed Brasstown Creek just north of the folk school property.

Visitors are welcome to stroll the Rivercane Walk at the John C. Campbell Folk School during daylight hours throughout the year. The walk actually begins in the uplands near the western edge of the folk school property; this beginning point is accessed on foot from the central parking area

Rivercane basket by Eva Wolfe. (Photograph by Rob Amberg)

Walker Calhoun making darts used in rivercane blowguns. (© 2000 Steve Wall)

located along Brasstown Road. The trail completes a loop of 1.5 miles and passes near the parking area at its end. Although the Rivercane Trail is generally smooth and well prepared, it is not recommended as handicapped accessible.

CONTACT: John C. Campbell Folk School, One Folk School Rd., Brasstown, NC 28902, 828-837-2775

LOCATION: The John C. Campbell Folk School is located approximately 8.6 miles southeast of Murphy in Brasstown, North Carolina. To reach the school from the Cherokee County Historical Museum, drive southeast on Peachtree Street 0.5 miles to the intersection with US 64. Proceed east on US 64 for 4.6 miles to Peachtree. Just past Tri-County Community College, bear left onto Old US 64 (which becomes Phillips Road) and continue south for 3.5 miles to Brasstown Road. Turn right onto Brasstown Road and cross the bridge over Brasstown Creek; the folk school is the first cluster of buildings west of the bridge.

■ US 64 through Peachtree to Hayesville

Some of the more important Cherokee sites accessible from the Murphy hub are located east along US 64 on the route toward Hayesville and can be visited in an afternoon's drive through the Hiwassee River Valley. All of this landscape is permeated by Cherokee history. Some of the key sites accessible from US 64 east of Murphy are the Peachtree Mound and Village area at Peachtree, the Valleytowns Baptist Mission site at Peachtree, and the Aquohee community area at Brasstown (where you may also visit the John C. Campbell Folk School). Farther east, at Hayesville, is the site of Fort Hembree (a removal-era military post), the Spikebuck mound and village site, and the Clay County Historical and Arts Council Museum.

From Peachtree, North Carolina, southeastward through Hayesville, US 64 follows the route of the eighteenth-century trading path that stretched from Charlestown, South Carolina, to the Overhill settlements of Tennessee. East of the Hiwassee River bridge in Clay County, US 64 also corresponds with the Unicoi Turnpike, traveling along Sweetwater Creek and crossing Sweetwater Gap to descend into Hayesville.

As visitors pass through the extensive river bottoms and terraces at Peachtree, they are in the midst of the old town site of Hiwassee, the largest of the Cherokee Valley Towns and the principal settlement of the region. This site (on the south side of US 64, next to the river), now known as the Peachtree Mound and Village, is on private property and is not open to public visitation, but the broad floodplains that once cradled the village can be appreciated from the roadside. Hiwassee was especially prominent during the early eighteenth century, when British traders and diplomats knew the town as a center of economic and political power. The height of Hiwassee's influence is evident in the archaeological record; Smithsonian Institution excavations of the mound and a portion of the village recovered vast quantities of early eighteenth-century British goods. These excavations also revealed a long, continuous sequence of occupation; the mound was constructed as a townhouse platform as early as A.D. 1000, and may have had a Middle Woodland period (ca. A.D. 100–A.D. 600) antecedent.

In 1761, Christopher French noted that Hiwassee was the largest of the Valley Towns and included fifty to sixty Natchez Indian families, refugees from a disastrous war with the French in Mississippi. The Rutherford expedition from North Carolina destroyed Hiwassee in 1776, but the town was

Stands of rivercane, often found along riverbanks near Cherokee village sites, are easily overlooked. (Photograph by Roger Haile)

soon rebuilt and was occupied until the Cherokee removal of 1838. During the 1820s, Hiwassee was the seat of the Aquohee District courthouse and by the 1830s, the settlement consisted primarily of Cherokee Baptist converts.

East of Peachtree, US 64 passes through another old town, Aquonatuste, which archaeologists from the University of North Carolina investigated during the 1960s. Here they found well preserved ruins of burned Cherokee homes believed to date to Rutherford's 1776 raid. Christopher French, who wrote about the town in 1761, noted that the settlement was only two years old, but that it had long been the residence of Cornelius Dougharty, the first British trader to live among the Cherokees. Later, probably around 1800, a community of Natchez Indians (perhaps from nearby Hiwassee) settled at Aquonatuste and remained there until the Baptists established Valleytowns Mission on a high terrace overlooking the town in 1820. Like the Peachtree Mound and Village site, Aquonatuste is privately owned and is not open to the public. Visitors traveling along US 64 pass through the river bottoms of Aquonatuste on the west side of the Hiwassee River.

About 1 mile from Aquonatuste, Settawig Road turns south from US 64 to run west along the south side of the Hiwassee River through the old nineteenth-century community of Aquohee. The road is named for Situ-wakee, a prominent pre-removal leader who lived on one of the river terraces north of the road. Settawig Road runs for 3 miles along the route

Site of Quanassee Village with Spikebuck Mound in Hayesville, N.C.
(Photograph by Roger Haile)

of the Unicoi Turnpike, and some segments are paved over the turnpike roadbed. Near the western end of Settawig Road stood the home and church house of Peter Oganaya, a Cherokee national councilman and Baptist preacher. Settawig Road intersects with Phillips Road near the John C. Campbell Folk School, where interpretive panels along the Rivercane Walk trail relate details of the Cherokee history of Aquohee.

From the eastern end of Settawig Road, US 64 follows the turnpike route through a landscape dotted with sites of nineteenth-century Cherokee farmsteads that belonged to folks like Spring Lizard, Nancy Timpson, and Aquallah. After crossing Sweetwater Gap, US 64 descends the Blair Creek Valley into Hayesville, passing the site of the Tusquittee townhouse and the nearby farms of Old Spikebuck and Tom Spikebuck. On the western outskirts of Hayesville, the turnpike diverged from present-day US 64 and ran uphill along modern-day Fort Hembree Road past Fort Hembree, the removal-era fort that gathered in the Cherokee residents of the upper Hiwassee River Valley east of Brasstown.

On the north side of Hayesville, a broad river bottom extends north to the Hiwassee River, where a large Mississippian mound stands on the riverbank. Present-day archaeologists call this the Spikebuck Mound and Village site, but Cherokees knew the place as Quanassee, a large seventeenth- and early eighteenth-century settlement that was home to a British trading

Shooting Creek valley near Hayesville, N.C. (Photograph by Roger Haile)

factorage. The town was abandoned in 1725 as a result of a devastating raid by a Coosa Indian war party. Old Quanassee was replaced in the early nineteenth century by the westward extension of Tusquittee Town, which occupied the Tusquittee Creek Valley on the north side of the Hiwassee River. Archaeological investigations at Quanassee (Spikebuck) in the 1970s recovered evidence of intensive Cherokee occupations dating from the sixteenth through early eighteenth centuries. Artifacts from these excavations are currently displayed at the Clay County Historical and Arts Council Museum in Hayesville. Most of the village site is privately owned, but the town of Hayesville owns the mound on the riverside, and visitors can access the mound via a trail leading from the town recreation park.

East of Hayesville, us 64 ascends the Shooting Creek Valley, once home to the nineteenth-century Cherokee communities of Shooting Creek and Nacoochee. The crossing at Hothouse Creek marks the location of the old Shooting Creek townhouse, burned by vindictive whites on the eve of the Cherokee removal. Near the head of Shooting Creek, us 64 begins its ascent of Chunky Gal Mountain (named for a Cherokee woman, the Chunkey [as in the chunkey game] Gal, who lived in Shooting Creek), and a spectacular view of the upper valley reveals the forks of Muskrat Creek, where Old Muskrat lived with his son Johnson Muskrat and his grandsons Thompson and Wilson Muskrat. Just across the mountain, in the Little Tennessee River Valley, us 64 descends another Muskrat Branch, where Old Muskrat lived before 1820. Here, visitors enter the old Middle Towns area and can continue east on US 64 to the Franklin hub.

■ Valleytowns Baptist Mission

Seven miles east of Murphy, US 64 crosses the old Valleytowns Baptist Mission Farm on the west side of the Hiwassee River near Peachtree, North Carolina. Here, in 1820, the American Baptist Foreign Mission Board founded a church, boarding school, and model farm to "civilize" and Christianize the Cherokees in the Aquohee District, the most remote and insular part of the Cherokee Nation. The missionaries built at old Aquonatuste town; a small community of Natchez Indians had lived there but abandoned the site when the Baptists arrived.

When the mission opened its doors in November 1820, Cherokee parents from the surrounding region placed almost fifty children under the care of the Baptist teachers. The missionaries first attempted to teach school by English language total immersion, but most of the students were quickly disheartened by lessons in an alien tongue. The teachers, particularly Evan Jones, resolved to learn the Cherokee language and conduct the school in the best interest of the monolingual, full-blood Cherokee population. Through the use of the Sequoyan syllabary as a primary teaching tool, the Valleytowns Baptist Mission school became the most successful and popular of the Protestant mission schools to operate in the Cherokee Nation.

The primary leader of the Valleytowns mission was Evan Jones, a native of Wales who served as teacher and minister from 1821 until 1836, when U.S. troops expelled him from the Cherokee Nation for supporting Cherokee resistance to removal. Under Jones's direction, the mission helped shape future Cherokee leaders such as John Timson, Peter Oganaya, John Wickliff, and James Wafford. Jones became a confidant of Chief John Ross and the National Committee, and he coached the Cherokee leadership in developing legal strategies to combat President Andrew Jackson's push for Cherokee removal. When the dreaded military removal became reality in the summer of 1838, Jones ministered to his congregations during their imprisonment at Fort Cass. During the Cherokee exodus, Jones assisted with the management of one of the emigration detachments, and later worked avidly to reestablish the Baptists' mission in Oklahoma.

Recent archaeological investigations have located some of the mission's original structures, and preliminary excavations have recovered materials from the earliest days of the mission. A brick-lined cellar appears to have underlain the primary school building. Discarded writing slates and pencils from this cellar attest to the students' lessons, while inexpensive tableware,

The First Time I Saw a White Man

I grew up in the time when there were no outside noises, there was nothing that interfered with the serenity of my childhood. I grew up with nature, see. But it was during that time, that storytellers would come into our home and tell stories and legends and history of what happened to their ancestors, on back. One of the stories was how the Indians had been gathered together and moved by force to leave their homes and have that trek to Oklahoma. I heard that so many times, the time came when I created a new hate in my heart, even as a child for the white man for what they did to my people. And that kept growing, that kept growing, but I had never seen a white man. To me, when they said white man, it was just like a snow man, white from head to foot, but just before I was six years old I saw a white man for the first time. And he was not white as I had imagined, he was just like anybody else only he was white.

We had a little chinking pushed out from between the logs in our little cabin and we devised it as a window because it looked down on the trail, where if somebody was coming up the trail you could see them. And one morning my mother said, "There's somebody coming up the trail." And I told her, "By horse, too." This is unusual, somebody unusual. So we looked through that little hole, and watched this white man on a white horse come up the trail. Fear seized me, because I knew what the white man had done to the Indian. My brother, who is only three years older, took me to the largest corner in the house, and then sat in front of me protectively.

And this lady came, and this gentleman came. The man stopped outside, and the lady came on in, and she was red-headed, she wore spectacles, she had wrinkles. I say that was the most ferocious thing I had ever seen in my life. And she came over to us, we could not understand what she was saying, but the tone of her voice told us she loved us.

And finally there came a time when we would be standing at that little hole in the wall, looking down, awaiting her appearance. And then I think after several days, or several months maybe of that, she decided we had graduated from that time, and she took us by the hand and led us to a small stream, and she led us across that stream, and she placed two yellow flint stones at the foot of the apple tree, and there we sat, and she talked. She taught us with those picture cards. Those old fashioned aprons they wore, they had pockets on the inside. She'd

Robert Bushyhead.
(Photograph by Bill Bamberger)

reach in there and pull out pictures. Especially one, and she would say, "Now this is Jesus. This is Jesus." Over and over again. I would see him, I would hear him, created a picture of Jesus. And then, "He loves you, he loves you, and because he loves you, I love you." You know, we could understand somehow, somewhat of what she was saying, and so we learned that, and one morning when she pulled out that picture, I beat her to the draw and I said "Jesus" before she did, and she said, "Yes, yes, yes, Jesus," and she gave me the card for saying "Jesus." And then when my brother noticed that I had gotten a card for saying "Jesus" he said "Jesus" too, so he got a card. Then from that point she showed us Jesus feeding the multitudes, Jesus healing the sick, Jesus, and that was her way of introducing the Bible to us. Jesus did this, Jesus did that, Jesus did such and such, and so I began to depend a lot upon those pictures.

Robert Bushyhead

pig bones, and eggshells reflect more mundane activities of daily life at the mission. Cherokee and Catawba ceramics hint at the traditional foods that native cooks prepared for the students' meals.

The mission site is situated on private property, but future plans call for a roadside overlook and interpretive station alongside US 64 at the Hiwassee River bridge. The earlier mission buildings were located on a high terrace about 0.25 mile northeast of the bridge; structures built after 1830 were situated on a lower terrace near a spring head.

CONTACT: Cherokee County Historical Museum, 87 Peachtree St., Murphy, NC 28906, 828-837-6792
LOCATION: At the eastern edge of Cherokee County, US 64 transects the original Mission Farm before crossing the Hiwassee River.

■ Fort Hembree

The site of Fort Hembree, a removal-era U.S. Army facility, is located on Fort Hill on the western side of Hayesville. The site fronts on Fort Hembree Road and occupies much of the hilltop flat across the western half of Fort Hill. The fort site is privately owned and is not open for public visitation, but a planned roadside exhibit at the junction of Fort Hembree Road and US 64 will provide visitors an opportunity to view the landscape from the ground.

The U.S. Army founded Fort Hembree in 1837 as part of its preparation for the forced removal of the Cherokee people from southwestern North Carolina. The hilltop location commands the basin area formed by Town and Blair Creeks and gave the army easy access to the densely populated communities of Tusquittee and Shooting Creek. The fort also controlled the Unicoi Turnpike and guaranteed the Army of the Cherokee Nation its primary line of supply and communication.

When the army began the removal operations on June 12, 1838, troops from Fort Hembree fanned out to cover communities from Hiawassee, Georgia, northward to the heads of Tusquittee and Shooting Creeks and westward to the mouth of Sweetwater Creek. They drew in almost a thousand prisoners in various contingents into the area surrounding the fort, then conducted the Cherokee deportees along the Unicoi Turnpike to Fort Butler. Although few of the prisoners spent more than a week at Hembree, claims records indicate substantial mortality around the fort. Celia Downing and several of her nieces perished of "fevers" at Fort Hembree; they, with dozens of others, are buried in unmarked graves on Fort Hill.

No contemporary drawings of the fort survive, but army sketch maps

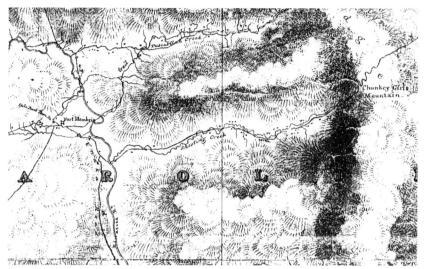

Detail from "Map of Part of the Cherokee Territory Situated among the
Mountains of N. Carolina, Georgia and Tennessee," by W. G. Williams, 1838.
(U.S. 125, Record Group 77, National Archives, College Park, Md.)

prepared in 1838 depict rows of hilltop barracks at the fort, and an 1847
account mentions the ruins of wooden palisades. Local tradition contends
that a large log house dismantled during the 1930s once served as the officers' quarters and mess area. Other fort buildings were reused after removal as a post office and store for the early white community of Fort Hembree, the precursor to Hayesville.

CONTACT: Clay County Historical and Arts Council Museum, P.O. Box 5,
Hayesville, NC 28904, 828-389-6814
LOCATION: The site of the former Fort Hembree is now on private
property. To drive by, take US 64 Bypass and turn onto NC 79 North.
Within 200 yards, turn left onto Fort Hembree Road. A wayside exhibit
is planned for the intersection of US 64 and Fort Hembree Road.

■ Clay County Historical and Arts Council Museum

The Clay County Historical and Arts Council Museum, located in the old
county jail in Hayesville, North Carolina, features exhibit panels that detail the nineteenth-century Cherokee landscape of Clay County. Panels to
be added will relate the role of Fort Hembree, and discuss the impact of
removal and the Trail of Tears on the Cherokee people of Clay County. Arti-

The Removed Townhouses

*Long ago, long before the Cherokee were driven from their homes in
1838, the people on Valley River and Hiwassee heard voices of invisible
spirits in the air calling and warning them of wars and misfortunes
which the future held in store, and inviting them to come and live with
the Nunnehi, the Immortals, in their homes under the mountains and
under the waters. For days the voices hung in the air, and the people listened until they heard the spirits say, "If you would live with us, gather
everyone in your townhouses and fast there for seven days, and no one
must raise a shout or a war whoop in all that time. Do this and we shall
come and you will see us and we shall take you to live with us." . . .*

*The people of another town, on the Hiwassee, at the place which we
call now Dustiyalvyi, where Shooting Creek comes in, also prayed and
fasted, and at the end of seven days, the Nunnehi came and took them
away down under the water. They are there now, and on a warm summer day, when the wind ripples the surface, those who listen well can
hear them talking below. When the Cherokee drag the river for fish the
fish-drag always stops and catches there, although the water is deep,
and the people know it is being held by their lost kinsmen, who do not
want to be forgotten.*

*When the Cherokee were forcibly removed to the West, one of the
greatest regrets of those along Hiwassee and Valley rivers was that they
were compelled to leave behind forever their relatives who had gone to
the Nunnehi.*

*Salili (Squirrel), blacksmith and patent holder
of a new rifle design, to James Mooney ca. 1890*

fact displays present materials recovered from excavations at the Spikebuck
village site, the old town seat of Quanassee, and reflect the late prehistory
and early history of the area that would become Hayesville. Other items
exhibited in the museum, such as antique farm implements, a moonshine
still, and an early telephone system represent the Anglo-American experience in Clay County.

Future plans call for exhibit panels that will relate vignettes about the
Cherokee inhabitants of the local area in the years leading up to the Cherokee removal. For instance, Judge Richard Walker, who lived west of Hayes-

Clay County Historical and Arts Council Museum, Hayesville, N.C. (Photograph by Roger Haile)

ville near Brasstown Creek, served as justice for the Cherokee Supreme Court. Walker, a full-blood reared by white adoptive parents, was a planter and entrepreneur who owned extensive properties outside the Cherokee Nation. An early patron of the Baptist Mission, he is immortalized by Walker Branch, a tributary of Brasstown Creek. Account records from Hyatt and Love's Store at Hayesville illustrate one panel. These records listing local Cherokee customers and their purchases survive as part of a settlement in a business scam that one of the partners attempted—the other partner harassed Cherokee debtors for years. Another panel will discuss the origins of local place names and their relations to the pre-removal Cherokee communities of the Hayesville area. For instance, Blair Creek is named for George Blair, a Cherokee planter deported to Oklahoma in 1838; Downing Creek and Jack Rabbit Mountain are named for individuals (Richard Downing and Jack Rabbit) who managed to avoid removal.

CONTACT: Clay County Historical and Arts Council Museum, P.O. Box 5, Hayesville, NC 28904, 828-389-6814
HOURS: Open Tuesday through Saturday, 10:00 A.M. to 4:00 P.M., June 1 until Labor Day weekend. Other times by appointment; call 828-389-6760 to arrange a schedule. Limited street-side parking is available, and the museum itself is equipped for handicapped accessibility.

Gathering Blessings

It's been the life of many families here—the baskets, the carving, the other crafts. And the land has put out that material all these years, it's helped a lot of families here. Whenever you go out looking for that material, you have to be very selective. You don't just go and get this tree, the first one you see. When they went to get a tree for baskets, or for carving, there was a prayer said. And then they might take the fourth one. And then they would get it on the east side. When they were getting medicinal herbs it was always on the east side.

And a prayer was said. Even today I think there's still prayer that goes with that, before getting a particular material. I think there was a lot of respect when that was done. And a lot of gratitude was shown before it was taken out.

I know when I go out there looking for something—something to eat or whatever I'm finding out there, or flowers, whatever, it just really touches my heart. It makes me realize the blessing that we get. And it fills me with gratitude to be in this place, this beautiful land. It's very touching because there's just so much that we need to be thankful for.

And do we return the blessing with gratitude? When the wind was blowing a couple days ago, you could almost see the Lord out there. I don't know how else to say it. He has just blessed us. He continues to bless us every day with this beautiful land, beautiful natural resources, the water, every little plant that comes up.

Marie Junaluska

LOCATION: From the west, take US 64 Business East into downtown Hayesville. At the stop sign, turn right. The museum will be just ahead on the right in a red brick building (a former jail) next to the sheriff's office.

SCENIC DRIVE

■ US 19 through the Valley Towns

Murphy, once known as Tlanusi-yi, is located near the southwestern corner of the old Valley Towns region, the breadbasket of the old Cherokee Nation. Upstream from Murphy, in the large river bottoms that spread northeastward along the Valley River toward Andrews, the Cherokee communities of Canasti, Nottely, Tomotla, Little Tellico, Neowee, Tasetsi, and Konahete once dotted the landscape like pearls on a strand. Fertile cornfields stretched for almost 20 miles through the Long Valley Place (in Cherokee, Konahete), which lends its name to the Valley River, Valley River Valley, and Valley River Mountains. When Cherokee emigrants arrived in Oklahoma in 1839, they carried the name Konahete to a new valley to remember the garden spot of the old nation.

Today, visitors can tour the old Valley Towns with a scenic twenty-minute drive through the center of the valley along US 19/74 from Murphy to Andrews. More leisurely drives are afforded by the older parallel roads that run along the valley's margins, such as the old Marble/Coalville Road on the northwestern side of the valley or Fairview Road on the southeastern side. From the Cherokee County Historical Museum, follow Peachtree Street south to the intersection with US 64 and US 19/74, then turn left on US 19/74 toward Andrews and proceed northeast.

Less than 1 mile along US 19, a river bottom is apparent on the left side next to Murphy High School. This is the site of the old town of Clenussee (Tlanusi-yi), a late-eighteenth-century settlement destroyed by the Rutherford expedition. Later, these bottoms were farmed by Elijah Sourjohn and his wife, Nancy Hawkins; the place is still known locally as the Sourjohn Farm. Upstream, the valley constricts for about 1 mile, then widens again into a series of river bottoms and older terraces. The southernmost of these, maintained as a cow pasture, marks the old town site of Tomotla, a former settlement that lends its name to a modern Cherokee community in the area. Tomotla was once home to James Maxwell, a resident trader who teamed with Cornelius Dougharty in a 1743 silver mining venture that left enigmatic mine shafts in the nearby hills; later writers thought these were Spanish mines. Farther upstream, an isolated traffic signal light on US 19 marks the entry of Vengeance Creek Road, where the old Charlestown Trading Path passed through low hills between Hiwassee Town (at Peachtree) and Nottely or Canasti on the Valley River before ascending Hyatt Mill Creek on the western edge of the Valley and continuing toward Hanging Dog Creek. This was once the primary commercial route through the region before the construction of the Unicoi Turnpike shifted traffic to the mouth of the Valley River. A right (east) turn onto Vengeance Creek Road (Vengeance was a Cherokee resident of this valley at the time of the 1838 removal) takes travelers across Valley River; an immediate left after the Valley River bridge places drivers on Fairview Road, a scenic two-lane country road that ascends the southeastern side of the valley to Andrews. A left turn (west) at the stoplight will direct visitors to the old Marble/Coalville Road, which runs along the northwestern edge of the valley to Andrews.

On us 19/23 north of Vengeance Creek, visitors will encounter signs for the Sanitary Landfill on the right. A turn into the landfill reception area allows access to the Old Parker Cemetery, located on a narrow ridge top in the woods immediately northeast of the landfill gates and weigh station. This cemetery was founded as part of the pre-removal Cherokee Baptist church that once held brush arbor meetings by the Valley River. Visitors can park in the gravel lot at the landfill entrance and walk into the woods to view a memorial to John Welch, a Cherokee leader and an unsung hero of removal. Welch, who lived nearby on the northwestern side of the valley, was a wealthy Cherokee planter who received a written exemption from removal. A fierce opponent of the New Echota Treaty and the removal policy, Welch, along with his friends and neighbors Gideon Morris, Nancy Hawkins, Wachacha, and Junaluska, encouraged the Cherokees of the Valley River Valley to hide from the removal troops and avoid deportation. Welch and Morris fed the fugitives and provided them with information on troop movements until Welch was arrested by the U.S. Army and held in the brig at Fort Cass until the conclusion of the removal operations. When he was released, Welch, blinded by disease during his incarceration, walked 80 miles back to his home on Valley River and began systematically buying land for the Cherokees who remained in the area. By 1842, the Welch family held over thirteen hundred acres of land in trust for their Cherokee neighbors and kinspeople, enabling the Cherokee community to remain and thrive in the Valley River region.

About 1 mile farther northeast, us 19 passes through the old town site of Little Tellico, then the river bottoms continue to the site of Tasetchee (Setsi), where construction of the Andrews-Murphy Airport leveled a townhouse mound during the 1960s. Another 2 miles northeast is the town of Andrews, built on the site of removal-period Fort Delaney. The river bottoms bordering Andrews were the seat of Konahete (Gunahita), Long Town or Long Valley Town, for which the Valley Towns are named. This was a thriving Cherokee settlement throughout the eighteenth century, and was still densely populated at the time of the 1838 removal. Here lived Culsatehee, the head priest-chief of the region who assisted Situwakee in leading the Valley Towns Cherokees over the Trail of Tears to Oklahoma. Brothers Wachacha, Junaluska, and Scoyah ("Worm") also lived in the neighborhood; Junaluska and Worm Creeks still mark their tenure here. Junaluska is well known as a hero of the Battle of Horseshoe Bend; his lesser known brother Wachacha was the defendant in a famous court case that determined whether Cherokees living on reserves were subject to removal. When Junaluska led his escape attempt from the Trail of Tears, Wachacha led a contingent that made it back to North Carolina to join Oochella's (Euchella) band in hiding.

Visitors to Andrews can continue northeast along US 19/74 to pass through the Nantahala River Gorge, once the impregnable hideout of Cherokee fugitives on the run from U.S. troops. At the head of the valley, where US 19/74 descends from Red Marble Gap to the Nantahala, a small river bottom marks the town site of Nantahala (Nunda-ayehli, "where the sun is in the middle"), a former settlement surrounded by steep cliffs and mountainsides. At the other end of the gorge at Wesser, near the Nantahala Outdoor Center recreation complex, was Chinleanatlee Town, the home community of Tsali and Oochella (Euchella). Visitors will pass a road sign for Euchella Cove; Oochella (Euchella) and Tsali lived near the mouth of this cove. Two miles northeast, US 19/74 intersects US 28, and travelers can chose to turn east on US 19/74 to reach Cherokee or go west on US 28 toward Fort Lindsay and Stecoah.

Visitors to Andrews can also choose to follow Tatham Gap Road across the Snowbird Mountains to Robbinsville; this is marked as the Old Robbinsville Road, which turns northwest off US 19/74. By turning northeast at the head of the valley on the northern edge of Andrews, travelers can trace Junaluska Creek Road (an old route constructed in 1837 by Cherokee workers) to Nantahala Lake at Aquone, the site of a nineteenth-century Cherokee community. From here, visitors can cross the Nantahala Mountains over Wayah Gap Road, a scenic but tortuously winding road that leads to US 64 en route to Franklin.

The Overhill Towns and Sequoyah

Vonore, Tennessee

5

Years ago, during the time when the whites were coming into this country, things were hard for the Cherokee. One day, an old man came to the city of Old Echota, and he called all the people into the townhouse to hear him speak. Before he spoke he took a wampum belt and threw it up over two of the crossbeams between the posts that held up the seven-sided council house. He told the people that times were hard for them, and that they would get harder. But they would survive as a people, he said, if they would follow the traditional way of the Cherokee people: *Duyuktv,* the path of harmony, of being in balance. They asked him what the wampum belt meant, and he explained.

"The man and woman on one end of the belt represent the Cherokee people. The white path of beads down the center of the belt represents *Duyuktv,* the path of harmony, of being in balance. The black beads on both sides of the white path represent all the things that you can do to stray from the path. The checkerboard of squares at the other end of the belt represents all the good things that will come to you at the end of life's journey if you stay on the path of harmony."

He said that as long as the Cherokee people stayed on the path of harmony and balance, and the wampum belt survived, the Cherokee would survive as a people. As he finished speaking, the wampum belt burst into flame. The people were horrified, thinking this signified the end of them as a people.

But when the flames died down, they saw that the belt was still intact: all of the beads, the threads, the deerskin backing. And they knew they would survive as a people if they would follow the path of harmony and balance.

— Lloyd Sequoyah, 1978, from his testimony
at hearings on the building of Tellico Dam

This story foretells the survival of the Cherokee people, and so it is no surprise that it is located at Old Echota (Chota), one of the Cherokee towns where the sacred fire burned. Although Chota and several Overhill Towns have been submerged under Tellico Lake (created by Tellico

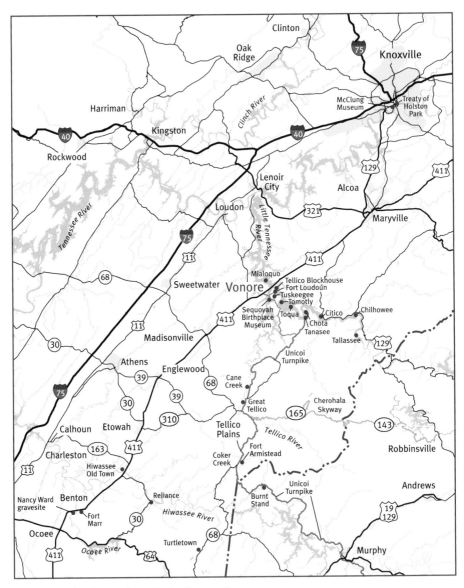

MAP 9. *Cherokee Heritage Trails, Vonore, Tenn.*

Dam), the Cherokee people still survive and are preserving Kituhwa, ancient mother town of the Cherokee Nation.

Cherokee Heritage Trails in Tennessee bear a markedly different character from those in North Carolina. Because Tennessee has no contemporary Cherokee communities, the living Cherokee heritage is not well

View from Whiggs Meadow off the Cherohala Skyway in the Cherokee National Forest. (Photograph by Murray Lee)

represented, although a number of venues offer works by Cherokee artists and craftspeople, and periodically scheduled events present Cherokee performers. Neither is the eastern Tennessee landscape well represented in traditional Cherokee stories, many of which derive from the Eastern Band and focus on locales in the North Carolina mountains. The majority of Overhill Cherokee inhabitants of eastern Tennessee were deported during the tragic Trail of Tears removal of 1838, effectively ending the Cherokee presence in much of the area. The disruptions of removal, and the long absence of the Western Cherokees from the Tennessee homelands, have dulled the collective cultural memories of the old Overhill country. As a result, the Heritage Trails sites in eastern Tennessee are primarily landscapes and locations known through the historical and archaeological records as places important to the Cherokee experience.

In Vonore, the Sequoyah Birthplace Museum, a tribally owned and operated facility, presents historical and archaeological exhibits about the eighteenth-century Overhill Cherokee towns and also features the life and accomplishments of Sequoyah, originator of the Cherokee syllabary. Although the museum is located on tribal land, it is not the center of a Cherokee community. In fact, since the Trail of Tears in 1838, only a few members of the Eastern Band live in Tennessee; many residents here, however, claim Cherokee ancestry through great-grandparents who stayed behind and intermarried, becoming integrated into Appalachian families and their communities.

From Vonore, home also to the Fort Loudoun State Historic Area, visitors can access sites that illuminate eighteenth-century Cherokee life in the eastern Tennessee River Valley. The small town of Vonore stands on the south side of the Little Tennessee River, now Tellico Lake. This controversial impoundment flooded some of the finest farmland in eastern Tennessee and, with it, many of the old Overhill Cherokee town sites that once formed the frontier stronghold of the Cherokee Nation.

Immediately north of town, Tellico Lake shrouds Mialoquo (Amayelegwa, "Great Island"), the home of the famed Chickamauga Cherokee leader, Dragging Canoe. Upstream, the lake covers the town sites of Tuskeegee, Tomotley, Toqua, Chota, Tanassee, and Citico. Farther upstream, Chilhowee Lake covers the next town sites of Chilhowee and Tallassee. These former settlements, together with Great Tellico and Chatuga on the Tellico River and Hiwassee, Chestuee, and Amohi on the Hiwassee River, comprised the Overhill Towns. This was the Cherokees' western frontier, and the Overhills were gatekeepers who guarded the nation against attack by the Iroquois, Shawnees, Illinois, and Wyandots from the north, the Choctaws and Chickasaws from the west, and the Muskogees from the south.

Early European travelers to the Overhill country found as many as five thousand Cherokees residing in the fertile bottomlands of the Little Tennessee, Tellico, and Hiwassee Rivers. Their farming villages consisted of twenty to seventy-five households clustered around a public plaza, a council house or townhouse, and a summer pavilion. Each family maintained a round, tightly built *asi*—an earth-covered house for a winter dwelling—along with a rectangular, partially open summer house and corn cribs for crop storage.

As much as three hundred acres of farmland surrounded each village, and Cherokee farmers, mostly women, produced large crops of corn, beans, pumpkins, and sunflowers. All of the towns were built within a half-day's walk of the Chilhowee and Unaka Mountains, a vast, uninhabited, reserve of game animals and wild plant foods accessible to Cherokee hunters and foragers.

Cherokee Architecture

*Two or more families join together in building a hot-house, about
30 feet Diameter and 15 high, in the form of a cone, with Poles, and
thatched, without any Air-hole, except a small Door about 3 feet high
and 18 inches wide. In the Center of the hot-house they burn fire of well
seasoned drywood, round the inside are Bedsteads fixed to the Studs,
which support the Middle of each Post; the Houses they resort to with
their Children in the Winter Nights.*

    *The Indians build their Houses of Posts, in which they lash in- and
out-side Canes and plaster them over with white Clay. . . . They are
about 12 feet wide, and 20 or more long, covered with a clapboard roof,
have no windows, but two doors on the opposite sides, sometimes only
one door; the fire place is at one end of the house, and two bedsteads
are on both sides of the fire; the bedsteads are made of canes, raised
from the ground about two feet, and covered with bears skin.*

        *William Gerrard DeBrahm, 1756, surveyor and architect,
        describing Cherokee homes in the Little Tennessee Valley*

*When there is a new temple building, there is commonly ten towns
about building one of them their butts of prodigious strong timber. . . .
Their temple is builded quite round with and is supported by great pillars of wood, a round hearth in the middle of the house. The fire never
goes out.*

        *Alexander Longe, 1725, "A small postscript on the ways
        and manners of the Indians called Cherokee"*

Each village was autonomous, with leaders and governing elders selected from the ranks of the town on the basis of their merits and accomplishments. Although the Overhill Towns were often unified in war,
diplomacy, and ritual affairs, intense rivalries also existed between towns
that sometimes followed drastically different policies. Such rivalries usually
played out in tribal political arenas or in the stickball game.

    Cherokee Heritage Trails sites here include two museums that inter-
pret eighteenth-century life. The Sequoyah Birthplace Museum provides information on Cherokee village life, and Fort Loudoun State Historic Area

chronicles the brief history of that French and Indian War outpost. At Fort Loudoun, a historical marker commemorates the Tellico Blockhouse, built in 1794 to protect Cherokees from local militia and later used by federal Indian agents.

Nearby, the Cherokee towns of Chota and Tanasi were flooded by Tellico Dam, but monuments mark their location, about 12 miles from Vonore. An important town in the eighteenth century, Chota was the home of Cherokee leaders Attakullaculla, Oconostota, and Nancy Ward. At the Chota Memorial site, seven markers were erected and are maintained by the Cherokees, and Oconostota's grave is marked.

Cherokee Heritage Trails sites in Knoxville, only forty-five minutes from Vonore, include the Treaty of Holston Park and the Frank H. McClung Museum on the University of Tennessee campus. The museum features a new, permanent exhibition, "Archaeology and the Native Peoples of Tennessee." On the newly developed Knoxville riverfront on the Tennessee River, the Treaty of Holston Park provides walking trails and interpretive materials at this historic site.

Scenic drives leaving from Vonore pass sites of former Overhill towns, travel part of the Trail of Tears route, and reveal panoramas from a newly built highway. To the south, the sites of Hiwassee Old Town, Turtletown, and the village at Coker Creek can be seen (see Chapter 6 for more details on this route). The Unicoi Turnpike, recognized as a national millennium trail, can be driven all the way from Vonore to Murphy, North Carolina, and follows part of the historic Trail of Tears. From Tellico Plains, Tennessee, the Cherohala Skyway ascends and then rides the ridge tops into Graham County, North Carolina, connecting with the Snowbird Community and the town of Robbinsville.

Outdoor recreation opportunities here center around Tellico Lake, where people fish, boat, and swim throughout the spring, summer, and fall. National forests and rivers in the area provide opportunities for hiking, horseback riding, camping, mountain biking, fishing, and canoeing.

To connect from Vonore back to North Carolina, the traveler can return to Graham County taking either the Cherohala Skyway or NC 129, admiringly dubbed "The Dragon" by motorcyclists. The most direct route back to Cherokee, North Carolina, is through the Great Smoky Mountains National Park on US 441, weather permitting. For those who don't mind some miles of gravel road and remote locations, the Unicoi Turnpike from Vonore to Murphy traces an ancient trading path and part of the Trail of Tears.

Events in this region include the Sequoyah Birthplace Museum Fall Festival and the Fort Loudoun Eighteenth Century Trade Faire, always held the weekend after Labor Day. These two institutions, less than a mile apart,

Visitors participate in the Cherokee Friendship Dance at the Sequoyah Birthplace Museum festival. (Photograph by Murray Lee)

collaborate on their festivals, offering discounts on tickets and parking for those who visit both. This weekend features Cherokee performances, craft demonstrations, and reenactments that illuminate Cherokee history and Colonial history, and the sale of Cherokee crafts and food. During the rest of the year, authentic crafts made by Cherokee people can be found at the gift shop of the Sequoyah Birthplace Museum and the McClung Museum.

SITES IN VONORE

■ Sequoyah Birthplace Museum

The Sequoyah Birthplace Museum provides an excellent interpretive overview of Overhill Cherokee history, culture, and archaeology. Visitors to the Cherokee Heritage Trail should consider the museum a point of departure for touring the Overhill Cherokee landscape of eastern Tennessee.

Owned and operated by the Eastern Band of Cherokee Indians, the museum is situated on the south end of a five-hundred-acre island created by Tellico Lake. In addition to the museum, the forty-seven-acre complex includes a three-hundred-seat amphitheater, a seven-sided open air pavilion, and picnic tables for visitors' use. From the museum, a 150-yard pathway

Sequoyah Birthplace Museum, Vonore, Tenn. (Photograph by Murray Lee)

leads southwest across a field to a grassy mound that serves as a mauso-
leum for the remains of Cherokees exhumed from the town sites excavated
for Tellico Lake; visitors may pay their respects to generations of Cherokees
who lived and died in the lower Little Tennessee River Valley.

Visitors to the museum can hear traditional Cherokee creation stories
and see exhibits on archaeology and archaeological interpretations of native prehistory from twelve thousand years ago to the dawn of the historic
era, circa A.D. 1700. A well-produced video outlines the Tellico Archaeological Project (1967–79). Other video presentations detail Cherokee occupation at the beginning of European contact and the mid-eighteenth-century
heyday of the Overhill Towns. Exhibits on postcontact Cherokee life combine historical and archaeological perspectives to illuminate the changes in
the Cherokee world.

The museum particularly commemorates Sequoyah, inventor of the
Cherokee syllabary, an ingenious writing system that transformed the
Cherokees into a literate people. Interpretive displays, a video, and a life-
sized diorama of Sequoyah and his daughter, Ayoka, detail the story of
Sequoyah's life and accomplishments as the centerpiece of the exhibit
space.

Sequoyah, also known as George Gist, was born in the nearby town of
Tuskeegee about 1776 and grew up in the turbulence of the American Revolution and Chickamauga conflict. Like many Overhill Cherokees, Sequoyah

The Story of Sequoyah

Well, in the eyes of the people, Sequoyah is a genius. Nobody has accomplished anything alone like he developed. He was an important man. And like for instance he decided one day that if white man could put talk on paper, so can the Cherokee. And how this came about was, he was sitting by the creek, and the wind blew a newspaper before him. He took it, he couldn't read it, and now that's where he said if white man can put talk on paper, so can the Cherokee. And then he began. Now here's the genius part: just by hearing people talk, he captured those sounds and gave them sentences. And how many sounds are there? So he set himself to capture those sounds. As we have said before that his wife thought it peculiar, busy man, sitting in dark corners, muttering strange sounds. And she begin to think that there was something wrong with him mentally, to the point that she drove him away, or out of her house. And he didn't give up. He went down to the creek, and on the side of the creek built a cabin, and there is where he worked on the dialect. And then, after two years of labor in that new cabin, all of his materials, such as he had, she burned the cabin and all of his works. So that meant a great loss to him, I'm sure. And then I suppose news began to get out of his queer activity, strange doings, and eventually the village ousted him, they put him out. Then he began to travel, and he had a little girl that stayed right with him. And she went with him when he left and as he went down in to the southern part of the United States—well, he went into Texas, and he went down into Mexico, working, still working on that Cherokee language. After twelve years he felt satisfied with what he had done. Come back to the village, and they were still leery about his activities. And he told them about how he had accomplished what he started. And they were leery, they didn't know. And then he said, "I'll tell you what we'll do. Send my daughter out and then, you come back and tell me what you want me to write on paper." And they sent the girl out, closed the door, and then they gave him a few sentences and he wrote them down in this alphabet. And then, when they gave him a few sentences they sent for the girl again, and Sequoyah said, "read this to the council." And she read it and it was word for word, what they had told him to write. And then they accepted that. There are seventy, or eighty-five, eighty-five characters in the dialect, and each one had a sound. Now he did not use any inflections at all because he was writing for a people that already knew

The Sequoyah syllabary.

how to say the words. To a non-speaker, we would have to put those inflections in so they can be pronounced properly, correctly, and so they could be understood because the inflections are those markings that give the sounds differently, and that even inflection can change the sound of the word as well as the meaning of the word.

When Sequoyah finished his work, he had an idea that he could work out his own symbols for sounds, but after twelve years he knew that it would take much, much, longer to work out a character or symbol for each sound. So he borrowed an English style, and you'll find a lot of English letters in that, and then he got a testament that was written in the Greek. A Greek testament and English speller and borrowed characters from each of those and you can find those in the setup. And now then, wherever he was accepted, Cherokees became very interested, they were reading, and they were writing, the Cherokee language. So he had accomplished his purpose, even though he suffered quite a bit of setbacks along the way.

Robert Bushyhead

and his family left the old towns on the Little Tennessee River to find refuge in the new Chickamauga settlements of north Alabama, where several of his kinsmen were leaders. As a young adult, Sequoyah proved himself a mechanical genius as a self-taught silversmith, blacksmith, and artist. While serving with American troops as a Cherokee Volunteer during the Creek War of 1813–14, Sequoyah was impressed with the ease and efficiency by which the Americans communicated through writing. He also recognized that his own nation's illiteracy was an enormous handicap to their legal struggle to preserve Cherokee homelands from American encroachment. After the war, he began to work diligently, even obsessively, to develop an effective means to render written Cherokee. By 1821, Sequoyah's efforts produced a simple, yet elegant phonetic syllabary that used eighty-six symbols to reduce the complex Cherokee language to written form. News of Sequoyah's invention spread like wildfire and electrified the Cherokee people. Use of the syllabary spread rapidly throughout the nation, and Sequoyah's system became a touchstone for Cherokee pride and nationalism, proof that Cherokees were intellectual equals of whites. Most important, the Cherokees' dramatic advance in "civilization" came on their own terms.

With the 1828 publication of a bilingual newspaper, the *Cherokee Phoenix,* the Cherokees founded a national press that introduced Sequoyah's

Sequoyah (ca. 1776–1843), painting by Henry Inman (1801–46) after Charles Bird King. Oil on canvas, ca. 1830. (National Portrait Gallery, Smithsonian Institution)

syllabary to the world. Sequoyah quickly became a national hero, a symbol of the Cherokees' remarkable cultural renaissance of the 1820s. About 1824, he joined the Cherokee Old Settlers in Arkansas and was welcomed as a venerated leader and advisor. After the 1838–39 removal, Sequoyah helped to reconcile the Old Settlers and the Ross Party emigrants to form a unified Cherokee national government. In 1843, Sequoyah led a party into Mexico in quest of a band of Cherokees rumored to live there. Sequoyah

Bo Taylor teaching the Cherokee Bear Dance at the Sequoyah Birthplace Museum during the museum's fall festival. (Photograph by Murray Lee)

died during the journey and rests in an unmarked grave in Taumalipas, Mexico.

The museum's exhibition space concludes with a multimedia treatment of the 1838 Cherokee removal and the tragic Trail of Tears journey that followed. This portion of the exhibit hall includes a video presentation, a map illustrating various emigration routes, and biographical sketches of persons important in this watershed episode of Cherokee history.

The museum features a gift shop, bookstore, and gallery that presents the works of Cherokee artists and craftspeople. The museum schedules guest lectures, crafts demonstrations, and special events throughout the year, including the annual Fall Festival, held in conjunction with the Fort Loudoun Eighteenth Century Trade Faire in September, on the first weekend after Labor Day. The Fall Festival is a celebration of Cherokee heritage and life, highlighting Cherokee craftspeople, artists, and demonstrators. The two-day event features traditional dancing, stickball games, blowgun demonstrations, and a variety of native foods such as fry bread and bean bread.

CONTACT: Scquoyah Birthplace Museum, P.O. Box 69, 576 Highway 360, Vonore, TN 37885, 423-884-6246, <www.sequoyahmuseum.org>, <seqmus@tds.net>

HOURS: Open Monday through Saturday from 9:00 A.M. until 5:00 P.M.; Sunday from 12:00 P.M. until 5:00 P.M.

LOCATION: The Sequoyah Birthplace Museum is located on the south side of TN 360, 1.2 miles southeast of its intersection with US 411 in Vonore, Tennessee.

■ Fort Loudoun State Historic Area

The great King George has ordered his children, the Cherrockees, and the English to love each other as Brothers and to live together as one people, to assist each other upon all Occasions and to go Hand and Hand together. All you Headmen and Warriors who are here present know this to be true. You sometime ago asked for a Fort to be built in the Upper Part of your Nation to be garrisoned by your Brothers the English, for the protection of your Women and children when your Warriors are out a Hunting, and yourselves in case of Need. You all see that we are . . . come up to you with Workmen and Artificers to build you a Fort and Warriors to garrison the same when finished. . . . what greater Marks of our Esteem could we possibly give you than serving you in this Particular?

—Captain Raymond Demere, commander of Fort Loudoun, 1757

After leaving the Sequoyah Birthplace Museum, visitors should tour nearby Fort Loudoun State Historic Area to become further acquainted with Anglo-Cherokee relations, diplomacy, and trade in the mid-eighteenth century. The state park, which fronts on the former Little Tennessee River channel, shares Great Island with Sequoyah Birthplace Museum and is located approximately 1 mile to the northeast. The park features a reconstruction of Fort Loudoun, a state-maintained visitor center with well-developed interpretive exhibits, walking trails, a large picnic area, and access to Tellico Lake. A reconstruction of an eighteenth-century Cherokee winter house, with a garden plot, helps convey the important Cherokee role in the history of Fort Loudoun.

Fort Loudoun (1756–60), the first British military outpost west of the southern Appalachians, was founded at the request of pro-British Cherokee factions at Chota, who needed the fort and garrison to deter raiding on the Overhill Towns by French-allied Indians, to regulate trade and police unscrupulous traders, and to discourage French sentiment in some Overhill Towns. The British considered the fort a much needed outpost against the French and "a strong curb upon the Upper Cherokees." Although relations between the Overhill Cherokees and the South Carolina Colonial troops were initially amicable, the situation gradually deteriorated, and the Cherokees laid siege to the fort at the outset of the Anglo-Cherokee War of 1760–61. The garrison surrendered after a long siege, under terms that allowed their return to South Carolina, but Cherokee warriors ambushed

Reenactors at Fort Loudoun. (Photograph by Murray Lee)

the garrison about 15 miles south of the fort, killing twenty-five men in retaliation for the earlier killing of Cherokee hostages at Fort Prince George.
After the surrender, the Cherokee warriors sacked the fort and a number
of Cherokee families moved in. When they abandoned the grounds after
nearly a year, local Cherokees burned the fort, a reminder of the British
military presence in their heartland.

Two-hundred and fifteen years after the destruction of Fort Loudoun,
the Tennessee Division of Archaeology completely excavated the old fort
site prior to its inundation by Tellico Lake. Evidence from these excavations
is the basis for an accurate reconstruction of the fort near the original location; the reconstructed fort includes a bastioned palisade, officers' quarters,
barracks, and a blacksmith's shop. The state-run visitor center features a
small theater with a video presentation on the history of the fort. Exhibits
in the visitor center deal primarily with military history and the experience of Colonial soldiers at the site, but they also include discussion of the
Cherokee presence, and of the military, diplomatic, and trade relations between the Cherokees and the British. Exhibits, including a fully uniformed
mannequin of a Colonial soldier, are well-illustrated with historically accurate replicas and actual archaeological materials from the site. A replica
eighteenth-century Cherokee winter house and garden plot were added in
2001.

The fort comes alive during the Eighteenth Century Trade Faire, an annual reenactment event held concurrently with the Sequoyah Birthplace Museum Fall Festival in September on the second weekend following Labor Day. Modern reenactors dressed in period costume as British Colonial soldiers, soldier's wives and children, traders, and Cherokee men and women stage a two-day bazaar, which features mid-eighteenth-century crafts, food, and music. Christmas at Fort Loudoun, another annual event, brings in reenactors to stage Christmas celebrations on the old southwestern frontier.

CONTACT: Fort Loudoun State Historic Area, 338 Fort Loudoun Rd.,
    Vonore, TN 37885, 423-884-6217, <www.fortloudoun.com>
HOURS: Open daily, year-round: visitor center—from 8:00 A.M. until
    4:30 P.M.; park grounds—from 8:00 A.M. until sunset.
LOCATION: On the north side of TN 360, 1.2 miles southeast of US 411 in
    Vonore, Tennessee

■ Tellico Blockhouse

Across the lake from Fort Loudoun is the site of Tellico Blockhouse, a fort built in 1794 by the U.S. government to preserve the fragile peace between the Cherokees and white Americans. Stone foundations of fort building exposed by archaeological investigations during the 1970s have been stabilized for public visitation, and the former wooden fortification walls are now represented by a low enclosure of creosote-protected pilings. Interpretive exhibits interspersed among these ruins tell the story of the Tellico Blockhouse and its role in maintaining order along the Cherokee frontier and promoting the "civilization" policy of the U.S. government. Visitors to the site can wander among the foundations and look across the river toward the old Cherokee Nation.

From 1794 until 1806, federal troops garrisoned at the Tellico Blockhouse guarded the northern Cherokee frontier against encroachment and attack by local white militia and posses. It was here at Tellico Blockhouse that the federal government initiated its new "civilization" program among the Cherokees, a plan to pacify Indian nations by transforming them into communities of yeoman farmers. Agents like Silas Dinsmoor and Return J. Meigs proffered farming equipment, spinning wheels, looms, and other goods to Cherokees throughout the Nation, disbursing such wares from their office and warehouse at Tellico Blockhouse. The government also established a trading factory at Tellico, a store that provided goods to Cherokee customers at cost, a policy designed to wean the Cherokees from their trade with the British. Tellico Blockhouse also became a gateway into the Cherokee Nation; all travelers had to stop there to apply to the agent for passports before entering tribal lands. Visitors at Tellico included Louis-Philippe, the future king of France, and Moravian missionaries Abraham Steiner and Frederich deSchweinitz (1799).

After the Cherokee Agency moved to Fort Southwest Point in 1801, Tellico Blockhouse gradually fell into disuse and was totally abandoned by the federal government by 1807. In 1813, Cherokee businessman John Lowery petitioned the government to take possession of the fort buildings, which by then were decayed and collapsing. By 1825, the Tellico Blockhouse was reduced to ruins.

During the 1970s, the Tennessee Valley Authority sponsored archaeological excavations at the Tellico Blockhouse site as part of its Tellico Reservoir Project. Archaeologists revealed the stone footers and foundations of the agency offices and other buildings, and recovered thousands of artifacts and food remains that illuminate the lives of soldiers on the early frontier. Cherokee pipes and ceramics found at Tellico Blockhouse hint at visits by people who came to trade, collect annuities, or confer with the agent.

CONTACT: Fort Loudoun State Historic Area, 338 Fort Loudoun Rd.,
   Vonore, TN 37885, 423-884-6217, <www.fortloudoun.com>
HOURS: Open daily, year-round, from 8:00 A.M. until sunset.
LOCATION: On the north side of the Little Tennessee River at the mouth of
   Nine Mile Creek, approximately 0.6 miles east of US 411. To visit the
   blockhouse site from the Sequoyah Birthplace Museum, turn left (west)
   onto TN 360 and proceed to the intersection with US 411. Turn right
   (north) onto US 411 and travel north. Approximately 0.25 miles north of
   the bridge over Tellico Lake, turn right onto Clearview Road, then turn
   right onto Blockhouse Road. This road dead-ends at the blockhouse
   parking area.

SIDE TRIP

■ Knoxville Loop

FRANK H. MCCLUNG MUSEUM

An easy forty-five-minute drive northeast from Vonore brings visitors to the regional center of Knoxville, where the Frank H. McClung Museum on the University of Tennessee campus features a permanent exhibition: "Archaeology and the Native Peoples of Tennessee." This state-of-the art, comprehensive exhibition showcases sixty-five years of archaeological research by the University of Tennessee, and presents a detailed chronicle of

Exhibit at the Frank H. McClung Museum, University of Tennessee, Knoxville.
(Courtesy of the McClung Museum)

native life in Tennessee (primarily eastern Tennessee) from the end of the Ice Age to modern times. The 3,200-square-foot exhibit hall is dominated by dramatic, life-sized murals by muralist Greg Harlin; these vignettes depict native life during the Paleoindian, Archaic, Woodland, Mississippian, and historic era Cherokee culture periods. The exhibits combine artifacts, images, and text to examine the changing lifeways of native peoples. The exhibit space is multi-tiered, with ramps and platforms defining different themes. Glass-covered cases at floor level re-create excavated archaeological contexts such as a rock-filled fire hearth and an Archaic period dog burial. Pull-out study drawers allow visitors to learn more about particular types of artifacts and topics such as plant domestication, cave art, and mound building. A scale model of the six-hundred-year-old village of Toqua can be explored with a fiberoptic key. An education area in the center of the gallery presents five hands-on interactive exhibits where visitors can learn more about archaeology. This open space is also used in docent-led school group instruction.

The archaeological collections of the McClung Museum are renowned, and the new exhibit features some of the most impressive examples of native art and craftsmanship in the eastern United States. The engraved shell gorgets, copper work, elaborate tobacco pipes, effigy vessels, and sandstone statues are fascinating for their aesthetic value as well as their

Joe Stout at Strawberry Plains

The Civil War? We've always been patriotic. When there's a crisis taking place where our country needs us, there's always Cherokee people there. World War I, our grandpas were there, World War II we were there, Vietnam, Korea, all those wars, Desert Storm, we had people there.

The Civil War took place, and my grandpa was there. He came home and he related to my dad that he was stationed in Knoxville, Tennessee. And at that time they had two stores that made up Knoxville, at one end, and a lot of houses scattered throughout the area. And they were stationed way out a ways at Strawberry Plains.

My grandpa, they called him Joe Stout. He wasn't a big man, in stature, but he was physically strong. He was just a young lad whenever he joined the Confederate Army. And he was a ball player, before he left here. He played the stickball, and they feared him.

During that time, he said, there was a big, big burly man who would come through every morning and challenge the troops in a wrestling match. And several had wrestled him, and he'd always defeat them. And whenever he defeated a man, when he had him down, he would do something to put an extra hurting on him, like twist his arm. And he wrestled just about all the troops in this company.

And he came to Joe's little pup tent and said "Joe, we haven't wrestled yet. Come on, let's wrestle."

And Joe told him, "No I'm not a wrestler." But he kept on and on and on.

And after while Joe said, "Well, I'm not a wrestler but I'll wrestle you."

They wrestled, and a signal went off and it was time to go to their details, and neither one had defeated the other.

And there were two old men visiting that camp, old Cherokee shamans, and they knew a lot of power. And one said to the other, "We're gonna have to do something for Joe, because that man will be back in the morning and challenge him again."

They told Joe they were going to give him some powers so that he could defeat that man. And they said, "We have some things that we have to say, some prayers calling on the spirits of the mountains and the valleys. And we have to do that just before you meet your opponent."

And sure enough next morning they heard that man coming, and he was yelling, "Joe, come on out now, I'm ready to wrestle, come on out."

Jerry Wolfe. (© 2000 Steve Wall)

And all the troops gathered to watch, because they were hoping that Joe would win over him.

When they met, they grabbed hands and this man jerked him, pulled him real hard and stuck his foot out to trip him and get him down on the ground. And Joe was fast enough to jump over the tripping, and that enabled him to come around from behind. And then he picked this big man up just as high as he could reach and body-slammed him to the ground.

And the man never got up. He lay there. And he called for a drink of water. And no one of the troops would get him a drink of water, because he did them so dirty. They didn't like him to start with. Anyway he crawled, under his own power, to the spring where they got their water, and he took a big gulp of water. And when he did, he died on the spot.

Then the shamans asked permission from the Captain to take Joe back into the mountains for seven days. They went, and they taught him the rituals that they knew for power. And when he came home from the Civil War he knew all that.

Jerry Wolfe

cultural meanings. The Duck River cache of eccentric chipped stone objects from the Mississippian period and a thirty-two-foot-long dugout canoe dating to 1797 are particularly noteworthy.

A small but well-designed portion of the exhibit deals with historic-era Cherokee life in eastern Tennessee. Text, contemporary graphics, maps, and artifacts combine to illustrate the Cherokee experience in the eastern Tennessee Valley during the eighteenth and nineteenth centuries. A mini-theater features a fifteen-minute video presentation that addresses the complex issues and events of Euro-American settlement and the response of native peoples. The video and other display components emphasize the continuing vitality of native life in the face of centuries of adversity.

A small gift and book shop in the lobby of the museum includes printed materials on the Cherokees and other southeastern tribes. Crafts by Eastern Band artisans are prominently displayed and available for purchase.

CONTACT: Frank H. McClung Museum, 1327 Circle Park Dr., Knoxville, TN 37996, 865-974-2144, <http://mcclungmuseum.utk.edu>

HOURS: Open Monday through Saturday from 9:00 A.M. until 5:00 P.M., and Sunday from 1:00 P.M. until 5:00 P.M. Closed on Independence Day, New Year's Day, Labor Day, Thanksgiving Day, and Christmas Eve and Day.

LOCATION: 1327 Circle Park Dr., University of Tennessee, Knoxville. From Vonore, drive north on US 411; merge with US 129 North at Maryville, Tennessee. Continue approximately 15 miles north on US 129, past McGhee-Tyson Airport. After crossing the bridge across the Tennessee River (Fort Loudoun Lake), exit right onto Neyland Dr. (also signed "James White Parkway"), then proceed east to the second stoplight at the south entrance to the University of Tennessee campus. Turn left onto Lake Loudoun Boulevard. At the second stoplight, turn right onto Volunteer Boulevard, then right onto Circle Park Drive. The McClung Museum is the first building on the right.

Visitor parking is available, by permit only, in Circle Park near the entry to the museum. When you enter Circle Park Drive, stop at the kiosk on the right and request a museum visitor's (two-hour) parking permit.

TREATY OF HOLSTON PARK

While in Knoxville, visit the Treaty of Holston Park on the newly developed Knoxville riverfront on the Tennessee River, a place the Cherokees once knew as Kuwanda ta lun yi, "the Mulberry Grove." Here, a new

Statue on the plaza at the Treaty of Holston Park in Knoxville.
(Photograph by Mark Finchum)

statue commemorates the 1791 signing of the Treaty of Holston between the Cherokee Nation and the United States government, an agreement that laid the foundation for relations between the Cherokees and the new federal government. This landmark treaty established the "civilization" program, an early federal policy for pacifying hostile tribes by encouraging farming and settled life.

The treaty ceded a large tract of Cherokee land (including present-day Knoxville) and was generally disadvantageous to the Cherokees, who felt that they had been duped by Governor William Blount, whom they knew as "The Dirt Captain." The agreement barely stemmed white encroachment on Cherokee land; frontier violence between whites and Cherokees continued unabated, and a lasting peace was not concluded for three more years.

The park features a plaza surrounding a massive marble statue that depicts the signing of the treaty. Included in the statue are signers Hanging

Maw, the Cherokee principal chief, and William Blount, governor of the territory south of the Ohio River. The varied poses and attitudes of the Cherokee participants reflect the range of sentiment about the treaty.

CONTACT: Public Affairs Office, City-County Building, Knoxville, TN 37901, 865-215-2065, <www.ci.knoxville.tn.us>

LOCATION: The park is situated at the east end of Volunteer Landing, on the south side of James White Parkway, in Knoxville. From the University of Tennessee south entrance, continue east along James White Parkway approximately 1 mile to the entrance to Volunteer Landing (on the right, south, side of James White Parkway).

The park shares a parking area with a number of riverfront businesses. During peak business hours, parking is difficult. Public parking is available in the garage of the City-County Building on the opposite side of James White Parkway. A pedestrian bridge provides access across this busy thoroughfare.

SCENIC DRIVES

■ Overhill Towns Driving Loop

After visiting the Sequoyah Birthplace Museum and Fort Loudoun, heritage trail guests are invited to tour the landscapes of the Overhill country by driving a 75-mile circuit that skirts many of the old town sites in the Little Tennessee, Tellico, and Hiwassee River Valleys. This driving tour is designed to follow eighteenth-century trails as closely as possible, routing visitors through the same hills and valleys that Attakullaculla, Oconostota, Nancy Ward, and thousands of other Overhill Cherokees traversed in their daily lives. Although the Anglo-American occupants of this landscape have wrought many changes over the past 180 years, much of the countryside retains a very rural character that recalls the heyday of the Overhill Cherokees and invites travelers to see the land as wayfarers did in the eighteenth century.

The complete circuit, from Vonore, Tennessee, to the Hiwassee River and back requires about two and a half hours of driving; this tour can be cut short at several junctures with access points to major highways. Many of the sites in this tour are located on private lands; these invite roadside viewing but not physical access. Most of the locations are currently unmarked and have no on-site interpretation, but their settings speak volumes about the Overhill world.

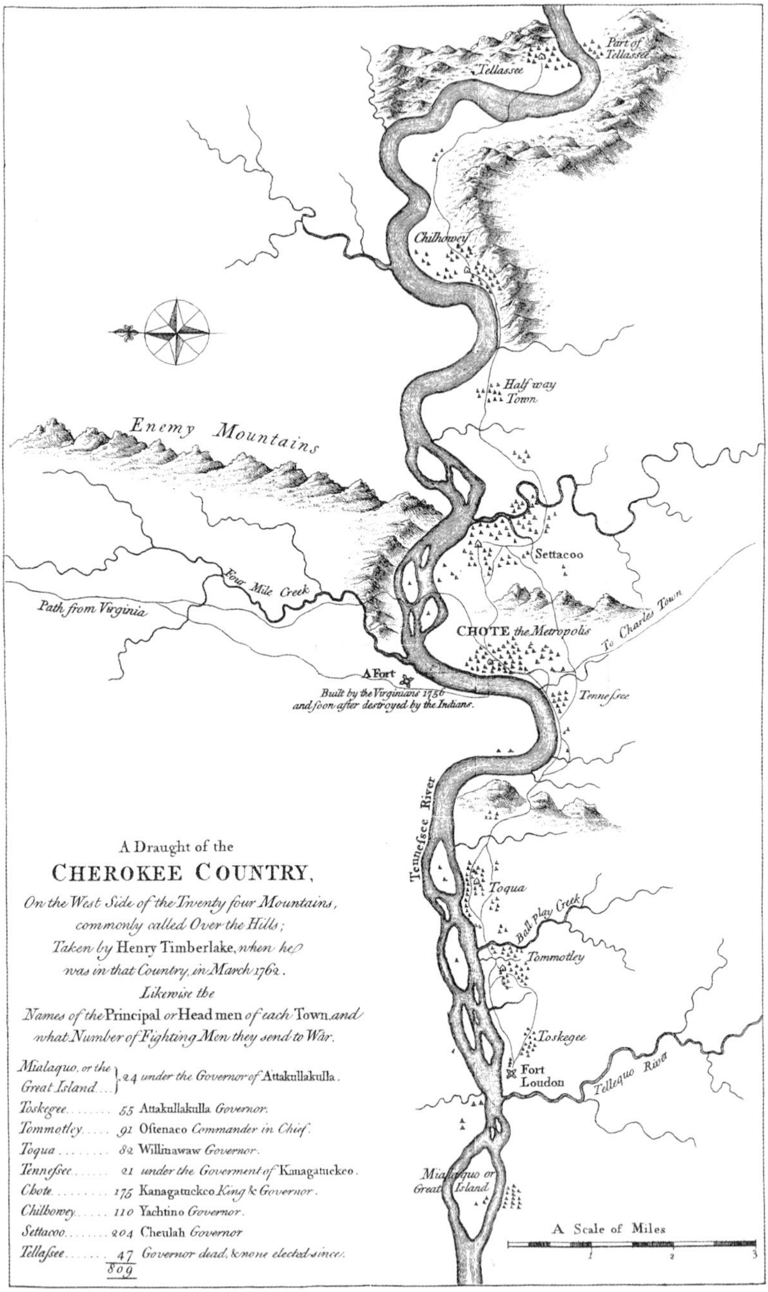
Part of Tellassee
Tellassee
Chilhowey
Half way Town
Enemy Mountains
Settacoo
Four Mile Creek
Path from Virginia
CHOTE the Metropolis
To Charles Town
A Fort
Built by the Virginians 1756
and soon after destroyed by the Indians.
Tennessee
Tennessee River
Toqua
Ball Play Creek
Tommotley
Toskegee
Fort Loudon
Telliquo River
Mialaquo or Great Island
A Scale of Miles
1
2
3
A Draught of the
CHEROKEE COUNTRY,
On the West Side of the Twenty four Mountains,
commonly called Over the Hills;
Taken by Henry Timberlake, when he
was in that Country, in March 1762.
Likewise the
Names of the Principal or Head men of each Town, and
what Number of Fighting Men they send to War.
Mialaquo, or the Great Island ... 24 under the Governor of Attakullakulla.
Toskegee .... 55 Attakullakulla Governor.
Tommotley ..... 91 Ostenaco Commander in Chief.
Toqua .... 82 Willinawaw Governor.
Tennessee ...... 21 under the Goverment of Kanagatucko.
Chote .... 175 Kanagatucko King & Governor.
Chilhowey ..... 110 Yachtino Governor.
Settacoo .... 204 Cheulah Governor
Tellassee ...... 47 Governor dead, & none elected since.
809

"A Draught of the Cherokee Country," by Henry Timberlake, 1762. (From Lieut. Henry Timberlake's Memoirs, 1756–1765, *edited by S. C. Williams [1762, rpt., Watauga Press, 1928])*

An artist's conception of the Cherokee town of Tuskeegee, ca. 1765.
Painting by Carlyle Urello, 1989. (Courtesy of the McClung Museum)

MIALOQUO

Start your tour at Mialoquo (Amayelegwa, "Great Island"), westernmost of the Overhill Towns on the Little Tennessee River and home to many of the refugees from the Lower and Middle Towns that were displaced by the Anglo-Cherokee War of 1760–61. The town site, now inundated by Tellico Lake, is visible northwest of the US 411 bridge over the reservoir; Bakers Creek Road, which turns northwest from US 411 on the northeast side of the lake, provides several views of the site.

Historical evidence suggests that Mialoquo was founded by Cherokee refugees who fled from Lower and Middle Towns to escape the Montgomery and Grant expeditions in 1760–61. In 1809, John Norton noted that when the Grant expedition destroyed Kituhwa, the inhabitants "removed to Big Island, where they built a town; and from that place to Chicamauga." Mialoquo was destroyed by the 1776 Virginia expedition, and Dragging Canoe moved the town to the Chattanooga area.

TUSKEEGEE

The next town site upstream was Tuskeegee, the birthplace and boyhood home of Sequoyah; today this location lies under the lake waters immediately south of Fort Loudoun and can be viewed from the grounds of the reconstructed fort and visitor center. This settlement was founded alongside Fort Loudoun to take advantage of the fort's protection and trade opportunities. A number of Cherokee women from Tuskeegee took soldiers as husbands, and protected these men during the 1760 siege and ambush.

TOMOTLEY AND TOQUA

From Tuskeegee, the driving tour continues along Citico Road (TN 360 and Monroe County Road 455), which closely parallels the original trail that linked the major Overhill Towns along the south side of the Little Tennessee River. As visitors continue southeast along Citico Road from Fort Loudoun, they will see a broad expanse of lake on the left, approximately 2 miles southeast of the Sequoyah Birthplace Museum.

Beneath these waters lie the old towns of Tomotley and Toqua; these locations can be viewed from the Toqua Beach Recreation Area, a well-marked public access point visible from TN 360, about 2.4 miles from the Sequoyah Birthplace Museum. Tomotley occupied the northwest end of this river bottom; Toqua was located on the southeastern side near Toqua Creek. Like Mialoquo, Tomotley appears to have been founded relatively late (ca. 1750) by Lower Town refugees, people seeking sanctuary from raids by Creek warriors. The town was razed by the 1776 Virginia expedition and never rebuilt. Toqua (Dakwa yi, "Dakwa Place") was the site of an ancient Mississippian town and mound center; the archaeology of this site is featured at the Frank H. McClung Museum in Knoxville. Until the establishment of Tomotley, Tuskeegee, and Mialoquo, the Cherokee town of Toqua represented the westernmost pale of the Cherokee Nation, a frontier outlier that bore the brunt of attacks by the Iroquois and French-allied tribes.

CHOTA AND TANASI MEMORIAL SITES

To reach the next town sites, Chota and Tanasi, continue southeast along TN 360 to the intersection of TN 360 and Monroe County Road 455. TN 360 turns right toward Tellico Plains; go straight at this intersection, following Monroe County Road 455 for 5 miles. Just past a brown-and-white sign for the Chota and Tanasi memorials, Bacon Ferry Road turns to the left, then skirts along the bend in the Little Tennessee River that was once home to the town of Tanasi and Chota. Bacon Ferry Road passes the Tanasi memorial (0.8 mile from Monroe County Road 455) and ends in a cul-de-sac with a parking lot at the Chota memorial pedestrian trailhead.

Throughout much of the eighteenth century, the Overhill Towns of Tanasi and, later, Chota, were recognized as "capitals" of the entire Cherokee Nation, beloved towns where Cherokees from all over the nation gathered for important national councils and religious events. The settlements were adjacent, and their intertwined history is complex. Tanasi (also written Tannassee, Tennessee, Tunasse, Tanassee, Tannassy, Tannassie, and Tennisse), which lends its name to the state and river, preceded Chota by decades as the Mother Town of the Overhill settlements and acknowledged capital of the nation. British Colonial diplomats, like Colonel George Chicken (1725) and Sir Alexander Cuming (1730), sought out Tanasi as the venue for negotiations with the tribe as a whole. On his mission to the Overhill Towns, Cuming obtained the "Crown of Tannassy, as an Emblem of universal Sovereignty over the whole Cherokee Nation," along with three eagle tails and four scalps to present to King George II as a purported gesture of Cherokee allegiance.

Chota apparently grew up on the northern outskirts of Tanasi during the 1730s; by 1746, it was "the mother Town Chote," although tribal business continued at the "Tennisse Town house." During the 1750s, Chota was "the beloved Town that all the other Towns in the Nation regards" a white town or peace settlement. James Adair noted, "Old Hop, who was helpless and lame, presided over the whole nation . . . and lived in Choàte their only town of refuge." The residence of the foremost priest-chief, or *uku,* of the nation, Chota was deemed a holy town of sanctuary, where fugitives were protected and no blood could be shed.

When Virginia militia invaded the Overhill country in 1776, they spared the beloved peace town of Chota, but the next expedition of 1780 destroyed Chota-Tanasi along with all the other settlements in the lower Little Tennessee River Valley. After the treacherous murder of the beloved man and principal chief Old Tassel in 1788, the Cherokee Nation moved its capital to Ustanali in northern Georgia. When Moravian missionaries visited Chota in 1798, they "could discover only five houses, which were well scattered over the plain. Besides some women or children, we met only one old man, in front of his house, Arcowee by name, who was the beloved man of Chota." In 1813, the Unicoi Turnpike Company built a wagon road through Chota along the route of the Warriors' Path, passing the home of Old Bark, the beloved man. When the Cherokee Nation ceded the old Overhill Towns in 1819, Old Bark of Chota and his son, Mink Watts, claimed two reservations that encompassed the old mother town. The few Cherokee families who remained at Chota were driven out by white settlers by 1823.

Before Tellico Lake flooded Chota and Tanasi in 1979, University of Tennessee archaeologists conducted extensive excavations, documenting much in the area of the eighteenth-century town sites. Among the more noteworthy discoveries were the remains of the great townhouse and its hearth, along with the grave of the great warrior and principal chief Oconostota, who died in 1783.

Tanasi Memorial, on the Little Tennessee River. (Photograph by Murray Lee)

Visitors to Tanasi will find a stone memorial erected by the Tennessee Historical Commission that commemorates the town as the source of the state name. The pavement in front of the marker is an octagonal slab representing a townhouse; in the center of the slab is a granite marker engraved with a seven-pointed star (representing the seven clans of the Cherokees) and a depiction of the eternal flame. The lakeside memorial, which overlooks the inundated town site, is located approximately one hundred feet east of Bacon Ferry Road; a small parking lot is provided for the convenience of visitors.

Almost a mile north of the Tanasi monument is the parking area for the Chota memorial. A gated gravel road leads approximately 550 yards south from the parking area to the Chota memorial, a full-scale representation of the townhouse erected by the Eastern Band of Cherokee Indians, which owns the memorial area. The townhouse monument is in the location of the original structure, on a raised surface built above the level of Tellico Lake. The outer wall of the townhouse is represented by a low concrete curb, with a walkway representing the door on the south side. Eight concrete pillars of different heights are positioned as the eight major roof supports; seven of these are topped with granite plaques representing the seven clans. In the middle of the memorial, an elliptical basin represents the central hearth, the repository of the sacred fire. Outside the doorway, a granite monument marks the former gravesite of Oconostota. The site, bordered on one side

Chota Memorial on the Chota Peninsula. (Photograph by Murray Lee)

by Tellico Lake and on the other by a large wetland alive with waterfowl and blackbirds, is quiet and peaceful and invites reverie and contemplation of the former glory of the great beloved town of the Cherokee Nation.

CONTACT: Sequoyah Birthplace Museum, P.O. Box 69, 576 Highway 360, Vonore, TN 37885, 423-884-6246, <www.sequoyamuseum.org>, <seqmus@tds.net>

CITICO, CHILHOWEE, AND TALLASSEE

Upstream from Chota and Tanasi lay the Overhill towns of Citico, Chilhowee, and Tallassee. Parts of Citico are accessible from the south side of the river; Chilhowee and Tallassee, which are inundated by Chilhowee Lake, are best viewed from the north side of the lake, where US 129 intersects the Foothills Parkway. To reach Citico from Chota, drive on the memorial road (Bacon Ferry Road) back to Monroe County Road 455. Turn left (east) onto Monroe County Road 455 and continue to Monroe County Road 464 (Mount Pleasant Road). Turn left and travel approximately 0.5 mile until Tellico Lake is in plain view (boat ramp/parking lot on left); this expanse of water covers the former town site of Citico.

Lieutenant Henry Timberlake, who visited the Overhill towns in 1762, wrote of his welcome to Citico: "I set out with Ostenaco and my interpreter in the morning and marched towards Settico. . . . About 100 yards from the town-house we were received by a body of between three hundred and four hundred Indians, ten or twelve of which were entirely naked, except a piece of cloth about their middle, and painted all over . . . six of them with eagle tails in their hands, which they shook and flourished as they advanced, danced in a very uncommon figure, singing in concert with some drums of their own make, and those of the late unfortunate Capt. Damere."

Across the Little Tennessee River from Citico is a rocky bluff called Tlanuwa-hi, where a pair of *tlanuwas,* or giant hawks, made their nest. Cherokee legend holds that the *tlanuwas* preyed on their towns, stealing dogs and children, until a great conjuror destroyed the nest and threw the young hawks into the river, where a giant Uk'tena serpent devoured them.

From Citico, you can retrace the ancient Warriors' Path to Great Tellico, the second mother town of the Overhills. In the eighteenth century, this route along Ballplay Creek and Tellico River became the Charlestown or Overhill Trading Path; in the nineteenth century, it was the Unicoi Turnpike Road from Toccoa, Georgia, to Chota, Tennessee. In the early eighteenth century, this corridor was uninhabited because "the Path [was] said to be lined with Enemies"—Iroquois and French-allied Indians who waylaid Cherokee and English travelers. When Moravian missionaries Abraham Steiner and Frederich C. deSchweinitz took this route in 1799, they passed through a pleasant parkland: "The roads in the Indian country are but narrow paths. . . . We rode mainly southward and soon came to high land, mostly level. Trees were scattered and we noticed Pine, Hickory, post-oaks, few black oaks and still less frequently, spanish-oaks. Underbrush we saw very little, other than very low Hickory and sourwood. Everywhere there was high grass, and we saw many low grape-vines. . . . Toward evening we passed women and children, who were setting fire to the grass in the woods; and soon after that we emerged in the great Tellico Plain, through which we rode some distance in the midst of high grass."

To reach Tellico Plains via this trace, backtrack along Monroe County Road 464 (Mt. Pleasant Road) to the Monroe County Road 455 intersection; turn right. Travel west on Monroe County Road 455 to intersection with TN 360; turn left. Proceed on TN 360 to a stop sign. (At this point TN 360 turns left.) Turn right onto Monroe County Road 401. Travel less than a mile to

Monroe County Road 701 (Belltown Road); turn left. You will be traveling south about 5 miles toward Cane Creek Baptist Church. Pass through a cluster of old 640-acre reservation tracts from the 1819 Calhoun Treaty, including the homeplaces of Smoke and Bell Rattle, a former leader who lent his name to Belltown. Immediately past Cane Creek Baptist Church, turn right onto Monroe County Road 701 (Belltown Mill Road). In 0.25 mile, cross the bridge over Cane Creek. Immediately to your right is the site of the ambush of the Fort Loudoun Garrison, in the middle of the old Katy Harlan reservation (this is private property). In about 3 miles, intersect with TN 360; turn right. In about fifty yards, TN 360 makes a sharp left curve toward the south. The old town sites of Great Tellico and Chatuga are located in the river bottom to your right. TN 360 intersects with TN 165 Bypass in Tellico Plains. Turn right onto TN 165 to reach downtown Tellico Plains and TN 68.

GREAT TELLICO AND CHATUGA

The broad river bottoms of Tellico Plains occupy almost fifteen hundred acres at the foot of the Chilhowee Mountains. Here, in the open farmlands of the Stokely estate (Stokely–Van Camp once had a cannery here) once stood Great Tellico, one of the largest and most powerful towns of the Cherokee Nation during the eighteenth century. When Sir Alexander Cuming (1730) installed Moytoy, the head warrior of Tellico, as a puppet "emperor" of the Nation for treaty negotiations, he asserted that Tellico was one of the seven mother towns of the nation. Tellico had an adjacent sister town, Chatuga, which allied itself with Tellico for mutual protection against enemy raids.

During the late 1730s, Tellico was home to Christian Gottleib Priber, a German intellectual who dreamed of setting up a utopian Cherokee republic called "the Kingdom of Paradise." Priber learned Cherokee, married a Cherokee woman, was adopted into the tribe, and earned a seat in the Tellico council as a Beloved Man. He advised his Cherokee friends on the workings of European governments and trade policies and warned them against the political schemes of both the English and the French. Priber's republican rhetoric crept into Cherokee addresses to the British. Colonial politicians and traders suspected that Priber was a French agent and conspired to capture him at Great Tellico. South Carolina sent a commissioner who demanded Priber's arrest, but the Cherokees refused to turn over their friend and severely rebuked the commissioner. The British finally took Priber prisoner in 1746 while he was on a diplomatic mission to the Creeks; he died in prison at Frederica, Georgia.

Although the 1780 Virginia expeditions against the Cherokees destroyed Great Tellico and Chatuga, the settlements were soon rebuilt and prospered in the waning years of the eighteenth century. When Moravian missionaries visited Tellico in 1799, they found a pastoral village that sprawled across the twelve-hundred-acre river bottoms.

In 1807, Great Tellico was the largest remaining Overhill settlement, with a population of 246 Cherokees, 1 white, and 22 black slaves. In 1819, the Cherokee Nation ceded Tellico as part of the Hiwassee Purchase, and two Cherokee families, the Phillips and the Riders, claimed reserves that covered most of Tellico Plains. The vast plains of Tellico quickly passed out of Cherokee hands, but were not quickly forgotten. When Cherokee emigrants to present-day Oklahoma reorganized their national government after their forced march along the Trail of Tears, they named their new capital Tahlequah, in honor of the seat of their long-lost utopia, the "Kingdom of Paradise."

CONTACT: Monroe County Tourism Council, 4765 Highway 68,
    Madisonville, TN 37354, 800-245-5428, 423-442-9147,
    <info@monroecounty.com>; Tennessee Overhill Heritage Association,
    P.O. Box 143, L&N Depot, Etowah, TN 37331, 423-263-7232,
    <www.tennesseeoverhill.com>
LOCATION: Ballplay Road (TN 360) on the eastern side of Tellico Plains,
    south of the intersection with Belltown Mill Road. The sites of Great
    Tellico and Chatuga are privately owned and are not available to public
    entry; these are best viewed as landscape sites during the driving tour.

■ Warriors' Path to Hiwassee Old Town

At Tellico Plains, the Overhill Trading Path and the Warriors' Path diverge. The Overhill Trading Path, and the later Unicoi Turnpike, climb Tellico Mountain and cross the Unaka Mountains to reach the Valley Towns of North Carolina. The Warriors' Path ran southwest to connect Great Tellico with the remainder of the Overhill Towns, the outlying frontier settlements of Hiwassee, Amohee, and Chestuee on the Hiwassee River.

To follow the Warriors' Path to Hiwassee, continue southward on TN 360 (Ballplay Road) to its juncture with TN 165 Bypass in the town of Tellico Plains. Turn right (west) on TN 165 Bypass to the intersection with TN 68. Turn right on TN 68 and drive northwest 0.5 mile to the intersection of TN 39 (Old Mecca Pike) and drive through the scenic Conasauga Creek Valley around the end of Starr Mountain, named for Caleb Starr, a Quaker trader and progenitor of a famous Cherokee family. Near the community of Mecca, TN 39 veers to the right; continue straight on TN 310 through the communities of Mecca and Conasauga to arrive at US 411 in Etowah, Tennessee.

In 1799, Moravian travelers Steiner and deSchweinitz took this route from Tellico to Hiwassee, passing "some miles in a southwestwardly direction through the great, dry plain . . . at the end of the plain there was a bog" in the location where Etowah now stands. Here, the route toward Hiwassee turns south along US 411; 7 miles southwest, US 411 crosses the Hiwassee River. Along the north side of the river, the highway passes through the town site of Hiwassee, known locally as Hiwassee Old Town or Savannah Farm.

■ Hiwassee Old Town — the Overhill Frontier

I passed the village of Hiyouwassee Equohigh, or Great Hiyouwassee, which is situated on a fertile plain at the foot of a lofty mountain washed by the Highyouwassee River. In the time of war, it was tolerably populous, but since that, Peace has done away with the necessity of living in collective bodies for mutual support, and they have separated and seated themselves on plantations suiting their fancies or convenience; so that there are only a few houses remaining.
— Major John Norton, 1807

Hiwassee Old Town, or Great Hiwassee, occupies a broad floodplain on the north side of the Hiwassee River, nestled at the foot of the Chilhowee Mountains. The name Hiwassee (Ayouwhasi) denotes just such a broad savanna or plain, and the Cherokee town gave its name to the river for its entire course. The old town site sits astride the great north-to-south Warriors' Path, which crossed the Hiwassee River at Savannah Ford near Jenkins Island. Great Hiwassee was a strategic entry point into the early Cherokee Nation, and for much of the eighteenth century, this frontier settlement guarded the flank of the Overhill region from attack by the Muscogee tribes to the south. Although the Hiwassee Cherokees abandoned the site after the devastating smallpox epidemic of 1738–39, a French-allied contingent of Cherokees from Great Tellico reoccupied Hiwassee in 1756.

When the 1776 Virginia expedition attacked the Overhill settlements on the Little Tennessee River, Cherokee refugees from across the nation streamed into Hiwassee for protection and support. Many of the displaced people took up residence at Hiwassee, then used the town as a base to launch raids against the American frontier. When Virginia militia again invaded the Overhill country in 1780, the expedition sought out Hiwassee, bent on punishing the northernmost "Chickamauga" town.

In 1788, John Sevier's Tennessee militia again destroyed Hiwassee, driving the town into a gradual decline. Throughout the 1790s, the Cherokee frontier shifted progressively southward, and the Hiwassee community gradually abandoned the old town site until the land was ceded to the

United States in the Calhoun Treaty of 1819. Nelly and Wally Paine, along with other Cherokee families residing at Hiwassee, attempted to preserve their homes by claiming life estate reserves under the terms of this treaty, but by 1821 they were displaced by the white settlers who flooded the region, and centuries of Cherokee occupation at Hiwassee Old Town came to an end.

Much of the site of Hiwassee Old Town, which is still known as Savannah Farm, is now a state-run tree seedling nursery. A forty-acre portion of this, which includes a Mississippian-period mound and village site, is now an archaeological preserve. Although the landscape has been modified by recent development, the old town site, in the expansive floodplains nestled at the foot of the Chilhowee Mountains, still evokes the feeling of the old Cherokee frontier.

The site of Hiwassee Old Town is best viewed from the Tennessee Division of Forestry offices at the tree seedling nursery.

CONTACT: Hiwassee/Ocoee Rivers State Parks, Spring Creek Rd., P.O. Box 5, Delano, TN 37325, 423-263-0050; Tennessee Department of Agriculture, Forestry Division, East Tennessee Nursery, P.O. Box 59, Delano, TN 37325

LOCATION: The old town site is located on the north side of the Hiwassee River along US 411, approximately 7 miles south of Etowah, Tennessee. The site occupies both sides of the highway, and covers an estimated 425 acres. The East Tennessee Nursery office is located in the midst of the site on the west side of US 411; the driveway entrance leading to the nursery office is clearly marked.

■ Unicoi Turnpike Trail

I left Fort Butler [on the Unicoi Turnpike] on the 19th in charge of 800 Cherokees. I had not an officer along to assist me, and only my own company as a guard. Of course I had as much to do as I could attend to, but I experienced no difficulty in getting them along other than what arose from fatigue, and the roughness of the roads over the mountains, which are the worst I ever saw. I arrived with about one hundred more than what I started with—many having joined me on the march. We were eight days in making the journey (80 miles) and it was pitiful to behold the women and children, who suffered exceedingly, as they were all obliged to walk, with the exception of the sick.
—Captain L. B. Webster, June 28, 1838

Just as our modern communities, states, and regions are integrated by the interstate highway system, the old Cherokee Nation was interconnected by a network of trails that linked town settlements. For Cherokee villages, these foot trails were conduits to the outside world; people, goods, and information moved constantly over the trail system. In traveling the Cherokee Heritage Trails, visitors follow many ancient pathways that have been supplanted by modern roads. Seldom are these native paths discernible; recent development and road building have obliterated all vestiges of most Cherokee trails. However, much of the Unicoi Turnpike path, one of the main arteries of the Cherokee trail system, can still be retraced across southeastern Tennessee, southwestern North Carolina, and northeastern Georgia. Major segments of this trans-Appalachian route, which was developed as a commercial wagon road in the early nineteenth century, survive intact on national forest lands and can be experienced by driving and hiking between the heritage trail interpretive hubs at Vonore, Tennessee, and Murphy, North Carolina.

During the eighteenth century, British travelers referred to the Unicoi Turnpike route as the "Tellico Path," the "Overhill Trading Path," or simply, the "great trading path." This ancient route spanned the Cherokee Nation, connecting the Lower Towns in the foothills of South Carolina and Georgia with the Overhill settlements of eastern Tennessee. European traders, soldiers, and diplomats from the Carolina coast who plied this path entered the Cherokee backcountry along the north side of the Savannah River in South Carolina. The northern branch of the trail passed through the Lower Towns of Keowee (now Lake Keowee, South Carolina) and Oconee, crossed Oconee Mountain, and passed through Chattooga Town (where US 28 crosses the Chattooga River). From the Chattooga River, the trail ascended Warwoman Creek, then descended Tuckaleechee Creek to Stecoah Old Town, near present-day Clayton, Georgia. Here, the path was joined by a southern branch, which ran through the Lower Towns of Tugaloo (now Lake Hartwell, near Toccoa, Georgia) and Tallulah to Stecoah. The area around Clayton is still known as "the Dividings," a place where paths join and diverge.

From the Dividings, the trail to the Middle and Out Towns ran northward through Estatoe (present-day Dillard, Georgia) toward Nequassee (present-day Franklin, North Carolina) along the present route of US 441. The Overhill Trading Path continued westward, near the present route of US 76, to Hiawassee, Georgia. Here the trail ran northwest along the Hiwassee River through present-day Hayesville, North Carolina (formerly Quanassee Town), then down the river to Peachtree (formerly Hiwassee Town) and across to present-day Marble, North Carolina (formerly Natali or Canostee Town). From here, the trail proceeded northwest to upper Hanging Dog Creek (formerly Ticotee), upper Beaverdam Creek, and Unicoi Gap at the North Carolina–Tennessee state line. From Unicoi Gap, the

Brett Riggs supervising excavations at the Burnt Stand site on the Unicoi Turnpike.
(© 2000 Steve Wall)

trail descended the Unaka Mountains to Coker Creek, then dropped over Chilhowee Mountain to Great Tellico (Tellico Plains, Tennessee), where it joined the Warriors' Path to Chota and the Overhill Towns on the Little Tennessee River.

During the first three-quarters of the eighteenth century, this path funneled steady commerce to and from the Cherokee Nation. British traders from the coastal settlements drove packhorse trains loaded with cloth, kettles, axes, guns, beads, and other manufactured goods over the trading path, taking their wares to the most remote Cherokee communities. They returned via the trading path to Charleston loaded with deer hides, furs, ginseng, baskets, and other Cherokee products for sale in the Colonies or export to Britain. The diplomatic missions of Colonel George Chicken (1725), Sir Alexander Cuming (1730), and Colonel George Pawley (1747) followed this route to the Overhills, as did Captain Demere with the garrison of Fort Loudoun (1756). When the Montgomery (1760) and Grant (1761) punitive expeditions invaded the Cherokee country, they followed the trading path from Keowee to the Dividings, then turned northward to harass the Middle Towns. The Williamson expedition took the same route in 1776.

Following the American Revolution, the westward expansion of American settlement in the Tennessee Valley opened new markets for commerce, and entrepreneurs began searching for ways to connect the markets of the seaboard states with the trans-Appalachian frontier. In 1813, a consortium of American businessmen with Cherokee partners formed the Unicoi Turnpike Company to build a commercial wagon road across the Cherokee Nation from the head of navigation on the Savannah River in Georgia to the Little Tennessee River near Maryville, Tennessee.

The Unicoi Turnpike, completed in 1816, generally followed the Overhill Trading Path to the head of the Hiwassee River, then took a more southerly route through the Nacoochee Valley, Clarkesville and Toccoa, Georgia, to Tugaloo on the Savannah River. The road opened a flourishing trade corridor across the Cherokee Nation; trains of freight wagons jostled northwestward against a tide of livestock driven from Kentucky and Tennessee to southeastern markets. Every fall, drovers herded tens of thousands of hogs and cattle, even geese, ducks, and turkeys down the turnpike; the herds and flocks swelled constantly as the drovers purchased more stock to resell in the hungry East. Stock stands, with inns and taverns, sprang up every 8 to 10 miles to serve this traffic, and Cherokee entrepreneurs reaped large profits by selling corn and other supplies to the drovers on the road.

The road also brought a vast new world of consumers' goods to the Cherokee heartland; Cherokee families could buy live oysters packed in seawater, India rubber boots, Panama hats, and Moet's champagne from stores along the turnpike.

By the time of the mass Cherokee removal of 1838, the Unicoi Turnpike was well established as the primary road into southwestern North Carolina from southeastern Tennessee and northern Georgia. In 1836, the U.S. Army established Fort Butler at present-day Murphy, and the Unicoi Turnpike served as the supply line and line of communications to Fort Cass, the Army headquarters for Cherokee removal at present-day Charleston, Tennessee. When the military roundup and deportation of Cherokee citizens began in North Carolina in June 1838, the turnpike was part of the route that the army used to conduct Cherokee prisoners from Fort Butler to the concentration camps at Fort Cass. Between June 19 and August 1, 1838, more than three thousand Cherokees marched along the Unicoi Turnpike from present-day Murphy to Tellico Plains in the first leg of their forced exodus to the West on the Trail of Tears.

After the Cherokee removal, the turnpike continued in use through the Civil War until the early twentieth century, when it was supplanted by modern roads built to accommodate automobile traffic. Although these newer roads have obliterated the turnpike in many areas, major sections of this historic trail and roadway were bypassed and remain accessible to modern visitors. In recognition of the historic significance of the Unicoi Turnpike, the White House Millennium Council designated a 68-mile segment of the old road from Chota, Tennessee, to Murphy, North Carolina, as a national millennium trail. Visitors to the Unicoi Turnpike National Millennium Trail can learn more about the road at the Sequoyah Birthplace Museum in Vonore, Tennessee, and the Cherokee County Historical Museum in Murphy, North Carolina.

Between these interpretive centers, visitors can tour the trail route by driving and hiking. Beginning at Vonore, follow the Overhill Towns Driving Loop (via TN 360) to Tellico Plains. Between Chota and Tellico Plains, traces of the old turnpike are most evident along Little Toqua Creek, Ballplay Road, and Belltown Road. At Tellico Plains, follow TN 68 south to the Coker Creek community. Once the highway ascends the grade, it coincides with the old turnpike route; near Long Ridge Baptist Church (about 6.9 miles from Tellico Plains) remnants of the turnpike roadbed are visible along the east side of TN 68. At the Coker Creek Baptist Church (8.6 miles south of Tellico Plains), the turnpike veers southeastward across private land at the site of old Fort Armistead (1832–38) and Merony's Stand to cross Coker Creek before rejoining Joe Brown Highway (Monroe County Road 618). Continue south on TN 68 another 0.6 mile to the intersection with Joe Brown Highway and Hot Water Road; turn left onto Joe Brown Highway and proceed southeast to follow the Unicoi Turnpike across the Unaka Mountains. The Joe Brown Highway begins as a narrow hard-surfaced road, but within 1 mile becomes a single-lane gravel track with occasional bedrock outcrops and other irregularities. It is easily passable to automobiles, but drivers should proceed carefully at low to moderate speeds. Vehicles larger than full-sized vans may have difficulty negotiating hairpin turns on the road.

The Joe Brown Highway crisscrosses the old Unicoi Turnpike as it passes through Cherokee National Forest on its ascent to Unicoi Gap at the Tennessee–North Carolina state line (2.9 miles from TN 68). Eighteenth-century British travelers knew the gap as "the Northwest Pass," a dangerous site that lent itself to ambushes. In 1788, five hundred Chickamauga Cherokee warriors pursued John Sevier's Tennessee militia from the Valley Towns, and the warriors attempted to trap the Americans in Unicoi Gap before chasing them into the Tennessee Valley. In the nineteenth century, turnpike operators maintained a toll gate on the Tennessee side of the gap; during the Great Depression, the Civilian Conservation Corps built Camp Rolling Stone where the gatekeeper's house had been.

A steep foot trail leads up the bank on the western side of the gap. A short climb up this trail rewards visitors with access to a well-preserved section of the turnpike, a deeply entrenched wagon trace leading down the Tennessee side.

On the North Carolina side of the gap, the turnpike diverges to the southeast of Joe Brown Highway (now North Carolina SR 1326), but recrosses the modern road about 1 mile below the gap. To parallel the turnpike, follow Joe Brown Highway approximately 3.4 miles to Shuler Creek, then bear left onto Burrell Mountain Road (SR 1325), another single-lane gravel track. About 2 miles northeast of Joe Brown Highway, the Unicoi Turnpike intersects, then parallels Burrell Mountain Road to the gap in Long Ridge, then diverges up North Shoal Creek and descends Bear Hug Ridge to rejoin Joe Brown Highway at Unaka, North Carolina. Follow Burrell Mountain Road south to its eastern intersection with Joe Brown Highway (where it becomes a two-lane, paved road); then travel Joe Brown Highway southeast toward Murphy (19 miles). Near Unaka, which was formerly known as Wacheesee's Town or "the Beaverdams," the turnpike rejoins Joe Brown Highway and closely parallels the modern road for several miles.

At the U.S. Forest Service Hanging Dog Recreation Area, visitors can hike accessible segments of the turnpike, which crosses the recreation area near the campground host's residence and runs southeast to Hiwassee Lake. The old road is submerged by Hiwassee Lake from the recreation area upstream to Murphy, but it reemerges on the south side of the Hiwassee River near the mouth of the Valley River and continues east along Lakeside Street past the former site of Fort Butler (on Hitchcock Street). This is the current western terminus of the Unicoi Turnpike National Millennium Trail, although the turnpike itself continues another 80 miles southeast to Toccoa, Georgia. Visitors can continue along the general route of the turnpike by following US 64 east to Hayesville, North Carolina, then NC 69 and GA 75 to Hiawassee, Georgia. Continue south on GA 75 toward Helen, where Unicoi State Park features interpretive displays on the Unicoi Turnpike. From Helen, continue on GA 75 to Nacoochee, then follow GA 17 southeast through Clarkesville to Toccoa, Georgia. At Toccoa, follow US 123 east for 6 miles to Traveler's Rest State Park, where an original inn and stock stand are preserved at the southern end of the Unicoi Turnpike. The Traveler's Rest Inn, started by James Wyly in 1815, and completed by Devereaux Jarrett after 1833, is maintained by Georgia State Parks to interpret the Unicoi Turnpike and the history of early commerce in the region.

Although the western end of the Unicoi Turnpike is designated a national millennium trail, there is currently very little interpretive development of the trail and associated sites, nor are public access points clearly delineated at present. The U.S. Forest Service, the Trail of Tears Association, the Cherokee Heritage Trail Initiative, and the Eastern Band of Cherokee Indians are collaborating to develop an integrated system of interpretive displays and a well-marked pedestrian and driving corridor along the 68-mile trail.

CONTACT: Tennessee Overhill Heritage Association, P.O. Box 143, L&N Depot, Etowah, TN 37331, 423-263-7232; Sequoyah Birthplace Museum, P.O. Box 69, Citico Rd., Vonore, TN 37885, 423-884-6246; Cherokee County Historical Museum, 87 Peachtree St., Murphy, NC 28906, 828-837-6792

LOCATION: Primary access points to the Unicoi Turnpike National Millennium Trail are the Sequoyah Birthplace Museum, Vonore, Tennessee, and the Cherokee County Historical Museum, Murphy, North Carolina. Numerous intervening access points include Tellico Plains and Coker Creek, Tennessee, and Unaka and Hanging Dog Recreation Area, North Carolina.

EVENTS

■ Sequoyah Birthplace Museum Festival

On the weekend after Labor Day, the Sequoyah Birthplace Museum and Fort Loudoun State Park both hold their annual festivals. Less than a mile apart, the two events illuminate both Cherokee life and eighteenth-century British military history.

At the Sequoyah Birthplace Museum, Cherokee performers tell stories, dance, and provide music. Some Cherokee crafts demonstrators from the Eastern Band also attend, as well as those from the powwow circuit and local people demonstrating and selling traditional Appalachian crafts. The museum exhibits and gift shop are open throughout the weekend of this annual fundraising event. There is an entrance fee, a parking fee, and usually a discount for attending both events.

CONTACT: Sequoyah Birthplace Museum, Citico Rd., P.O. Box 69, Vonore, TN 37885, 423-884-6246, <www.sequoyahmuseum.org>, <seqmus@tds.net>

■ Fort Loudoun Trade Faire

On the first full weekend in September, Fort Loudoun State Historic Areas hosts the Trade Faire. This annual event features a juried reenact-

Bumper sticker displays Cherokee pride on chair at Fall Festival.
(Photograph by Murray Lee)

ment of eighteenth-century life. More than two hundred reenactors camp on the grounds of the fort, and during the Trade Faire hours, 10:00 A.M. until 5:00 P.M. daily, provide performances and impromptu skits. Musicians, magicians, blacksmiths, traders, soldiers, Colonials, and Native Americans act in character throughout the weekend, while selling (for modern dollars) a wide array of clothing, tools, beads, jewelry, ironware, food, and drink. Educational and entertaining, the fair's highlight is the reenactment of a skirmish at the fort, with Cherokees and Frenchmen "attacking" from canoes on the lake, while British regulars fire a cannon from the fort, finally sallying forth with Colonial militia firing black powder rifles and muskets.

There is a minimal entry fee for the Trade Faire.

CONTACT: Fort Loudoun State Historic Area, 338 Fort Loudoun Rd., Vonore, TN 37885, 423-884-6217

■ Christmas at Fort Loudoun

Eighteenth-century Christmas traditions are featured at Fort Loudoun State Historic Area in December. Workshops and special events feature crafts, music, and holiday activities. Other events throughout the year include monthly musters of the reenactment unit associated with the fort. Call for more information or see the Cherokee Heritage Trails website.

CONTACT: Fort Loudoun State Historic Area, 338 Fort Loudoun Rd., Vonore, TN 37885, 423-884-6217

Cherokee Removal
Red Clay, Tennessee

Friends and Fellow Citizens, We have met again in Genl. Council and greeted
each other in friendship; for the enjoyment of this inestimable priviledge on the
present occasion, we are peculiarly indebted to the dispensations of an all wise
Providence, whose omniscient power over the events of human affairs is supreme,
and by whose judgements the fate of Nations is sealed.
— John Ross, opening the last Cherokee National Council meeting, Red Clay, 1837

Red Clay, Tennessee, became capital of the Cherokee Nation in
1832 after Georgia laws made it illegal to hold council meetings at New
Echota. The Cherokee National Council met at Red Clay through the fall of
1837. In 1984, when the Eastern Band of Cherokee Indians and the Cherokee
Nation from Oklahoma met together in council for the first time in nearly
150 years, they met at Red Clay, now a state park.

The visitor center at Red Clay State Historic Park illuminates nineteenth-
century Cherokee life in the early republic and details the federal removal
policy and the 1838 military removal of Cherokees from eastern Tennessee. The "Cherokee Days" festival in August brings members of the Eastern
Band here to demonstrate crafts and perform.

Red Clay is also convenient to nearby sites in the Chattanooga area:
Ross's Landing and the Brainerd Cemetery. At Ross's Landing, Cherokee
Principal Chief John Ross and his brother Lewis maintained a ferry and
warehouse that became one of three major emigration depots during the
Trail of Tears forced emigration. Just downstream, Moccasin Bend, a national landmark site, was important during the Civil War, the Trail of Tears
emigration, and Dragging Canoe's campaigns, and has been used by people
for more than ten thousand years. Brainerd Cemetery remains witness to
the mission and school of the same name.

Two scenic drives near Red Clay travel past old towns, the gravesite of
Beloved Woman Nancy Ward, and the Trail of Tears internment camp site
at Rattlesnake Springs. The first drive, on US 411, includes the Nancy Ward

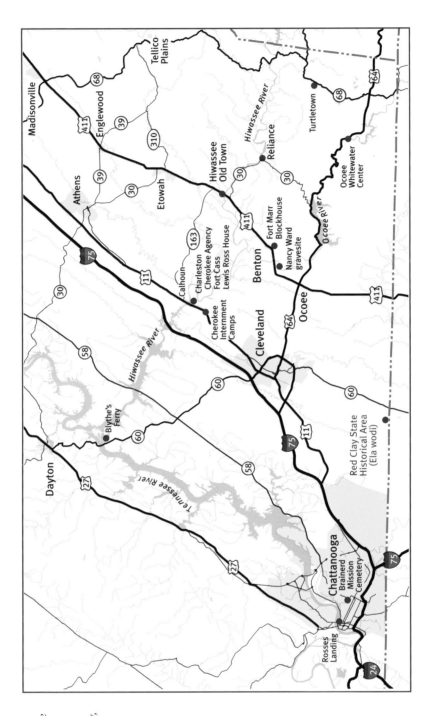

MAP 10 *Cherokee Heritage Trails, Red Clay, Tenn.*

Lake Ocoee covers the old Cherokee town sites of Silquo and Wakoee.
(Courtesy of Tennessee Overhill Heritage Association)

gravesite, the Fort Marr blockhouse, and the site of Cherokee internment camps around Charleston. The second drive, east along the Ocoee River, takes the traveler past inundated Cherokee towns, through the Ocoee River Gorge, and across a landscape of former Cherokee farmsteads near Turtletown, Coker Creek, and Reliance.

The Ocoee River Gorge has become world famous for whitewater recreation since it hosted 1996 Olympic events. Nearby, Cherokee National Forest offers hiking, camping, fishing, and other outdoor recreation.

The southeastern Tennessee region connects back with Cherokee Heritage Trails sites in North Carolina via US 64 from Ocoee to Murphy, or through a series of scenic two-lane blacktops through Cherokee National Forest.

■ Red Clay State Historic Park

The opposition to the treaty is unanimous and irreconcilable. They say it cannot bind them because they did not make it; that it was made by a few unauthorized individuals. . . . John Ross retains the post of principal chief. . . . The influence of this chief is unbounded and unquestioned. The whole nation of eighteen thousand persons is with him, the few, about three hundred, who made the treaty having left the country. It is evident, therefore, that Ross and his party are in fact the Cherokee Nation. . . . Were he [Ross], as matters now stand, to advise the Indians to acknowledge the treaty, he would at once forfeit their confidence and probably his life. Yet though unwavering in his opposition to the treaty, Ross's influence has constantly been exerted to preserve the peace of the country, and Colonel Lindsay says that he (Ross) alone stands at this time between the whites and bloodshed.

—John R. Mason, United States special envoy to the 1837 Council, September 25, 1837

This state historic area has been developed to preserve and commemorate the council grounds that served as the de facto capital of the Cherokee Nation from 1832 until 1837. The 260-acre park includes an interpretive center, reconstructed council building and Cherokee farmstead, hiking trails, a picnic area, an overlook tower, and a five-hundred-seat amphitheater. The focal point of the Red Clay park is the Council Spring, a large blue spring that issues more than a half-million gallons of water a day. In the early nineteenth century, the Council Spring was located in the midst of a dispersed community of Cherokee farmsteads known as Red Clay or Elawohdi, home to Charles Renatus Hicks, assistant principal chief of the Cherokee Nation. Beginning in 1816, Hicks hosted a series of national council meetings at Red Clay, establishing precedent for its later use. These general councils were often huge affairs; thousands of Cherokee citizens attended sessions and socialized at meetings that lasted days or weeks.

It was here at Red Clay that the Cherokee national government conducted some of its most important deliberations about the oppression of Cherokee rights by Georgia and repeatedly rejected the U.S. government's demands for total Cherokee land cession and removal. Four thousand Cherokees attended the August 1837 general council session at Red Clay, the last grand council of the Cherokee Nation in the east.

With federal troops watching, the Cherokee general council again unanimously rejected the Treaty of New Echota and appointed a delegation of Cherokee leaders to travel to Washington to attempt to renegotiate the treaty. The forced removal of 1838 prevented the next general council, and the nation never met again at Red Clay.

With the sale of the Ocoee District lands in 1838, the council grounds

Last Red Clay Council, 1837

Advancing through the grove, we began to perceive symptoms of an assemblage of Indians. Straggling horses, booths, and log tenements were seen at a distance through the trees, young Indian boys began to appear running in the woods, and the noise of men and animals was heard in the distance.

Hearing that a half-breed Cherokee named Hicks . . . had put up some huts for the accommodation of strangers, we found him out, and he assigned a hut to ourselves the floor of which was strewed with nice dry pine leaves. . . .

Having refreshed ourselves with a cup of tea, we walked out with General Smith, the Indian agent for the United States, to see the Council-house. Crossing the Cóoayhállay, we soon found ourselves in an irregular sort of street consisting of huts, booths, and stores hastily constructed from the trees of the forest, for the accommodation of Cherokee families, and for the cooking establishments necessary to the subsistence of several thousand Indians. This street was at the foot of some hilly ground upon which the Council-room was built, which was a simple parallelogram formed of logs with open sides, and benches inside for the councillors. The situation was exceedingly well chosen in every respect, for there was a copious limestone spring on the bank of the stream, which gave out a delicious cool water in sufficient quantities for this great multitude. What contributed to make the situation extremely picturesque, was the great number of beautiful trees growing in every direction, the underwood having been most judiciously cut away . . . and that which imparted life to the whole, was an unceasing current of Cherokee Indians, men, women, youths, and children, moving about in every direction, and in the greatest order . . . preserving a grave and thoughtful demeanor imposed upon them by the singular position in which they are placed, and by the trying alternative now presented to them of delivering up their native country to their oppressors, or perishing in a vain resistance. . . .

About 8 P.M., somewhat fatigued with the adventures of the day, I retired to our hut, from whence, through the interstices of the logs, I saw fires of the Cherokees, who bivouacked in the woods, gleaming in every direction; and long after I laid down, the voices of hundreds of the most pious amongst them who had assembled at the Council-house to perform their evening worship, came pealing in hymns through the now quiet forest, and insensibly and gratefully lulled me to sleep.

George Featherstonehaugh, 1847

International Indian Council (held at Tallequah, Indian Territory, in 1843),
by John Mix Stanley (1814–72), 1843. (Copyright © Smithsonian American
Art Museum, Washington, D.C./Art Resource, New York)

passed into private ownership and remained in private use until purchased
by the state and concerned citizens in 1971.

Visitors to the last capital of the Cherokee Nation in the East can learn
more about Red Clay and its role in nineteenth-century Cherokee life at
the James F. Corn Interpretive Center at the state historic park. The center features a brief video presentation that details the Cherokee Nation's
struggle for its homeland and eventual forced removal to the West. The
military removal and subsequent Trail of Tears are also depicted by a series
of stained glass images in an addition that overlooks the Council Spring
area. Interpretive exhibits in the center describe nineteenth-century Cherokee government, economy, recreation, and religion; these exhibits vividly
depict Cherokee assimilation of western lifeways and the cultural pluralism
of Cherokee society.

From the interpretive center, a paved, handicapped-accessible path leads
southward to the Council Spring, the tree-shaded, "copious limestone
spring . . . which gave out a delicious cool water" to the Cherokee national gatherings. The paved trail continues past a small reconstruction of
the national council house. This open-air shelter is based upon contempo-

Symbolic handshake between chiefs of the Eastern Band of Cherokee Indians and the western Cherokee Nation in the 1984 reunification meeting at Red Clay State Historic Site in Tennessee. (Photograph by Mark Finchum)

rary descriptions of the Red Clay council and an 1843 artist's painting of a similar building at Tahlequah, Oklahoma. Farther east along the trail are reconstructions of the log sleeping huts described by visitors in 1837 and log buildings that represent a Cherokee farmstead of the 1830s. The trail continues in a loop to the visitor center.

On a low knoll west of the Council Spring are benches and a large information panel near a stone monument that commemorates the symbolic reunification of the western Cherokee Nation and Eastern Band of Cherokee Indians at Red Clay in 1984. This knoll, or the adjacent hilltop where the amphitheater now stands, may have been the original location of the council house during the 1830s. A paved trail leads from the Council Spring westward past the monument to a parking area and picnic pavilion. A twenty-five-site picnic area with tables and grills extends southward from the pavilion. A 1.7-mile loop trail leads from the picnic pavilion to an overlook tower from which the entire grounds are visible.

Red Clay State Historic Park hosts two regularly scheduled events to commemorate the Cherokee heritage of the council grounds. Cherokee Days of Recognition, held annually on the first full weekend of August, features Cherokee craftspeople, artists, and performers in a two-day event. On the first Sunday afternoon in December, the park stages a "Nineteenth Century Cherokee Christmas" at the reconstructed farmstead; Cherokee dem-

Cherokee artist Alva Crowe performs at the Crane Days Festival near Blythe's Ferry. (Courtesy of Tennessee Overhill Heritage Association)

onstrators prepare traditional foods in the fireplace or over open fires, and re-create artisan crafts such as beadwork and finger-weaving.

CONTACT: Red Clay State Historic Park, 1140 Red Clay Park Rd. SW, Cleveland, TN 37311, 423-478-0339

HOURS: The park is open from 8:00 A.M. until sunset, March 1 through November 30, and 8:00 A.M. until 4:30 P.M., December 1 through February 28/29 (closed December 25). The museum and visitor center is open Monday through Saturday from 8:00 A.M. until 4:00 P.M., and Sunday from 1:00 P.M. until 4:15 P.M., March 1 through November 30; December 1 through February 28/29 it is open Monday through Friday from 8:00 A.M. until 4:15 P.M., and Saturday and Sunday from 1:00 P.M. until 4:15 P.M. (closed December 22 through January 1). There is no admission charge to the park or interpretive center.

LOCATION: At the Georgia state line, approximately 12 miles south of Cleveland, Tennessee. Access from Cleveland is via either Blue Springs Road or Dalton Pike (TN 60) from the US 64 Bypass on the south side of town. The park is accessible from the Chattanooga area via East Brainerd Road (Exit 3A on I 75); stay on TN 317 East and follow park directional signs.

Betty Maney demonstrates white-oak basket making.
(Photograph by Cedric N. Chatterley)

SITES NEAR RED CLAY

The heritage trail in southeastern Tennessee emphasizes themes of Cherokee life and culture in the early nineteenth century, and examines the tragic forced removal of the Cherokee people in 1838. Visitors traveling north from Red Clay cross the rolling hills and broad bottomlands of the old Amohee District to find Nancy Ward's grave at Womankiller Ford, the Fort Marr blockhouse at Benton, and Tennessee Old Town and Hiwassee Old Town at the Hiwassee River.

Visitors may also travel to Charleston, 25 miles north of Red Clay on US 11, to see the Lewis Ross Home and the sites of the old Cherokee Agency, Fort Cass, and the Cherokee internment camps where thousands of Cherokee prisoners spent the summer of 1838, awaiting their deportation over the Trail of Tears. The camps extended 12 miles southward from Fort Cass, up the valley toward Cleveland.

Twenty miles west of Cleveland, in Meigs County, is the Cherokee Memorial Park at the Blythe's Ferry site on the Tennessee River. It was at this point that Cherokee prisoners left their old homeland and crossed the river on their westward trek.

McMinn County Living Heritage Museum in Athens, Tenn. (Photograph by Murray Lee)

Fifteen miles north of Charleston on US 11 is Athens, Tennessee, location of the McMinn County Living Heritage Museum, where a small exhibit features information and artifacts about the legacy of prehistoric and historic Cherokee Indians in McMinn County and nearby areas. The Mississippian period Mouse Creek culture, local historic and post-removal Cherokee communities and families, and the Trail of Tears deportation point on the Hiwassee River at Charleston receive special attention.

Another trip northeastward from Red Clay leads visitors through the old Cherokee settlements of Turtletown and Coker Creek in the Chilhowee and Unaka Mountains. This two-and-a-half-hour trip leads to Cleveland, Tennessee, then east on US 64 through the Ocoee River Valley and the Ocoee River Gorge to the copper mining district at Ducktown, Tennessee. North from Ducktown, on TN 68, is Turtletown, where a Cherokee community hung on after removal until the late nineteenth century. Sixteen miles north of Turtletown is Coker Creek, site of the removal-era Fort Armistead on the old Unicoi Turnpike. From Coker Creek, visitors can descend the Chilhowee Mountains to Tellico Plains and access other interpretive hubs at Vonore (via TN 68 and US 411) or Robbinsville, North Carolina (via the scenic Cherohala Skyway). Travelers may also backtrack to Ducktown and follow US 64 east to the interpretive hub at Murphy, North Carolina.

The landscapes traversed by these tours present two different faces of the Cherokee Nation in the early nineteenth century, a period of great

The Cherokee Nation

In 1826, John Ridge, a prep-school-educated Cherokee, wrote a description of the Cherokee Nation in southeastern Tennessee and northern
Georgia to Albert Gallatin, an early linguist and ethnographer:

> Our Country is well adapted for the growth of Indian Corn, wheat,
> rye, oats, Irish and Sweet Potatoes, which are cultivated by our
> people. Cotton is universally raised for domestic consumption & few
> have grown it for market, and have realized very good profits. I take
> pleasure to state that there is not to my knowledge a solitary Chero-
> kee to be found who depends upon the Chase for subsistence. Every
> head of a family has his own farm and house. . . .
>
> The African Slaves are mostly held by half breeds & full blooded
> Indians of talents. The valuable portion of property is retained in
> this class. They have a few framed and brick houses, but their houses
> are usually constructed of hewed logs with brick chimnies & shingled
> roofs. Their furniture is better than the exterior of their buildings
> would induce a stranger to believe. Servants attend at their meals &
> the same rules and etiquette is observed at the table as in the first
> families of the whites.
>
> A great portion of Cherokee clothing is furnished from our own
> people and fancy goods such as silks, calicoes, cambrics, handker-
> chiefs & shawls etc. are introduced by native Merchants from the
> adjoining states. The principal portion of our trade consist in hogs
> and horned cattle. Skins formerly were sold in respectable quantities,
> but that kind of trade is fast declining and becomes less reputable.
> Cherokees on the Tennessee River already commenced to trade in cot-
> ton and grow it on large plantations for which they have experienced
> flattering profit.

change and resurgence for the Cherokee people. In the Tennessee Valley to the west of the Chilhowee Mountains, the Cherokee countryside
looked much like that of the white settlements in Tennessee, with large
plantations and small farms, roads, ferries, churches, schools, courthouses,
stores, mills, boat landings, and warehouses. The homes of Cherokees in
this region ranged from small log cabins to comfortable, two-story frame
houses. Large, well-maintained Cherokee farms produced corn, wheat, and
cotton for markets in Tennessee and New Orleans. Extensive orchards and

Replica Cherokee house at Red Clay.
(Courtesy of Tennessee Overhill Heritage Association)

vineyards yielded apples, peaches, and grapes. Beyond the fenced fields and orchards, much of the countryside was open, grassy parkland interspersed with groves of trees; many thousands of cattle and horses grazed across this open range, and extensive herds of hogs foraged through the woodlands.

In 1835, about 350 Cherokee families (totaling about 2,140 members) made their homes in this region. They tilled about ninety-eight hundred acres and operated eighteen ferries and eight gristmills. Fifty-seven families held a total of 480 black slaves. Half of the Cherokees in the Tennessee Valley had some white ancestry, and almost one-quarter of the families included white members. Many of the Cherokees in the Tennessee Valley attended Christian churches and camp meetings, and the Baptist and Methodist denominations boasted large Cherokee congregations. Many Cherokee families sent their children to church-sponsored schools; some sent their children to boarding academies in the East for advanced education. More than half of the families in the region were literate in English, Cherokee, or both languages.

This was one of the most prosperous and most westernized parts of the Cherokee Nation, a showcase for the foremost of the five "Civilized Tribes." The area was home to important Cherokee leaders and businessmen such

A Typical Cherokee Farmstead

Federal appraisers described a typical Cherokee farmstead in the Tennessee Valley in 1834:

No. 193
Isaac Bushyheads Impt. near Jack Walkers   Mouse Creek

1 Dwelling house 16 by 18 round logs but hewed down in the inside good well laid down under floor stick & clay chimney shed in front worth	$30.00
2 corn cribs shed between for thrashing floor etc.	20.00
1 old crib or house never cover'd	8.00
1 old cabin & small lot at the back of the field	3.00
5 apple tree @ $2.00	10.00
sixty seedling apple scions @ 6¼	3.75
48 young apple trees .25 & lot in which they are planted viz lot 2.50	14.50
20 acres uplnd @ 5 $100 30 do @ 4 $120	220.00
10 acres fenced but not cleared @ 2 $20 15 Do @ 1.50	42.50
1 cabbin about as the first only no front shade	30.00
1 kitchen 14 by 12 board roof ordinary chimney	16.00
1 smoke house 10 by 10 $10 2 small stables $12.00	22.00
1 dry house $10 Lot round the yard 5 ft tall 5	20.00
400 peach trees @ .50	200.00
	$639.75

as Charles Hicks, John Ross, Lewis Ross, David McNair, Joseph Vann, Hair Conrad, John Walker Sr., and John Walker Jr., people who pushed and pulled the Cherokee Nation to emulate American lifeways and organization. Such wealthy, English-speaking, mixed-blood leaders dealt effectively with American demands for land cessions; their influence in tribal politics frustrated Andrew Jackson and other proponents of Indian removal, and led Jackson to declare the Cherokees an oligarchy.

By contrast to the "civilized" Cherokees of the Tennessee Valley, the seventy-six Cherokee families who lived in Tennessee mountains to the east maintained a more traditional lifestyle. These full-blood families lived in small, inaccessible communities tucked away in mountain valleys along the Hiwassee and Ocoee Rivers and their tributaries. Their small farmsteads typically consisted of a hewn- or round-log cabin dwelling, a log corn crib, five to ten acres of farmland, and a few peach and apple trees. These subsistence farms yielded enough corn, fodder, beans, squash, potatoes, peaches, and apples to feed the families and their livestock, but little surplus was left over for market. The mountain families still hunted, fished, and gathered wild plant foods; for income, they sold hogs, furs, herbs, and baskets. Census records reveal that the mountain Cherokees of Tennessee owned no slaves and operated no gristmills. Only 15 percent of these people were literate in Cherokee; fewer than 5 percent could read English. They maintained the old township governmental organizations, and traditional native religion remained dominant in the mountain towns. The mountain Indians' conservatism was due partly to their isolation, but also reflected their conscious rejection of Western values and lifestyles, and their desire to keep a distinctly Indian identity.

In some ways, the Cherokees of the mountain towns and the Tennessee Valley lived worlds apart; their disparate lifestyles and beliefs constantly strained tribal cohesion. Yet they were held together by ties of kinship, common language, and the constant struggle to preserve their lands and rights against American encroachment. When the Cherokee Nation lost this struggle to the Treaty of New Echota in 1835, almost all of these people, rich and poor, Western and traditional, suffered the same fate—arrest, confinement, and exile in the 1838 forced military removal of the Cherokee Nation.

■ Nancy Ward Gravesite

Nancy Ward, the famed "Beloved Woman of Chota," rests in a small hilltop cemetery overlooking the Ocoee River, where US 411 crosses near the ancient ford of the Warrior's Path and the old Federal Road. Ward, an important councilor and diplomat for the Cherokee Nation, spent her last days at a nearby inn within sight of this cemetery. During her long life (ca. 1738–1822), Ward witnessed profound changes in Cherokee culture and was herself both innovator and conservator of Cherokee tradition. Oral tradition indicates that Nancy Ward was born in the Overhill settlement of Chota around 1738, a niece of the ascendant leader Attakullaculla. She married Kingfisher (Tsula) around 1752, and bore two children before Kingfisher

The Nancy Ward Gravesite near Benton, Tenn. (© 2000 Steve Wall)

was killed in the 1755 battle of Taliwa against the Creeks. She was with Kingfisher when he fell, and picked up his gun to continue the fight until the Cherokees had won a decisive victory. For her courage and tenacity, she was awarded the title of "War-Woman," a distinction that gave her an influential voice in the Chota council.

Nancy soon married a white trader named Bryant Ward and acquired the now famous name of Nancy Ward. Although they separated a few years later, she retained the surname until her death. By the time of the American Revolution, Nancy Ward had achieved the status of "beloved woman," a venerated elder who helped guide important affairs in the town and nation.

In the summer of 1776, warriors of the Overhill Towns staged a campaign to destroy the new American settlements west of the Appalachians. Ward, who was privy to the plans, sent messengers to forewarn the white settlers, a move that probably saved the whites from annihilation. Why Ward made this effort to save white interlopers and put her own kinspeople at risk is unclear, but she may have sought to prevent wholesale war that she knew would devastate the Cherokee people. When the warriors returned from their raids, they brought along two white prisoners; one was burned at the stake upon their arrival. Ward exercised her authority as beloved woman to save the second prisoner, Lydia Bean, from a similar fate. Throughout the eighteen-year Cherokee-American conflict, Ward continued to mediate

Cherokee Princesses and Petticoat Government

For the Cherokees, "respect" has always shaped their relationships with each other and with the natural and spiritual worlds. Cherokee towns functioned democratically, with everyone participating: men, women, children, and the elders. Men's power as war chiefs, peace chiefs, and priests was balanced by women's power as clan mothers and beloved women. Men's work as hunters and warriors was balanced by women's work as farmers, artists, and mothers. Children's family lineage was determined by their mother's clan, and the mother's house and fields passed to her daughters and granddaughters. Marriages could be dissolved by husband or wife, and both were free to remarry. Cherokee women participated in trade, and in all discussions affecting the life of the tribe. A "beloved woman," who was acclaimed by consensus for her outstanding service to the tribe, decided the fate of captives and prisoners; she could decree death, slavery, or adoption.

Men from eighteenth-century Europe could not comprehend or accept such a world. They ridiculed the Cherokees' "petticoat government" while they enjoyed Cherokee women's sexual freedom. Likewise, Cherokee men and women could not comprehend a society without men and women's participation. Cherokee women attended every treaty negotiation of the eighteenth century, and sent greetings (as well as baskets and other presents) to European women.

Perhaps Cherokee women were labeled "princesses" because their shocking, unfamiliar power compared only to that enjoyed by European royalty. Hernando DeSoto's chroniclers described "The Queen" of Cofitachiqui, whose main attribute was her treasure box of pearls, which he coveted. Following DeSoto, eighteenth-century Europeans ascribed royalty to Cherokee men and women, as a reflection of their own society. Nineteenth-century Victorian writers set "Cherokee princesses" in tales of star-crossed lovers whose breathless, doomed meetings— penned in overblown prose that sold books and pamphlets to tourists— stuck like legendary glue to places like Blowing Rock, Tallulah Falls, and Nacoochee Mound. Twentieth-century travelers stayed in the "Princess Motel" in Cherokee and continued to hold to these images. Some people today believe that their ancestors were "Cherokee princesses" because of stories handed down in their families.

The revolutionary reality is that Cherokee women were equals with Cherokee men long before any such notion became part of European

and American life. Even today, Cherokee women make most of the de-
cisions regarding their households and children. They participate in
politics, and they shape their communities by their actions. In fact,
Cherokee women have never been the princesses of popular imagina-
tion, but in both the Cherokee Nation in Oklahoma and the Eastern
Band of Cherokee Indians women have served as principal chief of their
nations.

between the Cherokees and whites. Virginia troops spared Chota, in part due to Ward's intervention. In 1780, Ward again warned white settlers of upper east Tennessee of impending raids, and when Virginia forces revisited the Overhill Towns, Ward made overtures for peace and pleaded for the preservation of Chota. She addressed the Long Island peace negotiations in 1781: "You know that women are always looked upon as nothing; but we are your mothers; you are our sons. Our cry is all for peace; let it continue. This peace must last forever. Let your women's sons be ours; our sons be yours. Let your women hear our words."

Ward probably left Chota about 1788 and moved south to the Hiwassee River Valley near her children and grandchildren. In 1819, U.S. treaty commissioner Joseph McMinn tricked, cajoled, bribed, and threatened Cherokee leaders into ceding the Hiwassee District lands, which included Ward's home on North Mouse Creek near Riceville, Tennessee. Ward, like many of her children and grandchildren, claimed a 640-acre reservation around her home. By 1821, Ward fled her reserve to escape the escalating conflicts between white settlers and the reservees. She moved back into the Cherokee Nation to live with her son, Fivekiller, near Womankiller Ford on the Ocoee River, south of Benton, Tennessee. Nancy Ward died there in 1822 and was buried in an unmarked grave on a nearby hilltop. Her brother, The Long Fellow, and her son, Fivekiller, are also buried here.

Nancy Ward has become so romanticized as the "Pocahontas of Tennessee" that her significance to Cherokee heritage is sometimes obscured. She is one of the few Cherokee women of the eighteenth century mentioned in male-centered histories, and she embodies the sometimes powerful role of women in traditional Cherokee society. She played a prominent part in the tumultuous evolution of Cherokee tribal society into a nation-state, and her numerous descendants shaped Cherokee history throughout the nineteenth century.

In 1923, the Daughters of the American Revolution memorialized Ward with a grave monument and an iron fence enclosing the small cemetery. Visitors to the site will find the graves overhung by large cedar trees, often festooned with offerings of small bags of cornmeal or tobacco hung by well-wishers and people seeking to connect with Indian identity.

CONTACT: Hiwassee/Ocoee Rivers State Parks, Spring Creek Rd., P.O. Box 5, Delano, TN 37325, 423-263-0050; Tennessee Overhill Heritage Association, P.O. Box 143, L & N Depot, Etowah, TN 37331, 423-263-7232

LOCATION: The Nancy Ward gravesite is situated on the east side of US 411 on the south side of the Ocoee River, 1.5 miles south of Benton, Tennessee, and 3.7 miles north of US 64 at Ocoee, Tennessee.

■ Fort Marr

I have the honor to report two hundred and fifty six Indians at this fort for voluntary emigration. From the report of my officers, who I have had out in various directions, I am induced to believe that nearly all the Indians in Tenn will be at the different places designated for their collection in the course of a few days.

— Captain John Morrow, June 4, 1838

The last surviving blockhouse of Fort Morrow (locally known as Fort Marr), a removal-era military post built on the old Federal Road near the Conasauga River, now stands on the southern outskirts of Benton, Tennessee, next to the Polk County jail on the east side of US 411. This cantilevered, hewn-log building is the last physical vestige of the forts that state and federal troops occupied during the infamous Cherokee removal of 1838. The blockhouse originally stood at Old Fort, Tennessee, where it was constructed in 1814 to serve as a supply depot for Tennessee troops serving in Jackson's Creek War campaigns. This long-abandoned post was re-garrisoned in 1837 by troops preparing for the forced Cherokee removal. Initially designated Camp Lindsay, the post was rechristened "Fort Morrow" after the addition of three blockhouses and a palisade enclosure. By May 1838, the fort housed one mounted company and two infantry companies under the command of Captain John Morrow. These troops were assigned the duty of collecting Cherokees from communities in the Tennessee mountains and the eastern edge of the Tennessee Valley, then transporting the Cherokee prisoners to the internment camps at Fort Cass, where they would await deportation.

Before the military roundup of Cherokees in Tennessee was slated to begin (June 12, 1838), more than 250 Cherokees voluntarily assembled at Fort Morrow to be conducted to the emigration depot at Charleston. When

The "Fort Marr" blockhouse is all that remains of Fort Morrow.
(Photograph by Mark Finchum)

Captain Morrow ordered patrols into the field on June 12, the Tennessee troops quickly gathered the Cherokees remaining in Ailaculsa, Wakoee, Silquo, Amohi, Springtown, and other communities and assembled them at Fort Morrow before continuing to the agency. It is likely that groups of Cherokee prisoners remained at Fort Morrow for only brief periods; the fort was never used for long-term internment. By early July 1838, Captain Morrow and the Tennessee troops had completed their task and were mustered out of service.

After the 1838 removal, Fort Morrow and its grounds passed into private ownership. The fort buildings gradually deteriorated until the single blockhouse remained, used as a chicken house. In 1922, the owners donated the old blockhouse to Polk County; it was moved twice before reaching its present location in Benton. Today, visitors to the blockhouse will find only this inconspicuous structural remnant as the sole physical reminder of the military operation that swept the Cherokee Nation from eastern Tennessee.

CONTACT: Hiwassee/Ocoee Rivers State Parks, Spring Creek Rd., P.O. Box 5, Delano, TN 37325, 423-263-0050

LOCATION: The Fort Marr (originally Fort Morrow) blockhouse is located on the east side of US 411 on the south side of Benton, Tennessee, immediately adjacent to the Polk County jail. The original fort location is in Old Fort, Tennessee, on US 411, 6.7 miles south of the intersection with US 64.

SIDE TRIPS

■ Athens, Tennessee, Sites

From the Fort Marr site in Benton, travel north on US 411 for 12 miles to Etowah, Tennessee. On the north end of Etowah, you will find the intersection of US 411 and TN 30. Turn left onto TN 30 West, and travel for approximately 12 miles to Athens, Tennessee.

Visit the McMinn County Living Heritage Museum at Athens to see an exhibit that interprets American Indian pre-history and Cherokee history in McMinn and surrounding counties, especially highlighting the Mouse Creek archeological culture, local Cherokee removal, and post-removal events and people.

CONTACT: McMinn County Living Heritage Museum, 522 West Madison Ave., P.O. Box 889, Athens, TN 37371, 423-745-0329, <www.livingheritagemuseum.com>

HOURS: Open Monday through Friday from 10:00 A.M. until 5:00 P.M., Saturday from 10:00 A.M. until 4:00 P.M.; closed Sundays and major holidays.

LOCATION: The McMinn County Living Heritage Museum is located at 522 West Madison Avenue. From Etowah, Tennessee, travel to Athens, Tennessee, on TN 30 West for approximately 12 miles. At Athens, turn left onto Jackson Street (which takes you to the McMinn Courthouse Square) and continue for two blocks. Turn left onto Washington Avenue and continue for two blocks. At this point, Washington Avenue will become West Madison Avenue and you will see the museum on the right-hand side of the street.

From the McMinn County Living Heritage Museum, return to the McMinn County Courthouse Square by following Madison Avenue until it intersects with Green Street (TN 30). Turn left onto Green Street and continue until you reach the intersection of TN 30 and Congress Parkway (US 11). Turn left onto Congress Parkway and continue south on US 11 for approximately 15 miles to Calhoun and Charleston.

■ Charleston, Tennessee, Sites

A number of sites important to Cherokee history during the era of the military removal are located in and around Charleston, Tennessee, situated on the south side of the Hiwassee River along US 11, 25 miles north of Red Clay. Here once stood the U.S. federal agency to the Cherokee Nation (1819–38) and its successor, Fort Cass, the army headquarters for the Cherokee removal of 1838. Still standing is Lewis Ross's house, once one of the finest homes in the Cherokee Nation, and the Cherokee government's headquarters during the nation's forced internment in the summer of 1838. The notorious internment camps, now fields and pastures, extend over 10 miles southward from Charleston to the northern edge of Cleveland.

THE CHEROKEE AGENCY

When the Cherokee Nation ceded the Hiwassee District to the United States in 1819, the federal Cherokee Agency relocated from Agency Creek in Meigs County to present-day Charleston, in Cherokee territory on the south side of the Hiwassee River. The agency functioned as an embassy; this was where the business of day-to-day relations between the United States and the Cherokee Nation was conducted. Official correspondence passed through the agency, as did annuity payments and federal aid linked to the "civilization" program. White businessmen and travelers applied at the agency for permits to pass through or trade within the Cherokee Nation. Cherokee citizens petitioned the agent for redress against American citizens and vice versa. First and foremost, the federal agents to the Cherokees were the representatives of American policy, and these agents fronted the push for land cessions and eventual removal of the Cherokee people. Agents who served at the Charleston agency were Joseph McMinn and Hugh Montgomery; after passage of the Indian Removal Act in 1830, the notorious Major B. F. Curry was stationed here as emigration agent. After Curry's death in 1837, Nathaniel Smith served as superintendent of removal.

The Cherokee Agency was situated along the east side of present-day US 11, near the intersection with Walker Valley Road. This location was well chosen; from Walker's Ferry landing emanated the main roads to Alabama, Georgia, and New Town, and the area around the new agency quickly developed as a center for Cherokee commerce. There remains no trace of the old agency, nor is there modern on-site interpretation for the place that was so important to the florescence and demise of the Cherokee Nation in the East.

View of the Hiwassee River Valley near Reliance. (Photograph by Murray Lee; courtesy of the Tennessee Overhill Heritage Association)

CONTACT: Cleveland/Bradley County, Convention and Visitors Bureau, P.O. Box 2275, Cleveland, TN 37320, 423-472-6587

LOCATION: Entering Charleston from Athens on US 11, visitors will see the site of the old Cherokee Agency along the east side of the road, about one block south of the bridge over the Hiwassee River.

LEWIS ROSS HOME

Lewis Ross, a Cherokee businessman, Supreme Court justice, and constitutional convention delegate, established his home, store, warehouse, and other enterprises across a small creek from the Cherokee Agency. From this base, Ross operated stores and other businesses within and beyond the Cherokee Nation, and grew to be one of the wealthiest men in eastern Tennessee. While much of the Cherokee Nation was held captive at Charleston in the summer of 1838, Lewis Ross's home was a center of operations for the tribal government, and most of the final arrangements for Cherokee emigration to the West were concluded here. Ross's former home, now privately owned, still stands at on Market Street in Charleston, 0.5 mile east of US 11. The original weather-boarded log structure is encased by early twentieth-century renovations that completely mask what was once the most elaborate Cherokee house in Tennessee.

CONTACT: Cleveland/Bradley County, Convention and Visitors Bureau, P.O. Box 2275, Cleveland, TN 37320, 423-472-6587, <www.clevelandchamber.com>. This site is not open to the public and should be viewed from the street or adjacent sidewalk.

LOCATION: Two blocks south of Water Street, on the northwest side of Market Street in Charleston, Tennessee

FORT CASS AND THE CHEROKEE INTERNMENT CAMPS

In 1835, the U.S. Army established Fort Cass at the Cherokee Agency. This post, founded at the suggestion of Emigration Superintendent B. F. Curry and named for Secretary of War Lewis Cass, was intended to intimidate the Cherokees into a total cession of their eastern lands. The fort was established along what is now Market Street in Charleston, less than two blocks from the Ross house; Curry aimed to force Lewis Ross away from his home and farm.

After Congress ratified the fraudulent Treaty of New Echota in May 1836, the army increased its presence at Fort Cass to protect the treaty party and to prevent Cherokee uprisings against the unpopular compact. The treaty specified May 23, 1838, as the deadline for the complete voluntary removal

Lewis Ross Property

Federal appraisers who valued Lewis Ross's home and farm at Charleston in 1836 found some of the most extensive and developed holdings in the Cherokee Nation:

No. 352
Lewis Ross, 1/8 Cherokee, Agency Reserve, Bradley Cty, Tennessee
Appraised 2d & 3d Oct 1836

250 acres low ground good fencing 9.00	$2250.00
160 acres do do do do 10.00	1600.00
35 do upland good fencing 8.00	280.00
Hewed log dwelling house 40[by]27 ft	
2 stories high weatherboarded 2 brick chimneys	
4 fire places 11[by]16 light windows sealed inside	
good floors & doors painted & all finished in	
workmanlike manner	$3500.00
yard log well enclosed with paling	200.00
Frame kitchen 20 20 20 brick chimney	300.00
Brick store house 40[by]26 story and a half high	
cellar good floors doors level counter & all finished	
& painted in good style	3000.00
Hewed log smoke house 18[by]18	150.00
* do do office 18[by]18*	150.00
3 Rnd log cabins 18[by]18 50$ each	150.00
* do do cabin 14[by]14*	25.00
* do do potato house 12[by]12*	20.00
Frame _____ 5[by]10	30.00
1 acre garden well paled in	200.00
Frame spring house 10[by]10	30.00
Hewed log barn 60[by]25 shingle roof	550.00
Rnd log cabin 16[by]18 (negro house)	30.00
Hewed log corn crib 21[by]21	45.00
Rnd log stable 16[by]16	35.00

do do stable 19[by]19	45.00
Hewed log corn crib 18[by]8	45.00
Rnd log corn crib 21[by]8	35.00
Double stable 48[by]18	60.00
Hewed log stable 21[by]21	50.00
3 Rnd log cabins 15[by]18 $50 each	150.00
Hewed log cabin 16[by]14 good floors & doors	150.00
Rnd log stable 16[by]16	35.00
2 Rnd log cabins 17[by]20 negro houses $45	90.00
do do smoke house 13[by]13	20.00
Hewed log cabin 20[by]16 shingle roof	120.00
Rnd log cabin 16[by]16	25.00
Old frame store house 11[by]22	150.00
Frame gin house 24[by]24 with gearing for gin	50.00
Gin screw and frame	50.00
3 acre lots 15.00 each	45.00
4 hen houses 5.00	20.00
Rnd log cabin 16[by]18 negro house	35.00
do do blacks[mith] shop 18[by]16	45.00
Rnd log cabin 16[by]18 (good floors & doors)	55.00
153 apple trees at 4.00 each	732.00
300 peach trees at 50c each	150.00
15 plum trees at 50c each	7.50
25 peach trees at 25c each	6.50
150 apple scions at 10c each	15.00
10 cherry trees at 50c each	5.00
Southern bank ferry at Calhoun Tenn settlement	1000.00
	——————
	24965.00

*Excerpted from ledger of Cherokee Property Valuations
in Tennessee, U.S. National Archives*

June 17, 1838, Petition by Cherokee Leaders

We your prisoners wish to speak to you. We wish to speak humbly for we cannot help ourselves. We have been made prisoners by your men, but we do not fight against you. We have never done you any harm. Sir, we ask you to hear us. We have been told we are to be sent off by boat immediately. Sir, will you listen to your prisoners. We are Indians. Our wives and children are Indians and some people do not pity Indians. But if we are Indians we have hearts that feel. We do not want to see our wives and children die. We do not want to die ourselves and leave them widows and orphans. We are in trouble. Sir, our hearts are very heavy. The darkness of the night is before us. We have no hope unless you will help us. We do not ask you to let us go free from being your prisoners, unless it should please yourself. But we ask that you will not send us down the river at this time of the year. If you do we shall die, our wives will die or our children will die. Sir, our hearts are heavy, very heavy. We want you to keep us in this country until the sickly time is over, so that when we get to the west we may be able to make boards to cover our families. If you send us now the sickly time is commenced, we shall not have strength to work. We will be in the open air in all the deadly time of sickness, or we shall die, and our poor wives and children will die too. And if you send the whole nation, the whole nation will die. We ask pity. Pity our women and children if they are Indians—do not send us off at the sickly time. Some of our people are Christians—They will pray for you. If you pity us we hope your God will be pleased and that he will pity you and your wife and children and do you good. We cannot make a talk, our hearts are too full of sorrow. This is all we say.

Cherokee leaders from the Aquohee Camps
to General Winfield Scott, Fort Cass, June 1838

of the Cherokee people, yet as time passed, it became clear that the majority of Cherokees would not move west of their own accord.

In April 1838, Brigadier General Winfield Scott assumed command of the "Army of the Cherokee Nation," headquartered at Fort Cass, and notified the Cherokees to prepare and submit to forced deportation by the military. Military operations began in Georgia on May 26, 1838, and continued in North Carolina, Tennessee, and Alabama on June 12, 1838. The primary "emigration depot" where Cherokee prisoners were interned for deportation was Fort Cass and the Cherokee Agency; other depots were located at Ross's Landing in present-day Chattanooga and Fort Payne, Alabama. By July 25, 1838, more than forty-eight hundred Cherokee prisoners were camped near the agency along Mouse Creek, Chatata Creek, and Chestuee Creek and around Rattlesnake and Bedwell Springs.

The army initially planned to transport all Cherokee prisoners from the emigration depots to the Arkansas country (present-day Oklahoma) without delay. Several parties of Georgia Cherokees departed Ross's Landing on the Tennessee River by boat in early June, but deepening drought lowered river levels, making water travel impossible for the remainder of the Cherokees. An overland march in the heat and drought of mid-summer invited great hardship and loss of life to cholera, and Cherokee leaders petitioned General Scott to postpone the emigration until fall. Scott granted a delay until September 1, 1838, and the Cherokees reached a further agreement to supervise their own emigration.

The Cherokee people settled uneasily into months of anxious waiting for their exodus. Although they received government rations, the prisoners lacked adequate food, shelter, and clothing, and diseases such as whooping cough and dysentery swept the camps. Cherokee children and old people died by the score; there were sometimes several deaths per day in the camps near the agency. White thieves, gamblers, bootleggers, and cutthroats descended upon the camps to wring the last penny from the captives, and the camps were near anarchy. Many Cherokees sank into total despair; some turned to whiskey for solace. Others, like Choihetee from Hanging Dog, took their own lives to escape the hellish conditions.

By the end of August 1838, detachments of Cherokee emigrants formed in the agency camps to begin their westward trek. Those who had spent the long summer near Charleston were joined by prisoners from Camp Ross near Cleveland and Ross's Landing; they organized into twelve groups and departed overland for "the Arkansaw" on a staggered schedule. The last Cherokee prisoners left the agency camps on December 5, 1838, to travel by boat into exile.

The area of the agency and the internment camps from Charleston to Cleveland witnessed some of the most traumatic scenes in the Cherokees' long and turbulent history. These sites are still permeated with a melancholy presence, a recollection of the thousands who suffered and the hundreds who perished here. Visitors who come to this area to honor the memory of the Cherokee prisoners and remember their travails will not find shrines or memorials; not even a roadside marker exists to denote the agency and its concentration camps. All that remains are the Lewis Ross

A Minister Describes the Internment

Reverend Daniel Butrick, a Congregationalist missionary to the Chero-
kees, remained with the Cherokee people through their hardships of
confinement and exile. He regularly toured the internment camps and
reported on the condition of the Cherokee prisoners:

> The sickness seems to increase so that in some families most of the
> members are sick. When we hear of their sickness, we start as usual
> for their relief, or comfort, but despair soon checks our zeal. Be-
> cause, first, they are houseless. They have only a few barks overhead,
> having lain all exposed to the damp night air, though they have
> been accustomed to warm houses. Second, they have no provisions
> suitable for a sick person. They have only meat and bread, and no
> bread neither only as they pound it in mortars, which sick women
> are poorly prepared to do. Third, they are afraid of white people and
> especially of physicians, so that in general they had much rather risk
> themselves with their own doctors. . . . Fourth, they can be station-
> ary but a short time. The officers are ordering them to their own
> detachments, and whether sick or well, they must obey these white
> commanders. . . .
>
> There seems to be no place, nor means, nor time, for the recovery
> of any who are now sick. Their death of course, seems almost inevi-
> table, unless prevented by a miracle of mercy. . . .
>
> About a week ago, a man killed himself. He had said that he
> would never go to the Arkansaw. Yet he joined Mr. Bushyhead's de-
> tachment, I think, and started towards the place of encampment. At
> length he stopped and remarked that he had gone as far toward the
> Arkansaw as he should ever go. He loaded his rifle, lay down at the
> foot of a tree, with his rifle by his side, the muzzle toward his head,
> and by means of his toe, discharged his gun, and thus put an end to
> his existence.

Journal of Rev. Daniel Butrick, 1838

Home and features of the physical landscape, such as Rattlesnake Springs, where the last Cherokee National Council in the East convened.

CONTACT: Cleveland/Bradley County, Convention and Visitors Bureau, P.O. Box 2275, Cleveland, TN 37320, 423-472-6587, <www.clevelandchamber.com>

LOCATION: To reach the site of Fort Cass, turn east from US 11 onto Water Street, the first intersection south of the Hiwassee River. Continue two blocks east, then turn right (south) onto Market Street. Fort Cass was located one block south, near the intersection of Market and Cass Streets. An 1840s-vintage brick building, the Henegar House, stands on the site of the Fort Cass barracks. This site is not open to the public and should be viewed from the street.

To visit the sites of some of the internment camps, continue on Market Street two blocks south of the Ross House, then turn left (east) onto Wool Street to cross over the railroad tracks. Turn right (south) onto Railroad Street, and continue southward 0.6 mile to the intersection with Dry Valley Road and Chatata Creek Road. Bear right onto Dry Valley Road and continue 2.1 miles to Beeler Ridge Road. Rattlesnake Springs, site of one of the main encampments and location of the last Cherokee National Council in the East, is located sixteen hundred feet south of this intersection and can be viewed from either Dry Valley Road or Beeler Ridge Road. Another trip south on US 11 from Charleston toward Cleveland takes the traveler along the east fork of South Mouse Creek, where the camps of Aquohee District Cherokees from North Carolina were located.

◼ Blythe's Ferry—Cherokee Memorial Park

The site of Blythe's Ferry, where thousands of Cherokee emigrants crossed the Tennessee River during the Trail of Tears deportation, is now home to Cherokee Memorial Park, a commemorative and interpretive area under construction. Future plans call for outdoor exhibits that chronicle the Cherokee experience across the rift of the 1838 removal. The park will feature a memorial on a bluff-top overlook of the former ferry crossing; this overlook provides a vista of Chickamauga Lake, Hiwassee Island, and the Hiwassee River Wildlife Refuge. The park is located at the old TN 60 crossing (recently bypassed by a new bridge installation) of the Hiwassee River between Cleveland and Dayton, Tennessee.

When Cherokee emigration detachments assembled to make the overland journey to Oklahoma in the fall of 1838, their first hurdle was the Tennessee River, the northwestern boundary of the old Cherokee Nation. The river was a real threshold for the emigrants; by crossing the Tennessee, the Cherokee prisoners truly left their homeland behind, and the permanent exile became reality. The emigration detachments from the agency camps and Camp Ross (at Cleveland) determined to make the crossing at John Blythe's Ferry, located just below the mouth of the Hiwassee near the old Cherokee town of Cayouka on Hiwassee Island. Between the first of September and mid-November 1838, almost nine thousand Cherokees, along with hundreds of black slaves and more than three hundred Creek deportees, passed through Blythe's Ferry. On the west bank of the Tennessee River, they resumed their trek to "the Arkansaw" by way of McMinnville and Nashville, Tennessee.

Because the emigration detachments consisted of seven hundred to more than fourteen hundred emigrants each, along with wagons and teams (approximately one wagon per twenty emigrants), the crossing at Blythe's required several days for each party. While they waited their turn to make the river crossing, groups of Cherokee emigrants camped around nearby springs and contemplated their fate. Faced with the arduous journey to an uncertain future in the West, small parties of prisoners hatched out escape plans and slipped away from their encampments on the east side of the Tennessee River. Lawlo, an old headman of Nottely, led a group of twenty back to the North Carolina mountains, where they were sheltered by sympathetic whites. Cheesquaneetah took his family back to Fighting Town in Georgia. Others waited until they had crossed the river to escape without immediate military pursuit. After Jesse Bushyhead's detachment crossed Blythe's Ferry and climbed the Cumberland Plateau, Junaluska led an escape attempt by fifty Cherokees who intended to return to the North Carolina mountains by way of Knoxville, Tennessee.

After the Cherokee removal, Blythe's Ferry developed as a primary link across the Tennessee River between the towns of Cleveland and Dayton, and the ferry continued in use as part of TN 60 until 1997, when it was replaced by a new four-lane bridge. Thanks to the efforts of a local citizens' group, the eastern ferry landing and the adjacent bluff are to be preserved as part of Cherokee Memorial Park, a facility devoted to the memory of the thousands of Cherokee emigrants who crossed the Tennessee River at Blythe's Ferry to leave their homeland forever.

The original ferry landing was flooded by the inundation of Chickamauga Lake during the 1930s; visitors to the memorial park will find a modern ferry slip at the end of Blythe's Ferry Road, where the Cherokee emigrants once awaited their turn to cross the river. A parking area is situated

Jesse Bushyhead (1804–44) led one of the Cherokee emigration detachments that crossed the Tennessee River at Blythe's Ferry during the Removal. Portrait by Charles Bird King, 1828.

approximately 0.1 mile east of the ferry slip; trails lead from the parking area to the bluff top overlooking the ferry landing. From the bluff top, visitors can see the ferry route across the Tennessee River and view the site of the old Cherokee Agency at Hiwassee Garrison on the western shore. To the north, remnants of Hiwassee Island, the site of old Cayouka Town, are visible above Chickamauga Lake. A separate wildlife viewing area to the north of the memorial affords visitors the opportunity to observe large flocks of sandhill cranes that overwinter in the area around the mouth of the Hiwassee River.

CONTACT: Meigs County Executive's Office, P.O. Box 156, Decatur, TN
  37322, 423-334-5850
LOCATION: Cherokee Memorial Park at Blythe's Ferry is located at the old
  TN 60 crossing on the east side of the Tennessee River, about 3 miles
  west of Birchwood, Tennessee. From I 75 at Cleveland, Tennessee,
  follow TN 60 west toward Dayton for 14 miles to Birchwood. From
  Birchwood School, proceed 3 miles to Blythe's Ferry Road (old TN 60);
  this turn is with directional signs for the Cherokee Memorial Park. At
  the next intersection (0.25 mile), turn left to follow Blythe's Ferry
  Road, and travel 0.5 mile northwest to the former ferry landing. The
  parking area and hiking trails are located approximately 0.25 mile
  southeast of the landing.

■ Chattanooga

The Chattanooga area, a forty-five-minute drive west of Red Clay, was once the stronghold of the Chickamauga band of Cherokees, a militant faction driven from the Overhill Towns by the 1776 Virginia expedition. Above the treacherous "Suck" and other rapids in the Tennessee River, Cherokee refugees established new settlements such as Chickamauga, Bull Town, Citico, Tuskeegee, and Toqua. Under the leadership of Dragging Canoe and, later, John Watts and Doublehead, these Chickamauga Cherokees ferociously contested American encroachment on tribal lands for almost eighteen years. Their struggle became the hub of a pan-tribal alliance that united Shawnees, Creeks, Miamis, Wyandots, and other nations in the fight to stem the American tide from the Great Lakes to the Gulf of Mexico. During the 1780s and 1790s, the Chickamauga Cherokees moved their towns farther downstream to more secure locations near the present-day Tennessee-Alabama state line; these settlements became known as the "Five Lower Towns," the center of Cherokee political and military power.

When the Chickamauga conflict subsided in 1794, the Chattanooga area was home to a number of Anglo-Cherokee families, British Loyalists with Cherokee wives and children who had cast their lot with the Chickamaugas. These families, including the Rosses, Shoreys, McDonalds, Lowerys, Taylors, and Browns, led a drive to revitalize the ruined Cherokee economy and remodel Cherokee life to mirror that of the American frontier. These Anglo-Cherokee planters, ranchers, merchants, and entrepreneurs embraced and promoted the U.S. government's "civilization" policy. They also believed that their children needed formal education, technical training, and religious instruction to survive and succeed in a world dominated by Anglo-Americans. The Anglo-Cherokee families welcomed and supported the Protestant mission schools that were established in their midst to train Cherokee children and evangelize the nation.

Among the businesses and institutions that sprang up in the old Chickamauga country during the early nineteenth century were Ross's Landing, a commercial port owned by Cherokee leaders John and Lewis Ross, and Brainerd Mission, a Congregationalist boarding school for Cherokee children. These early endeavors formed a nucleus around which Chattanooga later grew. Visitors can still find vestiges of the early landmarks of the Cherokee renaissance amid the bustle of the city's commercial districts.

BRAINERD MISSION CEMETERY

Eight new scholars have entered school this year. Part of them cannot talk English, and Miss Ames is obliged to have me interpret for her. I have a class of the younger children in

Sabbath school. I ask those children who do not talk English if they understood the sermon that was read and they say they do not but when my father comes on Sabbath days he talks in Cherokee. Then they tell me a great [deal] he says.

— Nancy Reece (a Cherokee student) describing Brainerd Mission, 1828

Northeast of Chattanooga, at the northern edge of the Eastgate Mall parking lot, stands the shady, wrought-iron-fenced Brainerd Cemetery, the last physical trace of a Congregationalist (Presbyterian) mission to the Cherokees that operated between 1817 and 1838. Within the fence are dozens of graves, some marked, most unmarked, of the Cherokee students and their white instructors who died in the service of Brainerd Mission. Among the graves is that of John Arch (Atsi), a celebrated Cherokee convert, teacher, and interpreter who walked from the remote mountains of North Carolina to become part of the Brainerd Mission family.

Brainerd was one of a dozen Protestant mission stations established in the eastern Cherokee Nation during the early nineteenth century. These missions sought to educate Cherokee children in "the rudiments of the English language, the principles of the Christian religion, and the industry and arts of civilized life." The federal government partially supported mission efforts to prepare the Cherokees for absorption and dissolution within American society. Most Cherokees had no intention nor desire to yield their sovereignty or identity, but many Cherokee parents sent their children to mission schools to learn English and arithmetic, so they wouldn't "be cheated by the whites." Among almost a thousand Cherokee children who passed through Brainerd and other mission schools, future leaders of the Cherokee Nation emerged with new skills to consolidate their people under a national government and challenge the Americans on their own terms in the halls of Congress.

When the missionaries and students vacated Brainerd during the forced Cherokee removal of 1838, one of the missionaries, Daniel S. Butrick, moved to the internment camps to continue his ministry to the Cherokee prisoners. When the Cherokee emigrants began their journey west in the fall, they asked Butrick, a trusted friend, to assist Richard Taylor's group in their arduous overland trek. Through Butrick's efforts, the legacy of the Brainerd mission continued across the Trail of Tears and took root in the new Cherokee Nation West.

CONTACT: Chattanooga Area Chamber of Commerce, 1001 Market St., Chattanooga, TN 37402-2690, 423-756-2121, <info@chattanooga-chamber.com>

LOCATION: Brainerd Mission Cemetery is situated between Eastgate Mall

Jeremiah Evarts's Description of Brainerd Mission, 1818

The place where the [Brainerd Mission] institution stands is two miles north of the line that divides the State of Georgia from the State of Tennessee, on the southwest side of a small river called Chick-a-mau-gah creek. On approaching it from the northeast, you come to the creek at the distance of fifty rods from the principal mission house. Immediately, you leave the woods, and crossing the stream . . . you enter an area of cleared ground, on the right of which appear numerous buildings of various kinds and sizes. At the distance of a few steps stand a grist mill and a saw mill, turned by a canal three quarters of a mile in length. . . . Following the lane, which runs across the cleared ground, you pass a large and commodious barn . . . and are conducted directly in front of a row of houses, which forms the principal part of the settlement and makes a prominent appearance in the view of Brainerd.

Nearly in the center of the row is the mission house, two stories high, having a piazza its whole length, with a pleasant court yard in front of it. It is occupied by the superintendent and other missionaries. Behind it, and immediately connected with it, is the dining hall and kitchen for the establishment. On your right, and at the distance of a few feet, stands another building of two stories, which is used for the instruction of the girls. . . .

Passing onward, about thirty rods, to the end of the land . . . you come to the school house for the boys, which stands in the edge of the woods, and is large enough to accommodate one hundred scholars. On the Sabbath, it is used also as a place of worship. . . .

The ground, on the south and east side of the land . . . is divided into a garden, an orchard, and several other lots. . . . In the corner of the orchard, next to the schoolhouse, is the graveyard, where lie the bodies of those who have died at the institution, and among them the remains of that great and good man, the Reverend Doctor Samuel Worcester. . . .

Jeremiah Evarts, 1818

and Brainerd Village Shopping Center on the east side of US 11/64, 2.7 miles southwest of Exit 3B (TN 320 West exit) off I 75, east of downtown Chattanooga.

ROSS'S LANDING

The modern city of Chattanooga grew up around a busy Cherokee river port known as Ross's Landing. In 1815, Cherokee entrepreneur and future chief John Ross, and his business partner, Timothy Meigs, established a landing, ferry, and warehouse on the bluffs of the Tennessee River to take advantage of the traffic that plied the waters between the Cherokee Nation and the state of Tennessee. Flatboats, keelboats, and, later, steamboats, unloaded their cargoes at Ross's; teamsters with wagons hauled these mercantile goods to stores throughout the western portion of the Cherokee Nation. After Meigs died in 1817, Lewis Ross entered the thriving business, and the Ross brothers grew wealthy as merchants with commercial interests in Tennessee, Georgia, and Alabama.

During the forced removal of 1838, Ross's Landing was an important point of departure for Cherokees headed west along the Trail of Tears. In June 1838, the U.S. Army forced more than sixteen hundred Cherokee prisoners from Georgia aboard flatboats and a steamboat at Ross's to send them down river toward Indian Territory. The chaos of their hurried departure led the national newspaper *Niles Register* to report that "The scenes of distress exhibited at Ross's Landing defy all description." Just upstream, almost two thousand Cherokee prisoners spent the summer of 1838 at Ross's Landing Camp, located along Citico Creek, 4 miles from the actual landing. When cooler weather marked the end of the "sickly season," overland emigration commenced, and several contingents of westward-bound Cherokees crossed the river at Ross's Ferry in their exodus from the old Cherokee Nation.

Ross's Landing is now the centerpiece of Chattanooga's revitalized downtown waterfront. Ross's Landing Plaza, an urban park surrounding the Tennessee Aquarium, features a walkway with inscriptions of historic quotations by and about Cherokee people. The words of leaders such as Old Tassel, Dragging Canoe, and John Ross chronicle the Cherokees' struggle to preserve their homeland against inexorable American expansion. The actual landing is submerged beneath the waters of Nickajack Lake between the Walnut Street and Market Street bridges; visitors can reach this waterfront via pedestrian walkways leading from the Market Street Bridge. Near the riverbank stands a bronze monument to the meteoric rise and tragic downfall of the Cherokee Nation in the East.

CONTACT: Chattanooga Area Chamber of Commerce, 1001 Market St.,
Chattanooga, TN 37402-2690, 423-756-2121,
<info@chattanooga-chamber.com>

LOCATION: On the eastern bank of the Tennessee River where it is
spanned by the Market Street and Walnut Street bridges. From
Brainerd Mission Cemetery, return to I 75 South; continue 9.8 miles to
the I 24 West exit (Exit 2). Merge onto I 24 West, then continue 6.1
miles to Exit 178 (US 27 North/Market Street) toward downtown.
Continue on US 27 North to Exit 1C; turn right onto Fourth Street, then
left onto Broad Street. Proceed two blocks; Ross's Landing Plaza is
located directly north.

■ Turtletown and Coker Creek

A scenic day trip eastward from Red Clay will lead visitors into the Chilhowee and Unaka Mountains, the most rugged terrain of southeastern Tennessee. At the eastern edge of the Tennessee Valley, lush valleys and rolling
hills strike the steep front of the Chilhowee Mountains. Beyond the Chil-
howees rise the Unakas, then range after range of mountains in the Appalachian summit. During the nineteenth century, these mountains were home
to some of the most conservative enclaves of the old Cherokee Nation.
In settlements such as Ailaculsa, Wakooe, Silquo, Fighting Town, Ducktown, Turtletown, Springtown, Mocking Crow's Town, and Coker Creek,
Cherokee families lived simple lives as subsistence farmers, and they still
hunted, fished, and gathered wild plants for food and medicine. Most of
these "towns" were small and dispersed; families sought out the scattered
patches of creek bottomland and coves for their homes and farms. Communities might spread over a 15-mile area but include only one or two hundred
people—just enough to keep a townhouse for ceremonies and dances.

The mountains of extreme southeastern Tennessee were some of the
most remote and least coveted lands in the old Cherokee Nation in Tennessee. Most of the Cherokee communities in this region coalesced in the late
eighteenth or early nineteenth centuries, after the dissolution of the old
Overhill Towns. The folk who moved into this mountain redoubt sought isolation to protect their old ways from encroachment by the white world, and
few whites intruded upon their stronghold until a gold rush swept southeastern Tennessee in 1831–32.

During the 1838 military removal, most of the Cherokees from the Tennessee mountains were taken into Fort Morrow; members of the Turtletown, Ducktown, and Coker Creek communities fell in with Cherokee prisoners from North Carolina. In Coker Creek, the Unicoi Turnpike directed

the line of march for North Carolina deportees past Fort Armistead, where it is likely that the Cherokee prisoners camped overnight before their descent of the Chilhowee Mountains into Tellico Plains.

A number of Cherokee families who escaped from military custody in 1838 fled back into the Chilhowee and Unaka Mountains and evaded their pursuers to remain with Cherokees left in the East. In the aftermath of the forced removal, some of these escapees established isolated farmsteads in the mountains, while others joined their kinspeople who remained in North Carolina. One group of families founded a thriving community at Turtletown, where they remained until the end of the nineteenth century.

Despite long decades of logging, mining, road building, and hydroelectric development, the landscapes of the Chilhowee and Unaka Mountains still retain a wild character that hearkens back to the heyday of the old Cherokee Nation. A drive through the Turtletown and Coker Creek localities will take visitors through these rugged lands into former strongholds of Cherokee tradition.

It is about 70 miles from Red Clay State Historic Park to Coker Creek; Turtletown is along the route. Visitors to this area can make the round-trip in four to five hours or travel on to interpretive hubs at Vonore, Tennessee, or Murphy, North Carolina. To reach Turtletown from Red Clay, leave Red Clay Park, turning left onto Red Clay Park Road. Turn right at Weatherly Switch Road (TN 317) and travel 1.1 miles to TN 60. Turn left onto TN 60 and proceed 8.6 miles to Red Food Drive. Turn right onto Red Food Drive and travel one block. Turn right onto TN 64/74 Bypass. Travel 1.5 miles, then take the TN 64/Ocoee River Exit. Turn east onto TN 64 toward Ocooee. Travel for 33.3 miles through the Ocoee River Gorge. At the TN 68 intersection, turn onto TN 68 toward Ducktown/Madisonville, then continue 7.8 miles north to Turtletown. Coker Creek is located another 16.5 miles north along TN 68.

East of Ocoee at the western edge of the Chilhowee Mountains, the Ocoee River is impounded by Parksville Lake; visitors can look across the waters over the flooded sites of the nineteenth-century settlements of Wakoee and Silquo. Farther east, US 64 retraces the Old Copper Road, a track built through the Ocoee River Gorge by Cherokee laborers in 1853. Portions of the old road are accessible to hikers and bicyclists at the Ocoee Whitewater Center, which features a garden of Cherokee medicinal plants. In the valley at the head of the Ocoee gorge was the Cherokee settlement of Ducktown (Kawonee), though the site is now obliterated by the mining wastes that surround Copper Hill, Tennessee. The Ducktown Basin Museum, which chronicles the copper mining heritage of the region, is located just off TN 68, in present-day Ducktown. The hours there are Mon-

Ocoee Whitewater Center with paddlers on the course below.
(Photograph by Murray Lee)

day through Saturday from 10:00 A.M. until 4:30 P.M. (phone 423-496-5778). To the north lie Turtletown and Coker Creek in the Hiwassee River Basin.

TURTLETOWN—ZION HILL BAPTIST CHURCH

After the Cherokee removal of 1838 and the Trail of Tears forced emigration, the Cherokees who remained in the East faced an uncertain future in a land that rapidly filled with the very whites who had demanded their removal. Eastern Cherokee families, many of whom had hidden or escaped the military dragnet, began the daunting task of rebuilding farms and communities to secure their livelihoods and maintain their connections to Indian society. The largest of the post-removal Cherokee settlements in the East were at Qualla (Cherokee), Buffalo Town (now Snowbird, near Robbinsville), and Valley River (near Marble, North Carolina), but a number of smaller enclaves were scattered over southwestern North Carolina, southeastern Tennessee, and northern Georgia.

One of the best known of these smaller, isolated Cherokee communities was Turtletown, located astride the North Carolina–Tennessee state line south of the Hiwassee River. Although Turtletown (Saligugi'hi) existed prior to the 1838 removal, the post-removal community was established by Cherokee families who evaded the troops or escaped the Trail of Tears.

Founders of the community included Young Bird (Cheesquaneetah) and Polly Bird, who escaped the emigration detachments at Blythe's Ferry, Bearmeat (Yonahchewayah) and James Catt (Teconesenaka), both of whom hid with Oochella's band during the removal. These and allied families (e.g., Mumbleheads, Walkingsticks) grew and prospered in the sparsely settled area around the foot of Little Frog Mountain, where they lived, worked, and worshipped among white neighbors. The Cherokee families of Turtletown helped found the Turtletown Baptist Church (now Zion Hill Baptist Church) in 1854, and worshipped there as part of a mixed Cherokee-white congregation for the next forty years. The Turtletown Cherokees were small farmers but also worked as colliers for the copper mines at Ducktown, Tennessee, cutting trees and burning them to make charcoal to run the smelters. They helped build the Old Copper Road, a wagon route through the seemingly impassable Ocoee River Gorge.

When the Civil War broke out in 1861, young Cherokee men from Turtletown joined their white neighbors in the Union Army rather than their kinsmen from Valley River and Qualla, who fought for the Confederacy. After the war, the Cherokee community at Turtletown began a gradual decline, until the last members moved away around 1905. Many of the Turtletown families joined Cherokee communities at Long Ridge (Violet, North Carolina) or Snowbird, then later moved to the Judson, North Carolina, area. By 1920, the descendants of the Turtletown Cherokees had rejoined their kinspeople on Qualla Boundary, where the families live today.

Among the last Cherokee residents of the Turtletown community were Johnson Catt and Sally Mumblehead Catt, who lived on Little Frog Mountain near Cold Springs in the early twentieth century. As late as the mid-1980s, older white residents of Turtletown fondly recalled the Catt, Walkingstick, and Mumblehead families living at Cold Springs, and the white rural community still senses a special connection to the Cherokees who lived in their area.

Today, Turtletown can be appreciated as a rural landscape that still echoes its Cherokee past. Visitors passing through Turtletown on TN 68 can stop at the Zion Hill Baptist Church (at present-day Harbuck) and stroll through its cemetery, where the graves of Cherokee and white church members are mingled in reflection of the old Turtletown congregation. One-half mile southwest of the church, Kimsey Highway (USFS Road 68, a gravel-surfaced road) leads from TN 68 up Little Frog Mountain to Cold Springs Gap, a drive which imparts an understanding of the hard lives and splendid isolation of the last Cherokee residents of Turtletown. The Little Frog Mountain Wilderness Area and several unmaintained trails at Cold Spring Gap offer hiking opportunities for the adventurous visitor.

Modern-day prospectors on Coker Creek, site of an 1800s gold rush. (Photograph by Murray Lee)

CONTACT: Tennessee Overhill Heritage Association, P.O. Box 143, L&N
   Depot, Etowah, TN 37331, 423-263-7232, <www.tennesseeoverhill.com>
LOCATION: The modern community of Turtletown is located along TN 68,
   approximately 8 miles north of US 64. Zion Hill Baptist Church is
   situated on the west side of TN 68 at Harbuck, 4.85 miles north of
   US 64. Kimsey Highway (USFS Road 68) joins TN 68 approximately
   4.3 miles north of US 64. All of this area was once part of Turtletown.

COKER CREEK

On the 14th of June ultimo General Armistead arrived at this place, and on the 17th we set
out for the gold region in the Valley Towns. On the 18th we passed the Coqua Creek gold
mines, which is in the chartered limits of Tennessee and about two miles north of the great
Unicoy Mountain. Here we found a large number of persons digging for gold; I notified
them to desist and be gone before I returned.

—Cherokee Agent Hugh Montgomery to Secretary of War Lewis Cass, July 12, 1832

Coker Creek, the site of a small, early nineteenth-century Cherokee community and a removal-era army fort (Fort Armistead) on the Unicoi Turnpike, is located just 16 miles north of Turtletown along TN 68. Eighteenth-
century accounts refer to this area as "Eunnaika," a level respite between
the Chilhowee and Unaka mountains along the Overhill Trading Path. By

the early nineteenth century, American travelers using the Unicoi Turnpike called the area Coker or Coqua (also Toqua) Creek, a name that may derive from *kuku,* the Cherokee word for pleurisy root. After the Hiwassee District cession in 1819, displaced Cherokee families from Old Cheohee in Cades Cove, Tennessee, moved along the Unicoi Turnpike to resettle at Coker Creek, which remained part of the Cherokee Nation. Among these Cherokee settlers were siblings Betsy, George, Ginnesa, and Winny, children of old Roman Nose of Cheoah. These families soon prospered from the commerce of the Unicoi Turnpike, and white travelers became familiar with Betsy Coker (or Coco Bet) and George Coker as providers of food and lodging to weary pilgrims. Other entrepreneurs soon established additional stands or "houses of entertainment" to serve this traffic, and Coker Creek grew as a bustling stopover point on the turnpike.

In 1831, American gold prospectors and outlaws overran the Cherokee community at Coker Creek in Tennessee's first gold rush. These brigands abused Cherokee citizens and plundered their property throughout the gold region from Coker Creek to Valley River, North Carolina. In June 1832, the Cherokee Agency dispatched a military expedition to bring order to the gold fields and expel white intruders. These troops, led by General Armistead, established their base at Meroney's Stand in Coker Creek. When the expedition withdrew from the region, a company of troops remained to build Fort Armistead in Coker Creek, the only army garrison in the Cherokee Nation until May 1835.

During the 1838 Cherokee removal, Fort Armistead saw limited use as an outpost for army express riders and as a way station and camping spot for parties of Cherokee prisoners who traveled the Unicoi Turnpike. In August 1838, U.S. troops occupied Fort Armistead while they scoured the Unaka Mountains for runaway Cherokees who had fled the internment camps at Fort Cass.

Fort Armistead once stood on a low knoll now on the east side of TN 68, three hundred yards southeast of the Coker Creek Baptist Church. This privately owned site still bears vestiges of the Unicoi Turnpike, the fort, and the stock stand. Local tradition asserts that a nearby hilltop just south of the church contains the graves of soldiers who died at the fort; this cemetery may also include the graves of the Cherokees who died on the trail at Coker Creek in 1838.

Local traditions have immortalized Betsy Coker in romantic legend as "Coco Belle," a winsome "princess" who died of a broken heart after losing her warrior lover. Some local residents can confidently point to her stone grave cairn in Coker Creek. The real Betsy Coker was a more believable tragic heroine. Forced from her home in Cades Cove by white intruders, the elderly Betsy rebuilt her life as the matriarch of the Coker Creek community until she was again cruelly uprooted by federal troops. After enduring months of internment at the Cherokee Agency, Betsy Coker joined the exodus to Indian Territory, only to perish on the trail in Illinois during the bitter winter of 1838. Like thousands of Cherokees who died on the Trail of Tears, Betsy Coker lies in an unmarked grave, hundreds of miles from her home and kin.

CONTACT: Tennessee Overhill Heritage Association, P.O. Box 143, L&N Depot, Etowah, TN 37331, 423-263-7232, <www.tennesseeoverhill.com>, <www.cokercreekvillage.com>

LOCATION: The Coker Creek community is located approximately 24 miles north of Ducktown, Tennessee, and 9 miles south of Tellico Plains, Tennessee, along TN 68.

EVENTS

■ Cherokee Days of Recognition at Red Clay

During the first weekend in August, Red Clay State Historic Park invites the public to a festival weekend. Performers and crafts demonstrators from the Eastern Band of Cherokee Indians participate in this event. The interpretive center is open at this time, as are the hiking trails and picnic facilities.

CONTACT: Red Clay State Historic Park, 1140 Red Clay Park Rd. SW, Cleveland, TN 37311, 423-478-0339

LOCATION: South of Cleveland, east of Chattanooga, near the Tennessee-Georgia state line

■ Nineteenth-Century Cherokee Christmas

The Nineteenth-Century Cherokee Christmas occurs annually on the first Sunday in December. This living history program features Cherokee people and is held in a replica 1830s Cherokee farmstead in the Red Clay State Historic Park.

CONTACT: Red Clay State Historic Park, 1140 Red Clay Park Rd. SW, Cleveland, TN 37311, 423-478-0339

LOCATION: South of Cleveland, east of Chattanooga, near the Tennessee-Georgia state line

Cherokee Renaissance
New Echota, Georgia

Resolved . . . That one hundred town lots, of one acre square, be laid off on the Oostenallah River, commencing below the mouth of the Creek, nearly opposite to the mouth of Caunausauga River. The public square to embrace two acres of ground, which town shall be known and called Echota. . . .

JNO. ROSS, Pres't, N.Com
MAJOR RIDGE, Speaker
Approved PATHKILLER (x) his mark
CH. R. HICKS
A. MCCOY, Clerk of Com.
E. BOUDINOTT, Clerk N. Council
November 12, 1825

Beginning more than a thousand years ago, the Cherokee culture that we recognize today existed across the landscape of all of what is now northeastern Georgia. Evidence of this culture is found in mounds, spear points, pottery, the names of rivers and creeks, and legends that are still told by Cherokee storytellers. Cherokee towns occupied the bottomlands along the Chattooga, Tugaloo, and Chattahoochee Rivers in north Georgia, adjoining their Lower Towns on the Keowee River. Established trading paths like the Unicoi Trail led north to the rest of the Cherokee Nation and south to the Creek Nation.

Northwestern Georgia, however, including the Coosawattee and Oostanula Rivers, was claimed by both the Creeks and the Cherokees. In 1755, the Cherokees' victory at the Battle of Taliwa gained this land for them. This area of rivers, rolling hills, and fertile farmland became home to thousands of Cherokees in the late eighteenth century as their lands were diminished by treaties and their towns were destroyed by British and American forces. Here in northwest Georgia between 1789 and 1838, Cherokee people transformed their society into a model "civilization" that surpassed the plans of George Washington, Thomas Jefferson, and missionaries to become at

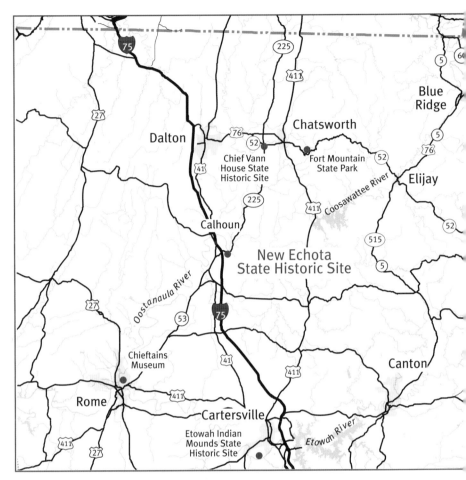

MAP II. *Cherokee Heritage Trails, New Echota, Ga.*

once uniquely American and uniquely Cherokee. Within sight of the mountains, the planned community and national capitol of New Echota became the geographical center of the Cherokee Nation and the focus of its renaissance. Here the Cherokee Nation reached a pinnacle of civilization before removal.

New Echota State Historic Site serves as the main interpretive center for Cherokee Heritage Trails in Georgia. The capital of the Cherokee Nation was here, constructed on the old village site of Gansagi-yi, also known as New Town, at the junction of the Conasauga and Coosawatee Rivers. The new capital was named for the beloved town of Old Echota, located in the Tennessee Overhills. Today reconstructed and relocated buildings along

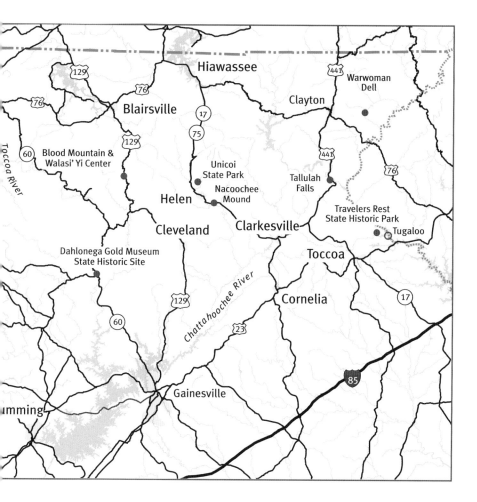

with an interpretive center mark the site where the Cherokee people developed a written constitution, a bilingual newspaper, a Supreme Court, and all the institutions making them as "civilized" as any other nation.

From this area, one can visit sites associated with the flourishing Cherokee Nation of the early nineteenth century, and with the tragedy of removal in 1838. In response to the federal initiative to assimilate the Cherokees, they became farmers and plantation owners, businessmen, and skilled tradesmen. Sequoyah's syllabary made them literate in their own language, and some had been educated to read and write English as well. They sang Christian hymns and played fiddle tunes as well as celebrated the Green Corn Ceremony with older traditional Cherokee dances and songs. This planned city and newly constructed capital became the center for Chero-

On the Shortness of Human Life

*John Ridge wrote this poem at sixteen, when he and Elias Boudinot
(Buck Watie) were students at the Foreign Mission School in Connecticut. Elected to the National Committee of the Cherokee Nation prior to
removal, he supported the Treaty of New Echota along with his father,
Major Ridge. As a result, his life was cut short by assassination June 22,
1839, at the age of thirty-six.*

> Like as a damask Rose you see,
> Or like the blossom on the tree,
> > Or like the morning to the day,
> > Or like the Sun,
> > Or like the Shade,
> > Or like the Gourd which Jonas had:
> Even such is MAN! Whose thread is spun,
> Drawn out and cut, and so, 'tis done.
> > Withers the Rose,
> > The blossom blasts,
> > The flower fades,
> > The morning hastes,
> The sun is set, shadows fly,
> The gourd consumes—so mortals die.

John Ridge, February 1819, Cornwall, Connecticut

kee optimism and enthusiasm for participating in the growth and building
of the new republic, the United States. This area became the geographical
and political center of the Cherokee Nation after treaty cessions left smaller
holdings in North Carolina and Tennessee.

In northwest Georgia, the Cherokee Nation grew and flourished as Cherokees created large farms, mills, blacksmith shops, and schools. Roads
through the Nation, like the Federal Turnpike built in 1805, provided income from travelers and drovers. In 1826, John Ridge, then in Washington,
wrote a description of the progress of the nation for Albert Gallatin, who
became the first director of the Bureau of American Ethnology. In his essay,
Ridge describes a nation with about ten million acres of land and more
than 15,000 inhabitants (including 147 white men and 73 white women

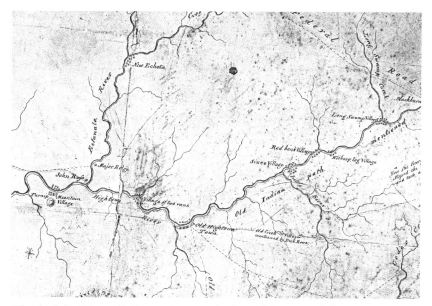

"Sketch of the [Disputed] Country between the State of Georgia and the
Cherokee Nation," by John Coffee, 1830. (Record Group 75, Map 144,
National Archives, College Park, Md.)

who had married Cherokees, and 1,277 African slaves). The Nation was divided into eight districts, each with its own courts and its own representatives to the National Council. He says, perhaps optimistically, that Cherokee people have completely given up communal village life and hunting
and have turned to farming on individual homesteads. He praises Cherokee women: "Duties assigned them as mothers and wives are well attended
to, and cheerfully do they prepare our meals, & for the family they sew,
they spin and weave and are in fact a valuable portion of our citizens." He
adds that Cherokee law "from time immemorial recognizes a separate property in the wife and husband, and this principle is universally cherished
. . . the law secures to the ladies the control of their own property." He
describes the Cherokee government and its "written and well-understood
laws." Acknowledging the existence of conjuring and "superstition" Ridge
adds that "The Standard of Religion is advancing with a steady march in
different parts of the Nation—and the Gospel is preached in eight organized churches by Presbyterians, Baptists, Moravians, and Methodists." He
states that there were thirteen schools, and he outlines plans to establish a
national academy of higher learning at New Echota.

Ridge concludes:

It is true, we enjoy self-government, but we live in fear, and uncertainty foretells our Fall. Strangers urge our removal to make room for their settlements, they point to the west and there they say we can live happy. Our National existence is suspended on the faith and honor of the United States alone. We are in the paw of a Lion—convenience may induce him to crush, and with a faint Struggle we may cease to be! But all Nations have experienced change. Mutability is stamped on every thing that walks the Earth. Even now we are forced by natural causes to a Channel that will mingle the blood of our race with the white. In the lapse of half a Century if Cherokee blood is not destroyed it will run its courses in the veins of fair complexions who will read that their Ancestors under the Stars of adversity, and curses of their enemies became a civilized Nation.

Ridge's concerns were justified. Two years after he wrote this essay, gold was discovered in north Georgia, Andrew Jackson was elected president of the United States on a platform that included removal of the Cherokees, and the immediate future of the Cherokee Nation was set in motion toward the Trail of Tears. The paw of the lion would indeed try to crush the Cherokees.

Many legends have arisen about "the first person to discover gold"— from the Cherokee boy who picked up a nugget on the Chestatee to the white pastor of the Yellow Creek Baptist Church, but the Cherokee had known about the presence of gold for centuries. Their name for the region, "Dahlonega" (*dalonige*), means yellow, and their oral history states that they allowed some Spanish mining of gold there in the 1600s. When the *Georgia Journal* in Milledgeville published the news in August 1829, however, a gold rush of major proportions followed. As many as ten thousand "twenty-niners" rushed illegally onto the lands of the Cherokee Nation in the "Great Intrusion," as Georgians characterized it at the time. Georgia laws already prohibited a Cherokee from testifying against a white man in court, and with no legal restraints to the "gold fever," squatters rushed onto Cherokee territory. By the end of 1832, more than half a million dollars worth of gold (in 1832 dollars) from Georgia had been deposited with the U.S. Mint.

Andrew Jackson was elected president of the United States on a platform that included Indian removal. By May 1830 he had pushed the Indian Removal Act through Congress, calling for the relocation across the Mississippi of all southeastern tribes. By this time, the situation of Cherokees and other tribes had been brought to the attention of the country, through their contact with missionaries from the Northeast and through speaking tours made by educated Cherokees to raise money for schools and a printing press. Indian removal was widely debated in newspapers and in public, and these debates reflected divisions between northern and southern states as well as issues of states' rights that foreshadowed the Civil War. The vote was close, but the Removal Act passed. David (Davy) Crockett, legislator from Tennesseee, voted against removal because of his friendship with the Cherokees, whom he fought with in the Creek War, including the Battle of Horseshoe Bend. Three days after the bill was passed, the state of Georgia took more than 4.6 million acres of Cherokee land, including their capital city of New Echota and six missionary stations. Cherokee courts were closed, the National Council was forbidden to meet, and their police were not allowed to function. Georgia surveyors began creating parcels to be given away in a fall land lottery. The Cherokee Nation ceased to exist, as far as the state of Georgia was concerned.

The first test of Georgia's assertion of its state's rights came in the fall of 1830, when the Georgia Guard arrested, tried, and sentenced Corn Tassel (George Tassel) for the murder of another Cherokee. This crime took place within the borders of what the Cherokee considered their nation, subject to their police, laws, and courts, so they challenged Georgia in federal court, with the intention of taking the case to the Supreme Court. Georgia authorities had Corn Tassel hung, in Gainesville, before the federal court could rule.

Lawyers for the Cherokee Nation next took a case to the Supreme Court as an independent foreign nation, arguing that Georgia had broken treaties with the federal government. In 1831, in *Cherokee Nation v. Georgia,* the court ruled that the Cherokee Nation could not bring suit as an independent foreign nation, because they were a "domestic, dependent nation." Justice John Marshall let his sympathies for the Cherokees be known at this time.

The Cherokee Nation's next opportunity to bring the case before the Supreme Court came quickly. Georgia had passed a law requiring all white men living within the bounds of the former Cherokee Nation to take an oath of allegiance to obey the laws of the state of Georgia, and if they did not do so, they would have to leave the state or be imprisoned. This law was aimed at the thirty-two missionaries living on Cherokee lands, many of whom had publicly expressed opposition to removal, often in nationally distributed newspapers like the *Christian Advocate,* printed in New York City. Reverend Samuel Worcester and Dr. Elizur Butler, both Congregationalists, were arrested and treated roughly by the Georgia Guard in July 1831. Worcester had a chain put around his neck and around the neck of a horse and was taken in that manner to Lawrenceville, where he and Butler were tried, convicted, and sentenced to four years hard labor in September 1831. Their lawyers appealed immediately, while Worcester and Butler began serving their sentences at Milledgeville Penitentiary.

In March 1832, John Marshall rendered the Supreme Court's decision in *Worcester v. Georgia.* "The Cherokee Nation is a distinct community occupying its own territory . . . in which the law of Georgia can have no right to enter but with the assent of the Cherokees." The court's decision established the Cherokees, and by extension, other tribes, as sovereign nations within the larger nation of the United States. President Andrew Jackson refused to enforce this ruling, however, and is said to have commented: "John Marshall has made his decision; let him enforce it now if he can." (Remark reported by Horace Greeley in *The American Conflict.*) When rumors spread about Jackson's attitude, John Ridge visited him in Washington and asked whether the United States would support the Supreme Court decision. Jackson confirmed that he would not.

Although the highest court in the land confirmed their rights as a sovereign domestic nation, the Cherokee Nation still could not prevail against the greed of gold seekers, land speculators, and politicians. Within three years, the Ridge Party, a small group within the Cherokee Nation, signed the Treaty of New Echota, knowing that they signed their death warrant for selling Cherokee land without the consent of the whole Cherokee Nation. They felt that the only way the Nation would survive was to remove to the West. The small Ridge Party, or "Treaty party," had already been repudiated by the Ross Party, the majority of the Cherokees, who followed Principal Chief John Ross. The act of signing the Treaty of New Echota irrevocably separated them. Even after the Treaty of New Echota was ratified in Congress in 1836, giving the Cherokees two years to remove to Oklahoma, John Ross and his party continued to resist removal with every legal and political strategy possible—to no avail. The renaissance of literacy, education, and Christianity that centered around New Echota gave way to the tragedy of removal—as the print shop, council house, and courthouse of the Cherokee Nation were burned to the ground to lie beneath the Georgia clay.

The reconstructed buildings of the New Echota State Historic Site sketch out the original ambitious design of this capital: council house, Supreme Court building, bilingual newspaper office, missionary's home, Cherokee farmsteads, and stickball playing field are set within wide streets laid out on a grid. A museum tells the story of this remarkable piece of Cherokee history. A few miles to the north, the Vann House has been restored as the showplace it once was—an antebellum mansion replete with white columns. A marker commemorating the Springplace Mission stands nearby.

The Council House at New Echota. (Courtesy of New Echota State Historic Site)

Southwest of New Echota, near Rome, the Chieftains' Museum preserves the house of Major Ridge, and the Etowah Indian Mounds State Historic Site preserves the earthworks of an earlier period of civilization. The Chieftains' Museum, a National Historic Landmark, provides interpretive exhibits within the house and on the grounds. At the Etowah Mounds, a museum interprets the culture that created the mounds almost a thousand years ago; many of the impressive earthworks still stand.

On Cohutta Mountain, a mysterious 855-foot-long rock wall looks to the south over the rolling piedmont where New Echota is located. Fort Mountain State Park preserves this antiquity, most likely built between A.D. 100 and A.D. 600. On this site, according to Cherokee legend, Agan-unitsi defeated the fearsome monster snake, the Uk'tena, and acquired the wonder-working crystal from its forehead.

In north-central Georgia, several sites add to the picture of the Cherokees in north Georgia. The Dahlonega Gold Museum State Historic Site provides information on the gold rush of 1829. Farther east the Nacoochee Mound marks the former site of a Cherokee village. Unicoi State Park stands on the original Unicoi Turnpike, an important trading path. For travelers wanting to explore a scenic route from central Georgia to Murphy, North Carolina, the road across Blood Mountain leads across another mountain gap described in the story of Agan-unitsi and the Uk'tena.

In northeast Georgia, the landscape of the Cherokees can be visited in former village sites, waterfalls, and trails. Near Clayton, Warwoman Dell Recreation Area provides recreation opportunities on an old Cherokee trail. Tallulah Gorge State Park includes a waterfall of legendary significance to the Cherokee. Traveler's Rest State Historic Site marks the old Unicoi Trail. Tugaloo State Park, at Lake Hartwell, links to the original Lower Towns of the Cherokee near the site of the old Tugaloo Town, now inundated.

Annual events in north Georgia include Christmas candlelight tours at New Echota and at the Vann House. Other events may be scheduled at other sites. The Etowah Mounds State Historic Site has presented Cherokee storytellers and craftspeople. New Echota and the Vann House sell some crafts made by members of the Eastern Band of Cherokee Indians as well as a selection of books.

North Georgia is known throughout the rest of the state for its many recreational opportunities. The Appalachian Trail begins here, and the Bartram Trail passes through. Unicoi, Tugaloo, and Fort Mountain State Parks, as well as other areas, offer camping, hiking, fishing, and boating. The Chattooga River offers trout fishing and world-class whitewater.

Works by many Eastern Band Cherokee artists can be found in gift shops featuring authentic Cherokee arts and crafts.

Louise Maney, potter. (Photograph by Cedric N. Chatterley)

Virgil Ledford, woodcarver. (Photograph by Cedric N. Chatterley)

Supreme Court at New Echota. (Photograph by Barbara Duncan)

■ New Echota State Historic Site

Built as prescribed by the Cherokee National Council, New Echota became the capitol of the Cherokee Nation. Near the geographical center of
the Cherokee lands remaining after the Treaty of 1819, New Echota symbolized the progress of the Cherokees toward "civilization," as mandated by
George Washington, Thomas Jefferson, and the federal government. Here,
with enthusiasm and idealism matching that of the young but growing
United States, the Cherokees planned and built a model city that included
a council house, Supreme Court building, newspaper office, houses, farmsteads, taverns, missionaries' homes, a traditional ball ground, and plans
for seminaries. This "capital" was located on the site of New Town, where
the Cherokee council had been meeting since 1819.

Here the *Cherokee Phoenix* (*Tsalagi Tsulehisanvhi*), was first published on
February 2, 1828. The official national newspaper of the Cherokee Nation,
the *Phoenix* was edited by Elias Boudinot (Buck Watie) who had been educated in Cornwall, Connecticut. With articles in English and "Sequoyan,"
the *Phoenix* circulated throughout the Cherokee Nation and beyond. When
Boudinot's wife's parents (from Cornwall) visited New Echota, they described it as follows:

> This neighborhood is truly an interesting and pleasant place. The ground
> is level and smooth as a floor; the center of the Nation, a new place,

The Samuel Worcester House, built in 1828. (Courtesy of New Echota State Historic Site)

laid out in city form; a hundred lots of an acre each. A spring, called the public spring, about twice as large as our sawmill brook, near the center, with other springs on the plat; six new framed houses in sight . . . which would be respectable in Litchfield . . . , besides a Council House, Court House, printing office and four stores, all in sight of Mr. Boudinot's house.

New Echota served as capital only through 1830, when conditions in Georgia made it too dangerous for the National Council to continue to meet there. The *Cherokee Phoenix* press was destroyed by the Georgia Guard in 1834 because of its anti-removal editorials, and the building was burned. In 1838, the U.S. Army made their headquarters for removal operations near the site of what was once the Cherokees' most enlightened city. All of New Echota's buildings were destroyed except for the house of Samuel Worcester, a white missionary, and the land became farmland once again.

No trace of New Echota remained. The location was marked in 1931 with a monument erected by the Women's Club of Calhoun, Georgia. Then, in the 1950s, a group of Calhoun citizens purchased two hundred acres at the site and deeded it to the state of Georgia, and the excavation of New Echota began. Using Cherokee documents, a Georgia surveyor's description, and archaeological research, the locations of buildings and streets were determined and artifacts were recovered. In 1962, the state of Georgia dedicated the New Echota State Historic Site, which included some restored buildings and other relocated ones. At the same time the Georgia legislature repealed the laws passed in the 1820s and 1830s that had oppressed the Cherokee Nation in Georgia.

Today, the New Echota State Historic Site includes a museum along with reconstructed buildings on the site. A walking tour of about an hour takes visitors past a Cherokee homestead, town center, reconstructed council house, reconstructed Supreme Courthouse, Cherokee cabin, and the original Worcester house, now restored. New Echota also includes the Vann Tavern, moved to this site in 1955; a reconstructed print shop; and the Boudinot house site, where the treaty of New Echota was signed in the early morning hours of December 29, 1835. In addition, a trail with natural history interpretation loops off of the main trail.

In the museum courtyard, plaques recognize New Echota as a Historic Site in Journalism (Sigma Delta Chi Professional Journalistic Society) and a National Historic Landmark (National Park Service). The Native American Journalists' Association also dedicated a bronze plaque here. Outside the courtyard, the original bronze marker from the Calhoun Women's Club has been reinstalled next to a marker from the state of Georgia.

CONTACT: New Echota State Historic Site, 1211 Chatsworth Highway NE, Calhoun, GA 30701, 706-624-1321, <www.gastateparks.org>

HOURS: Open Tuesday through Saturday from 9:00 A.M. until 5:00 P.M., and Sunday from 2:00 P.M. until 5:30 P.M. Closed Monday (except legal holidays), Thanksgiving, Christmas Day, and New Year's Day. Closed on Tuesday when open Monday. Small admission fee. Discount for groups with advance notice.

LOCATION: 1 mile east of I 75 Exit 317 on GA 225

■ Chief Vann House State Historic Site

Thus ended the life of one who was feared by many and loved by few in the 41st year of his life. . . . James Vann had been an instrument in the hand of God for establishing our Mission in this Nation. Never in his wildest orgies had he attempted to harm us. We could not but commend his soul to God's mercy.

—Springplace Diaries, February 21, 1809

Born in 1768, James Vann was the son of Wahli, a Cherokee woman, and a Scottish trader named Vann. He became successful and prosperous, and provided land for the first missionaries to the Cherokees, the Moravians. Vann further supported their efforts by sending his own children to be educated by them beginning in 1801. Several hundred yards from Spring-

James Vann House near Chatsworth, Ga., completed in 1805.
(Photograph by Brett Riggs)

place Mission, Vann built his brick mansion on a slight rise overlooking the countryside, near the Federal Road.

Designed by a German architect and constructed by brick masons, Moravians, Cherokees, and African American slaves, the Vann House was finished in 1805 and still stands as a landmark of Cherokee architecture. A three-story brick mansion with white pillars in the front and back, it incorporates Cherokee colors and details along with the American Georgian and Federal styles of the period. In its wide hallway, a "floating staircase" is the oldest remaining example of cantilevered construction in Georgia. Hand-carved Cherokee rose designs decorate the staircase and appear throughout the house. A large fireplace rises from the floor to the twelve-foot-high ceiling in a room now restored to its original paint colors (found under nineteen layers of paint): sky blue, light forest green, red clay, and sunny yellow. Most of the house materials were made on the plantation: bricks formed from local clay, nails and hinges forged in the blacksmith shops, and boards cut at one of Vann's sawmills.

In early 1809, James Vann was fatally shot as he stood at the bar of Buffington's Tavern; the unknown assassin fired through a crack in the door. In his will, he left everything to his son Joseph, then ten years old. Just the year before, the Cherokee National Council meeting at Broomes-

Joseph Vann (1799–1844), son of James Vann, had become a wealthy man when the Georgia militia forced him to flee in 1835. Painting by Frank Mack, 1950s. (Courtesy of the Vann House State Historic Site, Georgia Department of Natural Resources)

town had, at the urging of Vann and others, made it legal for Cherokee men to leave property to their sons, rather than having all property pass through the mother's lineage as in the old traditional ways. Vann's bequest was still controversial, however, and Vann's other children and wives received some property before most of the estate passed to Joseph in 1814.

Soon known as "Rich Joe" Vann, this young man prospered. By the time the Georgia Guard forced him to flee his house in 1835, his holdings included more than four thousand acres, 110 slaves, gristmills, sawmills, blacksmith shops, racehorses, taverns, ferries, farmsteads, whiskey stills, and orchards. He moved his family to a farm that he owned on Ooltewah Creek and the Tennessee River, one of the former Chickamauga towns (now under Chickamauga Lake). Rather than wait for removal, he moved to Indian territory in 1836 and built another, duplicate mansion at Webber's Falls. Joe Vann was killed in 1844 when his steamboat, the Lucy Walker, exploded on the Ohio River near Louisville, Kentucky. Many Vann descendants remain part of the Cherokee Nation today.

The Vann House has been completely restored and furnished with period furniture, artifacts, and textiles. Joseph Vann's fiddle, signet ring, and other effects on display have been donated by his descendants. An outstanding quilt on display, created about 1805—the "Indian Headdress"—was made by one of the Vann slaves. John Howard Payne, composer of "Home Sweet Home," spent several days in the cellar of the house, imprisoned by the

Georgia Guard during his visit to the Cherokee Nation. The house can be toured and is air-conditioned. A new visitor center provides interpretation of the house and its history.

The Springplace Mission stood down the road from the Vann house. A bronze plaque and a state historical marker have been erected on the edge of a field where their house, school, and farm buildings once flourished.

CONTACT: Chief Vann House State Historic Site, 82 Georgia Highway 225 N, Chatsworth, GA 30705, 706-695-2598, <www.alltel.net/~vannhouse/>, <vannhouse@alltel.net>

HOURS: Open Tuesday through Saturday from 9:00 A.M. until 5:00 P.M., and Sunday from 2:00 P.M. until 5:30 P.M. Closed Monday (except legal holidays), Thanksgiving, Christmas, and New Year's Day. Closed on Tuesday when open Monday. Small admission fee.

LOCATION: Just outside Chatsworth Georgia at the intersection of GA 225 and GA 52A.

SITES NEAR NEW ECHOTA

■ Chieftains' Museum—the Major Ridge Home

I am one of the native sons of these wild woods. I have hunted the deer and turkey here, more than fifty years. I have fought your battles, have defended your truth and honesty, and fair trading. I have always been the friend of honest white men. The Georgians have shown a grasping spirit lately; they have extended their laws, to which we are unaccustomed, which harass our braves and make the children suffer and cry; but I can do them justice in my heart. . . . I know the Indians have an older title than theirs. We obtained the land from the living God above. They got their title from the British. Yet they are strong and we are weak. We are few, they are many. We cannot remain here in safety and comfort. . . . There is but one path of safety, one road to future existence as a Nation. That path is open before you. Make a treaty of cession. Give up these lands and go over beyond the great Father of Waters.

—Major Ridge, to the Cherokee council at the Council House at New Echota, December 22, 1835, a week before he signed the Treaty of New Echota

A warrior, statesman, and orator, who was finally labeled a traitor, "The Ridge" was one of the leaders of the Cherokee Nation throughout his life (1771–1839). When he was a young hunter, he often returned to camp by following trails along the top of the mountain, and was given the name Gunvdalegi, "One who follows the ridge." This name also implied someone who was far seeing in other ways. "And those of us who knew his his-

Slavery and the Cherokees

Traditionally, the Cherokees, like other tribes, made slaves of people captured during war. Often these slaves became part of the tribe by marriage or adoption. This tradition fit not only with Cherokee cultural values of inclusion, but also with the enlightened philosophy and scientific views prevailing in the United States in the late eighteenth century, which held that all races of men were biologically and intellectually equal, made by the same Creator.

By the 1820s however, these views began changing for several reasons, including the widespread planting of labor-intensive cotton in the South. The efforts by Cherokees to become "civilized" included the expansion into plantation farming in north Georgia by a few prosperous businessmen such as John and Lewis Ross, descendants of Scottish traders. On the Coosa River, John Ross established a ferry and a plantation with a blacksmith shop and slave quarters. In 1835, nineteen slaves provided labor for growing corn, wheat, cotton, apples, and peaches. Lewis Ross owned forty slaves who helped operate a mill, ferries, stores, and his plantation. The Ridge owned about thirty slaves and his son John eighteen. Joseph Vann owned 110 slaves at the time of removal.

In other parts of the Cherokee Nation, however, more traditional Cherokees held to the older values of equality. In the mountains of western North Carolina, where large-scale plantation farming was impractical because of the terrain, Cherokees adopted patterns of slaveholding similar to those of their white neighbors. Landowners like Yonaguska owned one or two slaves who helped with farming. Many Cherokees maintained that they treated their slaves better than whites treated theirs. In 1825 David Brown, a young educated Cherokee, wrote to the Family Visitor (published in Richmond, Virginia): "You perceive that there are some African slaves among us. . . . They are, however, generally well treated and they much prefer living in the nation to residence in the United States."

During the Civil War, Cherokees in North Carolina fought for the Confederacy although they did not own any slaves at that time. When some of the Thomas Legion who had been captured in East Tennessee learned that they had been fighting to preserve slavery, they joined the Union Army. Cherokees in Oklahoma were divided along the lines of the Treaty Party and the Ross Party, which split at the time of removal. The Treaty Party, or Ridge Party, fought for the Confederacy, led by General Stand Watie (a nephew of Major Ridge), while the Ross Party followers fought for the Union. After the Civil War, both sides in Oklahoma suffered from the settlements made by the federal government.

Major Ridge (1771–1839) signed the Treaty of New Echota in 1835, ceding Cherokee land. (From Thomas L. McKenney and James Hall, History of the Indian Tribes of North America, with Biographical Sketches and Anecdotes of the Principal Chiefs, *1848)*

Major Ridge

tory from his own personal life are ready to agree that he walked along the mountain top in regard to integrity, high resolve, and purity of character," wrote Judge J. W. H. Underwood, an acquaintance. (After his leadership in the Creek War, when he led Cherokees to help Andrew Jackson defeat the Creeks at the Battle of Horseshoe Bend, he was known as Major Ridge.)

Sometime before 1800, Ridge settled with his wife Susanna on a bluff above the Oostanula River, near its junction with the Etowah and Coosa Rivers. Later he expanded their log cabin into a white frame mansion with the help of Moravian and Cherokee craftsmen. This plantation house stood two stories high, fifty-four feet by twenty-nine feet with four fireplaces, hardwood paneling, verandas, a balcony, and thirty glass windows. This house was the center of a thriving farm with log kitchens, smokehouse, and stables, and 280 acres under cultivation in corn, cotton, tobacco, wheat, oats, indigo, and potatoes. Cows, hogs, and sheep provided meat, milk, butter, and wool. Orchards held thousands of peach, apple, quince, cherry, and plum trees. Nurseries, vineyards, and gardens grew fruits, vegetables, and ornamental plants. Thriving businesses formed part of the Ridge estate: a ferry, a trading post that imported goods from Augusta, and a blacksmith shop. Ridge and Susanna sent their son John to be educated at the Congregational mission school in Cornwall, Connecticut, along with Elias Boudi-

Chieftains Museum, the restored home of Major Ridge in Rome, Ga.
(Photograph by Mark Finchum)

not, his cousin. John returned and settled near them with his wife from Connecticut on a smaller but similar estate, "Running Waters," in what became known as "Ridge's Valley." John Ross lived nearby.

In 1835 Major Ridge and his son John, Elias Boudinot, and others, designated as representatives of the tribe, signed the Treaty of New Echota, believing it the best course for their people, even though the majority of the Cherokee people opposed removal. As he made his mark, The Ridge said, "I have signed my death warrant." Major Ridge, John Ridge, and their extended families, along with a party of nearly five hundred Cherokees, left for Indian Territory in 1837 and established homes, stores, and a school there. Major Ridge was ambushed and fatally shot while riding horseback near the Arkansas state line the same day that his son John and Elias Boudinot were executed for their part in the Treaty of New Echota, on June 22, 1839.

His house on the Oostanula was given away in the Georgia land lottery of 1832 and was subsequently sold to Augustus Verdery, whose daughter described it as follows: "The mansion, two and a half stories high, was of hewn logs, weather-boarded and painted white. The ceilings, walls and floors were of hard wood; the windows were large and well placed. An arched triple window at the turn of the fine staircase looked out on a line of poplars, then on to the shining Oostanaula, with its fringe of reeds and lilies, and beyond to the spurs of the Blue Ridge mountains in the near distance."

The Ridge house has been restored and now operates as the Chieftains' Museum, a nonprofit organization. Exhibits tell the story of the Ridge family and extend through the Civil War. Artifacts unearthed in the area are on display, and archaeological research continues on the grounds.

CONTACT: Chieftains' Museum, 501 Riverside Rd. NE, Rome, GA 30162-0373, 706-291-9494, <www.chieftainsmuseum.org>, <chmuseum@bellsouth.net>

HOURS: Open Tuesday through Saturday, from 10:00 A.M. until 4:00 P.M. Small admission fee.

LOCATION: From Calhoun, take I 75 south about 12 miles. Take Exit 306 west (SR 140). Turn left onto SR 53 and left again onto GA 1 Loop to Riverside Road. Follow signs.

■ Etowah Indian Mounds State Historic Site

When you walk out on the place it's almost like you hear the people still there, you hear the happy sounds, the sound of children, and the sound of people playing games. All of a sudden you begin to cross the big ditch, and you begin to realize there were sounds there that were the sound of victory, the sound of defeat and agony. And it's hard to believe that there were so many people there at one time and only the mounds are left. And it's good that they're preserved.

It's a good place to sit and to think. It's almost like you're in touch with the past, almost like you're standing on holy ground.

—Freeman Owle

Located near the border of the original Cherokee homeland, the Etowah Mounds tower above the Etowah River and Pumpkinvine Creek. Built a thousand years ago or more, these mounds were the center of a palisaded town where more than three thousand Native Americans lived from A.D. 1000 to A.D. 1500. Often they are called "Moundbuilders" or the "Mississippian Indians," but these terms more accurately refer to architectural traditions and to a specific time period, respectively, than to people. The people who built and lived at these mounds were the ancestors of the Cherokees, the Creeks, and other tribes. In addition to being the focal point of a town, the Etowah Mounds supported the temples where priests practiced the ceremonies that made this an important religious center of its time, visited by many people from the surrounding region.

At what point the Cherokees lived at the Etowah Mounds is a question still debated by scholars. This area is part of territory long disputed be-

Etowah Mounds, Cartersville, Ga. (© 2000 Steve Wall)

tween the Cherokees and the Creeks. Scholars agree, however, based on archaeological evidence, historic documents, and Cherokee oral tradition, that Cherokees began moving back into this area in 1780, creating the town of Etowah. The Hightower Mission was established by the American Board of Commissioners.

Today, these mounds have been preserved by the state of Georgia on a fifty-six-acre site that includes six mounds, a village area with plaza, and a defensive ditch. The tallest mound stands 63 feet high with a base measuring 395 feet along two sides and about 335 feet along the other two sides. Structures were built on top of this mound, just as townhouses were built on smaller mounds in Cherokee villages throughout the southern Appalachians. Although one of the original mounds has been destroyed by archaeological excavation, the remaining mounds are intact and can be climbed by means of stairs built into the side of each mound.

A museum displays artifacts excavated from the site and provides information and interpretation of the site. A self-guided trail takes you around the three largest mounds, the village, plaza, borrow pit (which provided some of the dirt for mound construction), and fish weir. The park occasionally schedules programs by Cherokee storytellers and craftspeople.

CONTACT: Etowah Indian Mounds State Historic Site, 813 Indian Mounds Rd. SE, Cartersville, GA 30120, 770-387-3747, <www.gastateparks.org>

HOURS: Open Tuesday through Saturday from 9:00 A.M. until 5:00 P.M., and Sunday from 2:00 P.M. until 5:30 P.M. Closed Monday (except legal holidays), Thanksgiving, Christmas, and New Year's Day. Closed on Tuesday when open Monday. Small admission fee.

LOCATION: Take I 75 to Exit 288, then take GA 113 through Cartersville. Approximately 4 miles south of Cartersville on GA 113, turn left onto Indian Mounds Road.

SIDE TRIP

■ Fort Mountain State Park

East of Chatsworth, the road ascends in winding curves, climbing up the southern end of the Appalachians to the top of Cohutta Mountain. There, just below the ridge of the mountain, a stone wall of mysterious origin stretches 855 feet from east to west. Every thirty feet along the wall, round stone enclosures about six feet across protrude on the southern side. From this wall, one has an unobstructed view of sunrises and sunsets across the Piedmont to the south.

Archaeologists believe this wall to be a thousand years old or more. Theories about its purpose suggest that it might have been defensive or ceremonial. Its placement on the terrain makes one wonder what it was defending—the top of the mountain? Attackers could easily have reached around the ends of the wall. A ceremonial purpose seems more feasible, given the importance of the four directions in Cherokee prayer and the view from the wall over the surrounding Piedmont at the southern end of the Appalachians. Some stories claim that the wall's builders were "moon-eyed people" or even Welshmen led by Prince Modoc, as though the Cherokees lacked the technology for building a defensive wall. American Indian people throughout North America, including the Cherokees, built stone walls. Another, much smaller, stone wall snakes along the ridge above the Nantahala Gorge, a place Cherokee legends also describe as a haunt of the Uk'tena. The Cherokee legend of Agan-unitsi says that he built a defensive wall and ditch here on Fort Mountain in his struggle to kill the Uk'tena. (To read this myth in its entirety, see "Four Cherokee Stories" at the end of this book.) In 1900 James Mooney noted that several circular stone structures existed on hilltops near Clarkesville, Georgia, in the 1880s, and that legends about the Nunnehi were associated with them.

From the upper parking lot of Fort Mountain State Park, 190 stone steps

Reviving Old-Style Stamped Cherokee Pottery

Before the 1880s, most Cherokee pottery from the North Carolina Mountains was black and shiny on the inside and stamped with complex interlocking patterns on the outside. Pots were hand built in a variety of shapes, for different functions. Smudging with burned corncobs rendered the pottery waterproof, and it was used for cooking, making hominy, and carrying water. This style of pottery dates back more than six hundred years in the southern Appalachians, where potters have been at work for almost three thousand years.

At the beginning of the twentieth century, Catawba potters living in Cherokee influenced the way local people made pots, and the development of tourism brought visitors who preferred the Catawba-style pots, which are plain and shiny on the outside. The traditional forms were almost forgotten.

Recently, however, Cherokee people have been involved in an effort to revive the tradition. In the spring of 2002, at the Museum of the Cherokee Indian, Cherokee potters picked up carved wooden paddles and began stamping designs on large hand-built clay pots.

"It's a source of pride to be able to revive this tradition that's distinctly Cherokee," said potter Joel Queen, member of the Eastern Band of Cherokee Indians. "I've been wanting to do this style for a long time, to be able to turn a traditional style of work into a Cherokee art form that's not only functional but beautiful at the same time. This will be a part of Cherokee culture that won't be lost now."

"If we can bring this tradition back, we will really have accomplished something," said Ken Blankenship, executive director of the Museum of the Cherokee Indian. "All the pieces fell into place to revive the old style. This is something that the potters want to bring back, and the museum wants to help with this process."

Workshops teaching this style have been supported by the museum,

and short terraces (constructed in the twentieth century) lead up to one end of the wall and a round enclosure. A further climb up to the tower enables visitors to see a longer stretch of the wall, especially in winter when the trees are bare. Located in the Chattahoochee Forest near the Cohutta Wilderness Area, the wall is protected not only by U.S. Forest Service regulations but also by the Antiquities Act of 1906. Do not remove rocks from

Cherokee potters fire the pots they made in a workshop on old-style Cherokee pottery at the Museum of the Cherokee Indian. (Photograph by Brett Riggs)

the University of North Carolina–Chapel Hill Research Labs in Archaeology, the North Carolina Arts Council, and a grant from the W. K. Kellogg Foundation. Brett Riggs and Barbara Duncan helped organize the workshops, and ceramicist Tamara Beane provided hands-on instruction. Pots and sherds from the UNC–Chapel Hill collection as well from the museum were made available to the potters to handle and to replicate.

Shirley Oswalt, from Snowbird said, "In my community nobody else makes pottery, so it's important to me to learn this tradition to bring it back—not just so I can do it but so I can teach somebody else to do it. This is who we are: our language, our pots, our baskets."

the wall. Please leave this site as you find it, as with all sites on the Cherokee Heritage Trails.

South of Fort Mountain State Park, near the old Federal Road (now US 411), Carters Lake covers the old Cherokee town of Coosawattee. Principal town of the Coosawattee District established in 1820, this town was home to about six hundred Cherokees at the time of removal.

CONTACT: Fort Mountain State Park, 181 Fort Mountain Rd., Chatsworth,
GA 30705, 706-695-2621, <www.gastateparks.org>,
<fortmntpk@alltel.net>

HOURS: Open daily from 7:00 A.M. until 10:00 P.M. The park office is open
daily from 8:00 A.M. until 5:00 P.M.

LOCATION: 8 miles east of Chatsworth via GA 52, a scenic winding
two-lane blacktop. From I 75, take Exit 333 toward US 411.

SCENIC DRIVES

■ Sites in North Georgia

DAHLONEGA GOLD MUSEUM STATE HISTORIC SITE

The discovery of gold near here in 1828 led to a gold rush that hastened
the Trail of Tears for the Cherokee Nation. Georgia quickly passed laws pro-
hibiting Cherokees from mining gold on their own lands or from testifying
in court against a white man.

The Dahlonega Gold Museum tells the story of the gold rush, the founding of the towns of Auraria and Dahlonega, and the Georgia land lottery
that gave away Cherokee territory. Located in the old Lumpkin County
courthouse in the town square, the museum displays include artifacts, gold
coins, gold nuggets, and mining tools along with a video on the first gold
rush in America. Nearby, one of the North Georgia College buildings stands
on the site of the former U.S. Mint, which was burned during the Civil War.
Visitors can shop for gold nuggets and jewelry in stores around the square,
or learn to pan for gold at several locations just out of town. Gold from
Dahlonega covers the dome of the Georgia state house in Atlanta.

The southern Appalachians have their rugged ending near Dahlonega.
Mount Yonah ("bear" in Cherokee) can be seen on the horizon if one approaches Dahlonega from the east. North of town, the Appalachian Trail
has its southern terminus in the Chattahoochee National Forest near Ami-
calola Falls. From here, the Appalachian Trail covers some of the most
rugged terrain in its entire length before crossing into North Carolina near
Franklin.

CONTACT: Dahlonega Gold Museum State Historic Site, #1 Public Square,
Dahlonega, GA 30533, 706-864-2257, <dgmgold@alltel.net>

HOURS: Open Monday through Saturday from 9:00 A.M. until 5:00 P.M.,
and Sunday from 10:00 A.M. until 5:00 P.M. Closed Thanksgiving,

Dahlonega Gold Museum, Dahlonega, Ga. (Photograph by Mark Finchum)

Christmas, and New Year's Day. Small admission fee. Group rates available with advance notice.

LOCATION: Dahlonega can be reached via several state roads in central Georgia. GA 52 links it with Ellijay to the west. From the south, GA 400 and GA 60 provide easy access. From the north, US 19/129 provides an extremely scenic, winding route from Murphy, North Carolina, and Blairsville, Georgia.

To go east from Dahlonega to other Cherokee Heritage Trails sites, take GA 9/115 northeast to Cleveland. This route parallels the Chestatee River, where Cherokees mined gold, some of which financed the operation of the *Cherokee Phoenix* newspaper. From Cleveland, GA 75 leads to the Nacoochee Mound and Unicoi State Park along the old Unicoi Trail. Another route leads north from Dahlonega to Blairsville on US 19/129.

THE NACOOCHEE MOUND

The Nacoochee Mound, at the headwaters of the Chattahoochee River, marks the village site of Itsati, or Echota, located on Sautee Creek on the Unicoi Trail. (The name of Sautee Creek reflects the Kituhwa dialect pronunciation of the village name, It-sa-ti.) This village differs from and should not be confused with Old Echota on the Tennessee River in the Overhill Towns, or with New Echota in north Georgia. In the eighteenth century, this town on the Sautee was known as "Old Chota" or "Little Chota." The town of Nacoochee, or Nagutsi, stood farther south, at the junction of Sautee Creek and Soquee River.

The Cherokees considered these part of their Lower Towns, which stretched through present-day upper South Carolina. In 1915, the Museum of the American Indian, Heye Foundation, excavated Nacoochee Mound and concluded that it had been built and occupied by the Cherokees, thus laying to rest the theory of a separate race of "Moundbuilders." Artifacts from the mound still form part of the collection of the National Museum of the American Indian. Because of excavation and farming, the mound is much reduced from its original size. The Unicoi Trail ran through Nacoochee Valley here and crossed the Coosa Trail nearby. GA 75 roughly coincides with the Unicoi Trail's path from here north through the town of Hiawassee and on into North Carolina.

The legend of Princess Nacoochee and her tragic love affair does not come from Cherokee folklore but from the pen of a promoter who was trying to entice people to visit the mound and purchase his tract. Written shortly after removal, his story sets Shakespeare's star-crossed lovers in the

Nacoochee Mound, near Helen, Ga.
(Courtesy of the Convention and Visitors Bureau, White County, Ga.)

New World "where the white flowers of the climate, and the purple blossoms of the magnificent wild passion flower, mingled with the dark foliage of the muscadine." Cherokee women could marry and divorce freely, and legends of tragic love associated with places in the southern Appalachians come mainly from Victorian travel writers.

CONTACT: The Hardman family, the Trust for Public Land, and the state of Georgia are negotiating the ownership of the mound. Their goal is to make it part of the Georgia State Parks System, with an interpretive center to be created in the old farmhouse.

LOCATION: State roads are clearly marked, but the mound is not. If you are coming from Dahlonega and the west, take GA 115 to Cleveland, and from Cleveland take GA 75 north. (GA 75 is a two-lane blacktop and should not be confused with I 75, located farther west.) Where GA 17 enters and joins with GA 75, the Nacoochee Mound is located just off of GA 75.

If you are coming from the east, take US 76 west from Clayton. Just before reaching Hiawassee, Georgia, take GA 17/75 South. This takes the approximate route of the old Unicoi Trail as it turns south out of North Carolina, finding an easy route below Brasstown Bald. This road passes Unicoi State Park. To go to the Nacoochee Mound, proceed on to

Helen, Georgia. Go through Helen, and 2 miles south of town, the Nacoochee Mound stands on the east side of GA 75 where it splits from GA 17. To go on to Dahlonega, proceed on GA 75 to Cleveland. From there, take US 129 North, and then turn on US 19 South to Dahlonega. At the intersection for US 19 South, be sure to make that turn toward Dahlonega; US 19/129 North leads through the Chattahoochee National Forest as a scenic winding road through high mountains to Blairsville.

UNICOI STATE PARK

Unicoi State Park, located on GA 75 not far from the Nacoochee Mound, stands on the original Unicoi Trail, the trading path that connected Cherokee Overhill Towns and Lower Towns, reaching to Augusta, Georgia. At the park, some interpretive materials discuss the trail. The Unicoi Trail reaches this point in Georgia after turning south from the vicinity of Hayesville, North Carolina.

Unicoi State Park has more than a thousand acres of woods, streams, and mountains for hiking, biking, fishing, swimming, boating, and picnicking. A double waterfall, Anna Ruby Falls, is located near the entrance to the park. A lodge includes a restaurant, gift shop, and conference facilities, and the staff offer programs on natural history.

CONTACT: Unicoi State Park, P.O. Box 997, Helen, GA 30545, 706-878-3982; Ellen McConnell, Program Director, 706-878-3983. For rates and reservations, call 1-800-864-7275.

HOURS: Open daily from 7:00 A.M. until 10:00 P.M. The park office is open daily from 8:00 A.M. until 4:30 P.M.

LOCATION: On GA 75, 2 miles north of Helen in the Chattahoochee National Forest. From here, Cherokee Heritage Trail sites in northeast Georgia can be accessed by traveling to Clayton. From Unicoi State Park, continue north on GA 75/17 and take US 76 (designated a scenic route) east just before the town of Hiawassee.

BLOOD MOUNTAIN AND WALASI-YI CENTER

Another route north from Dahlonega along US 19/129 leads to DeSoto Falls, the Walasi-Yi Center and its trail to Blood Mountain, and Vogel State Park, finally connecting with Blairsville and with US 64 west of Murphy in North Carolina. About 14 miles north of Dahlonega, the DeSoto Falls Recreation Area includes five waterfalls on a 3-mile stretch of the DeSoto Trail. From here the road rises to cross Neel Gap, named for the engineer who brought the road through here in the 1930s.

The Cherokees call this gap Walasi-Yi, "Frog Place," because Agan-unitsi

Anna Ruby Falls. (Courtesy of the United States Forest Service)

found a giant frog here in this gap as he was traveling south, searching for the Uk'tena. (His search for the giant snake ended at Fort Mountain.) Later it was called Frogtown Gap. US 19/129 from Dahlonega curves and switchbacks up the mountain to reach the gap at 3,125 feet. From the gap, a 2-mile hiking trail leads to Blood Mountain, elevation 4,458 feet. According to Cherokee legend, the Nunnehi, the immortal spirit folk, had a townhouse underneath Blood Mountain, near the headwaters of the Nottely River. People downstream in the Nottely village told stories of visits to the other world of these beings, who helped them in times of trouble, just as the Nunnehi helped the village of Nikwasi on the Little Tennessee River.

The Walasi-Yi Center is a stone building erected by the Civilian Conservation Corps in 1934–38. Here the Appalachian Trail not only crosses the highway but goes through a breezeway at the Walasi-Yi Center, the only man-made structure on its entire length. The Mountain Crossings store in the center sells outdoor gear and camping equipment. Beyond Neel Gap to the north on US 19/129, Vogel State Park offers hiking, fishing, swimming, and boating.

CONTACT: Walasi-Yi Center, US 129, Rt. 1, Box 1240, Blairsville, GA 30512, 706-745-6095

HOURS: Open daily from 8:30 A.M. until 6:00 P.M. Closed on Christmas Day.

LOCATION: On US 19/129 between Dahlonega and Blairsville

■ Sites in Northeast Georgia

WARWOMAN DELL

In northeast Georgia, the trail from Clayton leads to Warwoman Dell, Tallulah Falls, Traveler's Rest, and the Tugaloo village site at Tugaloo State Park. Coming from the west into Clayton on US 76, you will intersect US 441, a four-lane highway. These roads approximate the old trails, and the Cherokees called the Clayton area "The Dividings" because of the intersection of trails here. From Clayton one can also travel north on US 441 to connect with Macon County, North Carolina, and the Middle Towns area along the Little Tennessee River, whose headwaters rise a few miles north of Clayton.

This scenic drive through northeast Georgia bridges the area between the old Middle and Lower Cherokee towns. Warwoman Dell is located on an old trading path and on Warwoman Creek, a tributary of the Chattooga River. This English name was used as early as 1730, but the story of its origin is unknown. Cherokee women were free to participate in war, and some did, although "warwoman" is not a Cherokee word. The Cherokees did have "beloved women" and "pretty women" who were acclaimed for their service to the tribe, and who made decisions of life and death over prisoners. The Warwoman Dell Recreation Area includes a nature trail and picnic tables. The Bartram Trail passes through the dell, leading to Becky Branch Falls and several other waterfalls.

CONTACT: Warwoman Dell National Recreation Area, Chattahoochee and Oconee National Forests, U.S. Forest Service, Tallulah Ranger District, 809 Highway 441 S, Clayton, GA 30525, 706-782-3320

LOCATION: To reach Warwoman Dell, go to Clayton on US 441 and turn east on Warwoman Road. Proceed 3 miles and watch for signs. A gravel road leads to Warwoman Dell.

TALLULAH GORGE STATE PARK

About 12 miles south of Clayton, Tallulah Falls thunders through a gorge nearly one thousand feet deep and 2 miles long, home to rare plants and diverse animal species. Known in Cherokee stories as a gateway to other worlds and the home of "little people," Tallulah Falls was called Ugv-yi (Ocoee), a word whose meaning is lost. (The myth associated with this place can be found at the back of this guidebook.) Talulu was the name of the ancient town on the river above the falls, and also the name of a town in present-day Graham County, on Tallulah Creek east of Robbinsville, North Carolina.

Georgia Department of Natural Resources and Georgia Power created this three-thousand-acre state park, which includes hiking trails, climbing areas, a lake, a beach for swimming, campsites, tennis courts, facilities for fishing and picnicking. The new Jane Hurt Yarn Visitor Center offers an award-winning video, an exhibit area on the Cherokees, an exhibit on the natural history and geology of the gorge, a three-story-high natural history diorama, and gift shop.

South of the visitor center and through the town of Tallulah Falls, on the loop road, the Tallulah Point Overlook sells snacks, crafts, books, and antiques and provides another view of the gorge. This two-story building has been a tourist shop since the 1920s, and its porch provides views of the gorge. It should not be confused with the official visitor center a few miles north.

CONTACT: Tallulah Gorge State Park, P.O. Box 248, Tallulah Falls, GA 30573, 706-754-7970, <www.gastateparks.org>, <tallulah@alltel.net>

HOURS: Open daily from 8:00 A.M. until sunset. The park office is open from 8:00 A.M. until 5:00 P.M.

LOCATION: 12 miles south of Clayton off of US 441, a four-lane road. Going south, turn left on Jane Hurt Yarn Drive, just before the five-lane bridge over Tallulah Lake. (Approaching from the north, this is the third turn marked for Tallulah Gorge.) This leads to the state park, rim trails, and interpretive center. To reach the Tallulah Point Overlook, a tourist stop built in the 1920s on the gorge rim, proceed through the town of Tallulah Falls and take either of the roads to the left marked "Tallulah Gorge." These are actually the same road, Tallulah Gorge Scenic Loop 15.

TRAVELER'S REST STATE HISTORIC SITE

Traveler's Rest State Historic Site is located on the old Unicoi Trail. The Cherokee Nation made an agreement for the development of this ancient trail into a modern turnpike in 1813, and the beginning of those improvements in the east started near the entrance of Toccoa Creek into the Tugaloo River (a tributary of the Savannah River). This site was near the old Tugaloo village site, and also near Traveler's Rest, which became a stagecoach inn on the new turnpike. This area passed out of Cherokee ownership in 1819.

In 1833 Devereaux Jarrett bought this land and created a thriving plantation, including the two-story structure that became an inn on the stagecoach route and which is the only remaining original structure on the entire length of the Unicoi Turnpike. English traveler and author George W. Featherstonaugh, who described the Cherokee council meetings at Red Clay, stayed here in 1837 and commented: "I got an excellent breakfast of coffee, ham, chicken, good bread and butter, honey, and plenty of good new milk for a quarter of a dollar. . . . What a charming country this would be to travel in if one was sure of meeting with such nice clean quarters once a day."

CONTACT: Traveler's Rest State Historic Site, 8162 Riverdale Rd., Toccoa, GA 30577, 706-886-2256, <www.gastateparks.org>
LOCATION: 6 miles east of Toccoa on US 23

TUGALOO STATE PARK

Tugaloo (Dugilu-yi), one of the Lower Towns, was an important Cherokee town located at the junction of Toccoa Creek and the Tugaloo River. This town site was inundated in 1963 by the creation of Lake Hartwell, but it is commemorated with a historic marker on the Georgia side of the lake. Along with Kituhwa in the Middle Towns and Echota in the Overhill Towns, Tugaloo was important in Cherokee religion and ceremony because priests kept the sacred fire burning here.

Because this area lies closer to the coast of South Carolina than any other part of the original Cherokee Nation, the Lower Towns were the first visited by colonists and traders, beginning about 1700. The Colonial Records of South Carolina chronicle the visits and activities of Colonel George Chicken, John Herbert, trader Theophilus Hastings, and others. This proximity, however, also led to the repeated destruction of Tugaloo along with the other Lower Towns—by Colonel Archibald Montgomery (1760), Colonel James Grant (1761), and American commander Andrew Williamson (1776). As a result, many Cherokee families moved from here to Willstown in northern Alabama, and a generation later their stories of the destruction remained so vivid that Cherokee children ran away screaming when they first saw a white man.

It should be noted that the sacred fire of the Cherokee Nation was carried on the Trail of Tears to Indian Territory, now Oklahoma. In 1951, the "eternal flame" was brought back to the East. It now burns at the entrance to the Mountainside Theater in Cherokee, North Carolina.

CONTACT: Tugaloo State Park, 1763 Tugaloo State Rd., Lavonia, GA 30553, 706-356-4362

HOURS: Open daily from 7:00 A.M. until 10:00 P.M. The park office is open daily from 8:00 A.M. until 5:00 P.M.

LOCATION: To get to Tugaloo State Park from Traveler's Rest, retrace the route along SR 123 almost back to Toccoa, then go south on GA 17. Follow park signs to Gerrard Road, turn right. Go 1.5 miles to GA 328 and turn left. Proceed 3.3 miles to the park, and turn right into the park entrance.

EVENTS

■ Christmas Candlelight Tours at New Echota and the Vann House

Luminaries and candles cast their glow on these historic buildings and reproductions of historic Cherokee buildings the first or second weekend in December. Summer programs also are available. Call for more information on events and times or see the Cherokee Heritage Trails website.

CONTACT: New Echota State Historic Site, 1211 Chatsworth Highway NE, Calhoun, GA 30701, 706-624-1321, <www.gastateparks.org>; Chief Vann House State Historic Site, 82 Georgia Highway 225 N, Chatsworth, GA 30705, 706-695-2598, <www.alltel.net/~vannhouse/>, <vannhouse@alltel.net>

LOCATION: Near Calhoun, Georgia (see information above in the sections on these two state historic sites)

A Connection to Place

Among Native Americans, you don't come from a place, you are of a place. Our name for ourselves is Kituhwa-gi, the people of Kituhwa. A connection to place designates who you are.

Many years ago I was in Los Angeles attending a summer institute there on Native American studies. One day a guy took a bunch of us down to the Greyhound bus station in Los Angeles. So we sat around, nothing happened. And he said, "Be patient, I want to show you all something." We sat in that huge waiting area, drinking Cokes and just watching people. After a while they began to announce buses, going down the list. They announced one bus leaving with connections to Barstow, Flagstaff, Gallup, to Albuquerque, to points east, Amarillo, Oklahoma City. And he stood up and said "Come with me, watch this."

There were some Navaho guys, in cowboy hats, dressed like that, and they'd been passing around a bottle. And of course, this is down-town Los Angeles, in 1969. They had gotten up at the same time, so we stopped and we followed them, where the docking area was, and they went out to the place where that bus that they just called, was leaving. And my thought was, we're going to watch these guys get on this bus and go home, cause it was headed for Gallup. And we sat there and watched for a few minutes.

When no one was watching — the driver was taking tickets, and others were boarding — they each took turns walking up and touching that bus. And then they turned around and came back in.

And then we left, and he said, "I just wanted you guys to see that." He said "These boys can't go home right now." He said, "Maybe they'll go home next week, or a year from now, but right now they can't."

Young fellow I met here from Snowbird, Tommy Chekelelee, he told me the other day that they have a basket in their family, given to them several years ago, that went to Oklahoma on the Trail of Tears. I said, "How did it get here, if it went over the Trail of Tears?"

He said that his mother was in Oklahoma some years back, and this lady came up to her and gave her that basket. She said, "This has been handed down in our family. Our great-great grandmother brought it from North Carolina." And this lady gave it to Tommy's mom.

And I immediately thought of that story. Here were these people, only eight hundred miles away — a day's drive — but even at that, they wished the basket to go home. After 160 some years, they still know where they come from. And it's why the lady gave the basket to her—to somehow make a connection, just like those Navaho boys touching that bus. They knew that that bus was going to go home. It was going to be driving through Navaho country. And that basket was coming home.

So you want to know how important our feelings are about where we come from? We are of *a place, not just* from *a place.*

Tom Belt

CALENDAR OF EVENTS

Events along the Cherokee Heritage Trails connect visitors with Cherokee people and their living traditions. From April through December, in North Carolina, Tennessee, and Georgia, people demonstrate traditions that are part of their lives today: basket weaving, pottery making, beadwork, carving, dance, storytelling, and singing. Visitors are welcome, and Cherokee people are usually prepared to talk and to answer questions. Through these events, visitors can meet Cherokee people and experience Cherokee traditions. Some traditions have been practiced for millennia, like rivercane basket making and flint knapping. But all of these folkways are made new with each generation—and they come alive with each performance, with the fleeting smile of a dancing child, the quavery voices of the elders raised in hymns, and the sure touch of a potter smoothing her work with a river stone.

At these events Cherokee people often demonstrate traditional crafts. Basket makers use rivercane, white oak, honeysuckle, and maple. People gather these from the woods, taking care to choose only those that will yield good basket materials, and they also collect herbs and barks for dyeing the basket splints: bloodroot, walnut, yellowroot, and butternut. The whole process, from finding a tree to weaving a finished basket, can take months of hard work. And good basket materials keep getting harder to find. Potters also say that the clay deposits known to older generations have become unavailable because of road building and development. The most traditional Cherokee potters coil or form their pots without the use of a wheel, and then smooth the outside with a stone or antler. Using carved wooden paddles, they stamp designs on the pots. This technique has been used by Cherokee potters for more than a thousand years; it has been one of the distinguishing characteristics of Cherokee culture. Potters also use corncobs, peach pits, and fabric to impress designs, and recently, some have begun incising the Sequoyan syllabary as decoration on pots. Bead workers decorate clothing, ball caps, bags, and barrettes with designs, as well as making wampum belts. Carvers render figures, masks, and tools from wood and stone, and some practice flint knapping, the creation of arrowheads

Shopping for baskets at the Fading Voices Festival. (Photograph by Murray Lee)

and spear points. Others make blowguns from rivercane and fashion the darts from locust sticks and dried thistle blossoms. Cherokee artisans create flutes from wood and rivercane as well as drums from a variety of materials.

Cherokee music and dance traditions range from ancient rivercane flutes to gospel quartet singing to rock and roll. Cherokee people make and play traditional flutes, which has become more popular in the last decade, throughout Indian country. Cherokee flute playing was described by William Bartram in the late eighteenth century and is surely much older — cane flutes simply do not survive as part of the archaeological record in the Southeast because they decompose. Drumming or the use of a hand-held rattle accompanies traditional Cherokee dance songs; women dancers wear terrapin shells tied below their knees to provide rattle accompaniment to dancing. Ceremonial dancing at stomp grounds continues as a sacred Cherokee tradition in North Carolina and in Oklahoma. Cherokee people have played fiddles since before 1800, and their twentieth-century fiddlers like Manco Sneed influenced Appalachian fiddling styles. In addition to fiddling, Cherokee instrumentalists play banjo, blues, and rock and roll. Cherokee people have been singing hymns and gospel music in English and Cherokee for two hundred years, and this tradition has evolved into today's quartets and groups who sing shape note hymns and gospel songs in both languages. Usually accompanied by guitar and bass, these groups sing in

Indian dinners are popular at Cherokee festivals. (Photograph by Murray Lee)

quiet four-part harmony and perform at their churches, their communities, at special "singings," and throughout the region.

Cherokee storytellers also perform at festivals and events. The tradition of storytelling lives on in families and in the community, in both English and Cherokee language, but has come to be shared with outsiders as well. Storytelling performances include humorous stories about the misadventures of possum, scary myths of the horrible Spearfinger, legends of local places, and reminiscences about family, friends, and Cherokee history.

"Indian dinners" at some events offer visitors a chance to sample Cherokee food. A typical meal might include fried chicken, greens, hominy, bean bread with fatback, potatoes, cabbage, herb tea, and blackberry dumplings. Fry bread comes from powwow traditions rather than Cherokee foodways, but can be found also, served with chili as an "Indian taco" or served with honey as dessert.

Events listed here occur annually, and have happened for at least three years. New events or special one-time events and exhibits will be posted on the Cherokee Heritage Trails website at

<http://www.cherokeeheritagetrails.org>.

All of the Cherokee Heritage Trails events involve Cherokee people who are enrolled members of the Eastern Band of Cherokee Indians, who represent authentic traditions. For more information about Cherokee artists who are willing to present traditions publicly, consult the *Cherokee Artist Direc-*

Rachel Watty, Senior Miss Cherokee, at the Cherokee Fall Fair. (Photograph by Roger Haile)

tory published in conjunction with the Cherokee Heritage Trails project. It can be found online at the above Internet address, or a copy can be obtained from the North Carolina Arts Council.

Cameras are generally allowed at festivals and events, but it is considered good manners to ask permission to take photographs. Any further use of photographs, video, or audio tapes for commercial purposes requires a signed release form from the people whose images and material are being used.

Powwows and powwow-related events are not part of the Cherokee Heritage Trails project because powwow traditions represent many native tribes as well as some emergent traditions of their own—they do not represent Cherokee tradition. Cherokee people often do participate in powwow dancing and drumming, but they recognize that these dances and songs come from other tribes or from the powwow traditions that have evolved since World War II. The straight dance, the fancy dance, the grass dance, or the jingle dance common at powwows differ markedly in music, language, regalia, and style from traditional Cherokee dancing. Still, powwows have an important place in the life of many Native Americans as a way to meet and socialize and to affirm their Indian identity. The ceremonial grounds at Cherokee hosts weekend powwows on Memorial Day, Fourth of July, and Veterans Day, where Cherokee people, other native people, and visitors of all races participate.

Spring events include two festivals and the opening of a living history museum. In April, the Cherokee Ceremonial Grounds hosts the annual Ramp Festival, celebrating the return of the wild green that combines the flavor of garlic and onion with a particularly strong, lingering, leek. In May, the Snowbird community holds their Fading Voices Festival at Little Snowbird Baptist Church, featuring music, dance, stickball, foods, and crafts demonstrations. This month also heralds the opening of the Oconaluftee Indian Village.

Summer provides festivals, outdoor drama, and gospel "singings." In June, the Museum of the Cherokee Indian hosts the Cherokee Voices Festival, which includes many elders from the community who do not travel to events farther afield. The outdoor drama *Unto These Hills* begins its summer production this month. The Cherokee Heritage Weekend at Swannanoa provides an opportunity for visitors to learn language, music, and arts and crafts from Cherokee people. In July, the Snowbird community hosts several "singings," outdoor events with gospel music by Cherokee and white groups. The Cherokee History and Culture Institute combines experiential learning and academic learning for educators. August brings "Cherokee Days" at Red Clay State Park.

Fall leads to festivals, including the Cherokee Fall Fair, which began in 1914. In September, festivals at Sequoyah Birthplace Museum and Fort Loudoun State Historic Area happen the same weekend. Mountain Heritage Day combines Cherokee and white Appalachian traditions. The first week in October, the Cherokee Fall Fair celebrates Cherokee heritage: arts and crafts, food, music, dance, and the stickball game. The whole community participates in creating exhibits of garden produce, art, and quilting as well as basket making, beadwork, carving, and other Cherokee traditions. In November, Junaluska's life is honored at the Annual Wreath Laying Ceremony at his gravesite.

The Christmas season gets celebrated in historical ways at Red Clay State Park, Fort Loudoun State Historic Area, and the New Echota State Historic Site.

Year round, events on Cherokee Heritage Trails connect visitors with Cherokee people and places. Other, less regular programs take place at sites on the trails, like storytelling at Cataloochee Ranch, art exhibits at the Museum of the Cherokee Indian, and demonstrations and workshops at state parks. Check with individual sites for their listings.

CALENDAR

FOUR CHEROKEE STORIES

■ KANATI AND SELU

This sacred story was told to James Mooney by Swimmer (Ayuini) and by John Ax (Itagvnahi), near present-day Cherokee, North Carolina, in the 1880s (and published in Mooney's *Myths of the Cherokee*). Mooney notes that in the old days, this story was considered so sacred that a person had to go through a cleansing ceremony, "going to water," before hearing it. The story of Kanati and Selu living at Shining Rock provides the beginning for many other stories in this mythic cycle: the story of the origin of hunting; the story of the origin of growing corn and beans; the story of the origin of strawberries; the stories of the adventures of their two sons as they journey to find their parents and finally go to live in the west, becoming the thunder boys. As in other Cherokee sacred stories, out of tragic events comes something good for the people: from the death of Selu comes corn and beans. (The names of the main characters are pronounced "Ga-NA-di," with a short "a" like "ah," and "di" pronunced like "dee"; and "She-lu," with the "e" like a long "a" and the "u" like a long "u".)

Readers may find some similarities between this origin myth and the story of the Garden of Eden in the book of Genesis, but that does not mean that the Cherokee story was influenced by the Bible. Many myths in different cultures around the world describe a time of harmony and plenty destroyed by the curiosity or foolishness of human beings. Perhaps we can interpret this not only as a literal past, but also something that we humans reenact over and over again. This story is still told in several different versions among the Eastern Band.

Long years ago, soon after the world was made, a hunter and his wife lived below Pilot Knob with their only child, a little boy. The father's name was Kanati (The Lucky Hunter) and his wife was called Selu (Corn). No matter when Kanati went into the wood, he never failed to bring back a load of game, which his wife would cut up and prepare, washing off the blood from the meat in the river near the house. The little boy used to play down by the river every day, and one morning the old people thought they heard laughing and talking in the bushes as though there were two children there. When the boy came home at night, his parents asked him who had been playing with him all day. "He comes out of the water," said the boy, "and he calls himself my elder brother. He says his mother was cruel to him and threw him into the river." Then they knew that the strange boy had sprung from the blood of the game which Selu had washed off at the river's edge.

Every day when the little boy went out to play the other would join him, but as he always went back again into the water, the old people never had a chance to see him. At last one evening Kanati said to his son, "Tomorrow, when the other boy comes to play, get him to wrestle with you, and when you have your arms around him hold on to him and call for us." The boy promised to do as he as told, so the next day as soon as his playmate appeared he challenged him to a wrestling match. The other agreed at once, but as soon as they had their arms around each other, Kanati's boy began to scream for his father. The old folks at once came running down, and as soon as the Wild Boy saw them, he struggled to free himself and cried out, "Let me go; you threw me away!" But his brother held on until the parents reached the spot, when they seized the Wild Boy and took him home with them. They kept him in the house until they had tamed him, but he was always wild and artful in his disposition, and was the leader of his brother in every mischief. It was not long until the old people discovered that he had magic powers, and they called him Inage utsv hi, "He who grew up wild."

Whenever Kanati went into the mountains he always brought back a fat buck or doe, or maybe a couple of turkeys. One day the Wild Boy said to his brother, "I wonder where our father gets all that game; let's follow him next time and find out." A few days afterward Kanati took a bow and some feathers in his hand and started off toward the west. The boys waited a little while and then went after him, keeping out of sight until they saw him go into a swamp where there were a great many of the small reeds that hunters use to make arrow shafts. Then the Wild Boy changed himself into a puff of bird's down, which the wind took up and carried until it alighted upon Kanati's shoulder just as he entered the swamp, but Kanati knew nothing about it. The old man cut reeds, fitted the feathers to them, and made some arrows, and the Wild Boy—in his other shape—thought "I wonder what those things are for?" When Kanati had his arrows finished he came out of the swamp and went on again. The wind blew the down from his shoulder, and it fell in the woods, when the Wild Boy took his right shape again and went back and told his brother what he had seen. Keeping out of sight of their father, they followed him up the mountain until he stopped at a certain place and lifted a large rock. At once there ran out a buck, which Kanati shot, and then lifting it upon his back, he started for home again. "Oho!" exclaimed the boys, "he keeps all the deer shut up in that hole, and whenever he wants meat he just lets one out and kills it with those things he made in the swamp." They hurried and reached home before their father, who had the heavy deer to carry, and he never knew that they had followed.

A few days later the boys went back to the swamp, cut some reeds, and made seven arrows, and then started up the mountain to where their father kept the game. When they got to the place, they raised the rock and a deer came running out. Just as they drew back to shoot it, another came out, and then another and another, until the boys got confused and forgot what they were about. In those days all the deer had their tails hanging down like other animals, but as a buck was running past, the Wild Boy struck its tail with his arrow so that it pointed upward. The boys thought this good sport, and when the next one ran past, the Wild Boy struck its tail with his arrow so that it stood straight up, and his brother struck the next one so hard with his arrow that the deer's tail was almost curled over his back. The deer carries his tail this way ever since. The deer came running past until the last one had come out of the hold and escaped into the forest. Then came droves of raccoons, rabbits, and all the other four-footed animals—all but the bear, because there was no bear then. Last came great flocks of turkeys, pigeons, and partridges that darkened the air like a cloud and made such a noise with their wings that Kanati, sitting at home, heard the sound like distant thunder on the mountains and said to himself, "My bad boys have got into trouble; I must go and see what they are doing."

So he went up the mountain, and when he came to the place where he kept the game, he found the two boys standing by the rock, and all the birds and animals were gone. Kanati was furious, but without saying a word he went down into the cave and kicked the covers off four jars in one corner, when out swarmed bedbugs, fleas, lice, and gnats, and got all over the boys. They screamed with pain and fright and tried to beat off the insects, but the thousands of vermin crawled over them and bit and stung them until both dropped down nearly dead. Kanati stood looking on until he thought they had been punished enough, when he knocked off the vermin and made the boys a talk. "Now you rascals," said he, "You have always had plenty to eat and never had to work for it. Whenever you were hungry all I had to do was to come up here and get a deer or a turkey and bring it home for your mother to cook; but now you have let out all the animals, and after this when you want a deer to eat you will have to hunt all over the woods for it, and then maybe not find one. Go home now to your mother, while I see if I can find something to eat for supper."

When the boys got home again, they were very tired and hungry and asked their mother for something to eat. "There is no meat," said Selu, "but wait a little while and I'll get you something." So she took a basket and started out to the storehouse. This storehouse was built upon poles high up from the ground, to keep it out of the reach of animals, and there was a ladder to climb up by, and one door, but no other opening. Every day when Selu got ready to cook the dinner she would go out to the storehouse with a basket and bring it back full of corn and beans. The boys had never been inside the storehouse, so wondered where all the corn and beans could come from, as the house was not a very large one; so as soon as Selu went out of the door the Wild Boy said to his brother, "Let's go and see what she does." They ran around and climbed up at the back of the storehouse and pulled out a piece of clay from between the logs, so that they could look in. There they saw Selu standing in the middle of the room with the basket in front of her on the floor. Leaning over the basket, she rubbed her stomach—so— and the basket was half full of corn. Then she rubbed under her armpits— so—and the basket was full to the top with beans. The boys looked at each other and said, "This will never do; our mother is a witch. If we eat any of that it will poison us. We must kill her."

When the boys came back into the house, she knew their thoughts before they spoke. "So you are going to kill me?" said Selu.

"Yes," said the boys, "You are a witch."

"Well," said their mother, "when you have killed me, clear a large piece of ground in front of the house and drag my body seven times around the circle. Then drag me seven times over the ground inside the circle, and stay up all night and watch, and in the morning you will have plenty of corn."

The boys killed her with their clubs, and cut off her head and put it up on the roof of the house with her face turned to the west, and told her to look for her husband. Then they set to work to clear the ground in front of the house, but instead of clearing the whole piece, they cleared only seven little spots. This is why corn now grows only in a few places instead of over the whole world. They dragged the body of Selu around the circle, and wherever her blood fell on the ground, the corn sprang up. But instead of dragging her body seven times across the ground, they dragged it over only twice, which is the reason the Indians still work their crop but twice. The two brothers stayed up and watched their corn all night, and in the morning it was full grown and ripe.

When Kanati came home at last, he looked around, but could not see Selu anywhere, and asked the boys where was their mother. "She was a witch, and we killed her," said the boys. "There is her head up there on top of the house."

When he saw his wife's head on the roof, he was very angry, and said, "I won't stay with you any longer. I am going to the Wolf people." So he started off, but before he had gone far the Wild Boy changed himself again to a tuft of down, which fell on Kanati's shoulder. When Kanati reached the settlement of the Wolf people, they were holding a council in the town house. He went in and sat down with the tuft of bird's down on his shoulder, but he never noticed it. When the Wolf chief asked him his business, he said, "I have two bad boys at home, and I want you to go in seven days from now and play ball against them." Although Kanati spoke as though he wanted them to play a game of ball, the Wolves knew that he meant for them to go and kill the two boys. They promised to go. Then the bird's down blew off from Kanati's shoulder, and the smoke carried it up through the hole in the roof of the townhouse. When it came down on the ground outside, the Wild Boy took his right shape again and went home and told his brother all that he had heard in the townhouse. But when Kanati left the Wolf people, he did not return home, but went on farther.

The boys then began to get ready for the Wolves, and the Wild Boy— the magician—told his brother what to do. They ran around the house in a wide circle until they had made a trail all around it excepting on the side from which the Wolves would come, where they left a small open space. They made four large bundles of arrows and placed them at four different points on the outside of the circle, after which they hid themselves in the woods and waited for the Wolves. In a day or two a whole party of Wolves came and surrounded the house to kill the boys. The Wolves did not notice the trail around the house, because they came in where the boys had left the opening, but the moment they went inside the circle, the trail changed to a high brush fence and shut them in. Then the boys on the outside took their arrows and began shooting them down, and as the Wolves could not jump over the fence, they were all killed, excepting a few that escaped through the opening into a great swamp close by. The boys ran around the swamp and a circle of fire sprang up in their tracks and set fire to the grass and bushes and burned up nearly all the other Wolves. Only two or three got away, and from these have come all the wolves that are now in the world.

Soon afterward some strangers from a distance, who had heard that the brothers had a wonderful grain from which they made bread, came to ask for some, for none but Selu and her family had ever known corn before. The boys gave them seven grains of corn, which they told them to plant the next night on their way home, sitting up all night to watch the corn, which would have seven ripe ears in the morning. These they were to plant the next night and watch in the same way, and so on every night until they reached home, when they would have enough corn to supply the whole people. The strangers lived seven days' journey away. They took the seven grains and watched all through the darkness until morning, when they saw seven tall stalks, each stalk bearing a ripened ear. They gathered the ears and went on their way. The next night they planted all their corn, and guarded it as before until daybreak, when they found an abundant increase. But the way was long and the sun was hot, and the people grew tired. On the last night before reaching home they fell asleep, and in the morning the corn they had planted had not even sprouted. They brought with them to their settlement what corn they had left and planted it, and with care and attention were able to raise a crop. But ever since the corn must be watched and tended through half the year, which before would grow and ripen in a night.

As Kanati did not return, the boys at last concluded to go and find him. The Wild Boy took a gaming wheel and rolled it toward the Darkening Land. In a little while the wheel came rolling back, and the boys knew their father was not there. He rolled it to the south and to the north, and each time the wheel came back to him, and they knew their father was not there. Then he rolled it toward the Sunland, and it did not return. "Our father is there," said the Wild Boy, "let us go and find him."

So the two brothers set off toward the east, and after traveling a long time they came upon Kanati walking along with a little dog by his side. "You bad boys," said the father, "have you come here?"

"Yes," they answered, "we always accomplish what we start out to do— we are men."

"This dog overtook me four days ago," then said Kanati, but the boys knew that the dog was the wheel which they had sent after him to find him. "Well," said Kanati, "as you have found me, we may as well travel together, but I shall take the lead."

Soon they came to a swamp, and Kanati told them there was something dangerous there and they must keep away from it. He went on ahead, but as soon as he was out of sight the Wild Boy said to is brother, "Come and let us see what is in the swamp." They went in together, and in the middle of the swamp they found a large panther asleep. The Wild Boy got out an arrow and shot the panther in the side of the head. The panther turned his head and the other boy shot him on that side. He turned his head away again and the two brothers shot together—*tust, tust, tust!* But the panther was not hurt by the arrows and paid no more attention to the boys. They came out of the swamp and soon overtook Kanati, waiting for them. "Did you find it?" said Kanati. "Yes," said the boys, "we found it, but it never hurt us. We are men." Kanati was surprised, but said nothing, and they went on again.

After a while he turned to them and said, "Now you must be careful. We are coming to a tribe called the Anada dvntaski ("Roasters," i.e., cannibals) and if they get you they will put you into a pot and feast on you." Then he went on ahead. Soon the boys came to a tree which had been struck by lightning, and the Wild Boy directed his brother to gather some of the splinters from the tree and told him what to do with them. In a little while they came to the settlement of the cannibals, who as soon as they saw the boys, came running out, crying, "Good, here are two nice fat strangers. Now we'll have a grand feast!" They caught the boys and dragged them into the townhouse, and sent word to all the people of the settlement to come to the feast. They made up a great fire, put water into a large pot and set it to boiling, and then seized the Wild Boy and put him down into it. His brother was not in the least frightened and made no attempt to escape, but quietly knelt down and began putting the splinters into the fire, as if to make it burn better. When the cannibals thought the meat was about ready, they lifted the pot from the fire, and that instant a blinding light filled the townhouse, and the lightning began to dart from one side to the other, striking down the cannibals until not one of them was left alive. Then the lightning went up through the smoke hole, and the next moment there were the two boys standing outside the townhouse as though nothing had happened. They went on and soon met Kanati, who seemed much surprised to see them, and said, "What! Here you are again?"

"Oh yes, we never give up. We are great men!"

"What did the cannibals do to you?"

"We met them and they brought us to their townhouse, but they never hurt us." Kanati said nothing more, and they went on.

He soon got out of sight of the boys, but they kept on until they came to the end of the world, where the sun comes out. The sky was just coming down when they got there, but they waited until it went up again, and then they went through and climbed up on the other side. There they found Kanati and Selu sitting together. The old folk received them kindly and were glad to see them, telling them they might stay there a while, but then they must go to live where the sun goes down. The boys stayed with their parents seven days and then went on toward the Darkening Land, where they are now. We call them Anisgaya Tsunsdi (The Little Men) and when they talk to each other we hear low rolling thunder in the west.

■ **STORY OF THE TERRAPIN AND THE HARE**

The race in this Cherokee folktale started at Black Mountain. Standing on its peak (now Mount Mitchell), one can see the three ridges of the story extending northward.

The Rabbit was a great runner, and everybody knew it. No one thought the Terrapin anything but a slow traveler, but he was a great warrior and very boastful, and the two were always disputing about their speed. At last they agreed to decide the matter by a race. They fixed the day and the starting place and arranged to run across four mountain ridges, and the one who came in first at the end was to be the winner.

The Rabbit felt so sure of it that he said to the Terrapin, "You know you can't run. You can never win the race, so I'll give you the first ridge and then you'll have only three to cross while I go over four."

The Terrapin said that would be all right, but that night when he went home to his family he sent for his Terrapin friends and told them he wanted their help. He said he know he could not outrun the Rabbit, but he wanted to stop the Rabbit's boasting. He explained his plan to his friends and they agreed to help him.

When the day came all the animals were there to see the race. The Rabbit was with them, but the Terrapin was gone ahead toward the first ridge, as they had arranged, and they could hardly see him on account of the long grass. The word was given, and the Rabbit started off with long jumps up the mountain, expecting to win the race before the Terrapin could get down the other side. But before he got up the mountain he saw the Terrapin go over the ridge ahead of him.

He ran on, and when he reached the top he looked all around, but could not see the Terrapin on account of the long grass. He kept on down the mountain and began to climb the second ridge, but when he looked up again there was the Terrapin just going over the top. Now he was surprised and made his longest jumps to catch up, but when he got to the top there was the terrapin away in front going over the third ridge. The Rabbit was getting tired now and nearly out of breath, but he kept on down the mountain and up the other ridge until he got to the top just in time to see the Terrapin cross the fourth ridge and thus win the race.

The Rabbit could not make another jump, but fell over on the ground, crying *mi, mi, mi, mi* as the Rabbit does ever since when he is too tired to run any more. The race was given to the Terrapin and all the animals wondered how he could win against the rabbit, but he kept still and never told. It was easy enough, however, because all the Terrapin's friends looked just alike, and he had simply posted one near the top of each ridge to wait until the Rabbit came in sight and then climb over and hide in the long grass. When the Rabbit came on he could not find the Terrapin, and so thought the Terrapin was ahead, and if he had met one of the other terrapins he would have thought it the same one because they looked so much alike. The real Terrapin had posted himself on the fourth ridge, so as to come in at the end of the race and be ready to answer questions if the animals suspected anything.

Because the Rabbit had to lie down and lose the race, the conjurer now when preparing his young men for the ball play, boils a lot of rabbit hamstrings into a soup, and sends someone at night to pour it across the path along which the other players are to come in the morning, so that they may become tired in the same way and lose the game. It is not always easy to do this, because the other party is expecting it and has watchers ahead to prevent it.

■ AGAN UNI TSI'S SEARCH FOR THE UKTENA

This story was noted by Lieutenant Henry Timberlake in 1762, and it was written down by James Mooney, as it was told by Swimmer (Ayuini) in western North Carolina in the 1880s, and by James Wafford in Oklahoma about the same time.

In one of their battles with the Shawano, who are all great magicians, the Cherokee captured a great medicine-man whose name was Agan uni tsi, the Groundhog's Mother. They had tied him ready for the torture when he begged for his life and engaged, if spared, to find for them the great wonder worker, the Ulvsuti. Now the Ulvsuti is like a blazing star set in the forehead of the great Uktena serpent, and the medicine man who could possess it might do marvelous things, but everyone knew this could not be because it was certain death to meet the Uktena. They warned him of all this, but he only answered that his medicine was strong and he was not afraid. So they gave him his life on that condition, and he began the search.

The Uktena used to lie in wait in lonely places to surprise its victims, and especially haunted the dark passes of the Great Smoky Mountains. Knowing this, the magician first went to a gap in the range on the far northern border of the Cherokee country. He searched and found there a monster blacksnake, larger than had ever been known before, but it was not what he was looking for, and he laughed at it was something too small to notice.

Coming southward to the next gap he found there a great moccasin snake, the largest ever seen, but when the people wondered, he said it was nothing. In the next gap he found a greensnake and called the people to see "the pretty *salikwayi*," but when they found an immense greensnake coiled up in the path they ran away in fear. Coming on to Utawagvta, the Bald Mountain [Now Joanna Bald, above Andrews], he found there a great *diyahali* (lizard) basking, but although it was large and terrible to look at, it was not what he wanted, and he paid no attention to it.

Going still south to Walasiyi, the Frog place, [now Blood Mountain, south of Murphy] he found a great frog squatting in the gap, but when the people who came to see it were frightened like the others and ran away from the monster he mocked at them for being afraid of a frog and went on to the next gap. He went on to Duniskwa'lgvyi, the Gap of the Forked Antler, and to the enchanted lake of Atagahi [Newfound Gap and Clingman's Dome], and at each he found monstrous reptiles, but he said they were nothing. He thought the Uktena might be hiding in the deep water at Tlanusi'yi, the Leech Place [Murphy] on Hiwassee, where other strange things had been seen before, and going there he dived far down under the surface. He saw turtles and water snakes, and two immense sun perches rushed at him and retreated again, but that was all.

Other places he tried, going always southward, and at last on Gahuti Mountain [Cohutta] he found the Uktena asleep. Turning without noise, he ran swiftly down the mountainside as far as he could go with one long breath, nearly to the bottom of the slope. There he stopped and piled up a great circle of pine cones, and inside of it he dug a deep trench. Then he set fire to the cones and came back again up the mountain.

The Uktena was still asleep, and, putting an arrow to his bow, Agan uni tsi shot and sent the arrow through its heart, which was under the seventh spot from the serpent's head. The great snake raised his head, with the diamond in front flashing fire, and came straight at his enemy, but the magician, turning quickly, ran at full speed down the mountain, cleared the circle of fire and the trench at one bound, and lay down on the ground inside.

The Uktena tried to follow, but the arrow was through his heart, and in another moment he rolled over in his death struggle, spitting poison all over the mountain side. The poison drops could not pass the circle of fire, but only hissed and sputtered in the blaze, and the magician on the inside was untouched except by one small drop which struck upon his head as he lay close to the ground; but he did not know it. The blood, too, as poisonous as the froth, poured from the Uktena's wound and down the slope in a dark stream, but it ran into the trench and left him unharmed. The dying monster rolled over and over down the mountain, breaking down large trees in its path until it reached the bottom. Then Agan uni tsi called every bird in all the woods to come to the feast, and so many came that when they were done not even the bones were left.

After seven days he went by night to the spot. The body and the bones of the snake were gone, all eaten by the birds, but he saw a bright light shining in the darkness, and going over to it he found, resting on a low-hanging branch where a raven had dropped it, the diamond from the head of the Uktena. He wrapped it up carefully and took it with him, and from that time he became the greatest medicine man in the whole tribe.

When Agan uni tsi came down again to the settlement, the people noticed a small snake hanging from his head where the single drop of poison from the Uktena had struck; but so long as he lived he himself never knew it was there.

Where the blood of the Uktena had filled the trench, a lake formed afterwards, and the water was black and in this water the women used to dye the cane splits for their baskets.

■ THE MAN WHO MARRIED THE THUNDER'S SISTER

In the old times the people used to dance often and all night. Once there was a dance at the old town of Sakwi-yi ["Soquee place"] on the head of Chattahoochee, and after it was well started two young women with beautiful long hair came in, but no one knew who they were or whence they had come. They danced with one partner and another and in the morning slipped away before anyone knew that they were gone; but a young warrior had fallen in love with one of the sisters on account of her beautiful hair, and after the manner of the Cherokee had already asked her through an old man if she would marry him and let him live with her. To this the young woman had replied that her brother at home must first be consulted, and they promised to return for the next dance seven days later with an answer, but in the meantime if the young man really loved her he must prove his constancy by a rigid fast until then. The eager lover readily agreed and impatiently counted the days.

In seven nights there was another dance. The young warrior was on hand early, and later in the evening the two sisters appeared as suddenly as before. They told him their brother was willing, and after the dance they would conduct the young man to their home, but warned him that if he told anyone where he went or what he saw he would surely die.

He danced with them again and about daylight the three came away just before the dance closed, so as to avoid being followed, and started off together. The women led the way along a trail through the woods, which the young man had never noticed before, until they came to a small creek, where, without hesitating, they stepped into the water. The young man paused in surprise on the bank and thought to himself, "They are walking in the water; I don't want to do that." The women knew his thoughts just as if he had spoken and turned and said to him, "This is not water, this is the road to our house." He still hesitated, but they urged him on until he stepped into the water and found it was only soft grass that made a fine level trail.

They went on until the trail came to a large stream which he knew for Tallulah River. The women plunged boldly in, but again the warrior hesitated on the bank, thinking to himself, "That water is very deep and will drown me; I can't go on." They knew his thoughts and turned and said, "This is no water, but the main trail that goes past our house, which is now close by." He stepped in, and instead of water there was tall waving grass that closed above his head as he followed them.

They went only a short distance and came to a rock cave closed under Ugv-yi (Tallulah Falls). The women entered, while the warrior stopped at the mouth; but they said, "This is our house; come in and our brother will soon be home; he is coming now." They heard low thunder in the distance. He went inside and stood up close to the entrance. Then the women took off their long hair and hung it up on a rock, and both their heads were as smooth as a pumpkin. The man thought, "It is not hair at all," and he was more frightened than ever.

The younger woman, the one he was about to marry, then sat down and told him to take a seat beside her. He looked, and it was a large turtle, which raised itself up and stretched out its claws as if angry at being disturbed. The young man said it was a turtle, and refused to sit down, but the woman insisted that it was a seat. Then there was a louder roll of thunder and the woman said, "Now our brother is nearly home." While they urged and he still refused to come nearer or sit down, suddenly there was a great thunder clap just behind him, and turning quickly he saw a man standing in the doorway of the cave.

"This is my brother," said the woman, and he came in and sat down upon the turtle, which again rose up and stretched out its claws. The young warrior still refused to come in. The brother then said that he was just about to start to a council, and invited the young man to go with him. The hunter said he was willing to go if only he had a horse; so the young woman was told to bring one. She went out and soon came back leading a great *uktena* snake, that curled and twisted along the whole length of the cave. Some people say this was a white *uktena* and that the brother himself rode a red one. The hunter was terribly frightened and said, "That is a snake; I can't ride that." The others insisted that it was no snake, but their riding horse. The brother grew impatient and said to the woman, "He may like it better if you bring him a saddle and some bracelets for his wrists and arms." So they went out again and brought in a saddle and some arm bands, and the saddle was another turtle, which they fastened on the *uktena*'s back, and the bracelets were living slimy snakes, which they got ready to twist around the hunter's wrists.

He was almost dead with fear, and said, "What kind of horrible place is this? I can never stay here to live with snakes and creeping things." The brother got very angry and called him a coward, and then it was as if lightning flashed from his eyes and struck the young man, and a terrible crash of thunder stretched him senseless.

When at last he came to himself, he was standing with his feet in the water and both hands grasping a laurel bush that grew out from the bank, and there was no trace of the cave or the Thunder People, but he was alone in the forest. He made his way out and finally reached his own settlement, but found then that he had been gone so very long that all the people had thought him dead, although to him it seemed only the day after the dance. His friends questioned him closely, and, forgetting the warning, he told the story; but in seven days he died, for no one can come back from the underworld and tell it and live.

FOR FURTHER READING

Adair, James. *History of the American Indians.* New York: Promontory Press, [1974?]. Reprint of 1775 edition.

Bartram, William. *The Travels of William Bartram.* Edited by Mark Van Doren. New York: Dover Publications, 1955. Reprint of 1791 edition.

Bird, Traveller. *The Path to Snowbird Mountain: Cherokee Legends.* New York: Farrar, Straus, and Giroux, 1972.

Chapman, Jefferson. *Tellico Archaeology.* Knoxville: University of Tennessee Press, 1985.

Crow, Vernon H. *Storm in the Mountains: Thomas Confederate Legion of Cherokees and Mountaineers.* Cherokee, N.C.: Museum of the Cherokee Indian Press, 1982.

Duncan, Barbara R. *Living Stories of the Cherokee.* Chapel Hill: University of North Carolina Press, 1998.

Duncan, Barbara R., ed. *Where It All Began: Cherokee Creation Stories in Art.* Cherokee, N.C.: Museum of the Cherokee Indian Press, 2001.

Ehle, John. *Trail of Tears.* New York: Anchor Books, 1988.

Finger, John R. *Cherokee Americans: The Eastern Band of Cherokees in the Twentieth Century.* Lincoln: University of Nebraska Press, 1991.

Finger, John R. *The Eastern Band of Cherokees, 1819–1900.* Knoxville: University of Tennessee Press, 1984.

Hill, Sarah H. *Weaving New Worlds: Cherokee Women and Their Basketry.* Chapel Hill: University of North Carolina Press, 1997.

Journal of Cherokee Studies, 1976–2002.

King, Duane. *The Cherokee Nation: A Troubled History.* Knoxville: University of Tennessee Press, 1979.

Lord, William G. *Blue Ridge Parkway Guide: Grandfather Mountain to Great Smoky Mountain National Park 291.9–469 Miles.* Birmingham, Ala.: Menasha Ridge Press, 1997.

McLaughlin, William. *Cherokee Renascence in the New Republic.* Princeton, N.J.: Princeton University Press, 1986.

Mooney, James. *History, Myths, and Sacred Formulas of the Cherokees.*

Bureau of American Ethnology Annual Report 1900, Part 2. Reprint, Asheville, N.C.: Historical Images, 1992.

National Park Service. *Comprehensive Management and Use Plan: Trail of Tears National Historic Trail.* Denver, Colo.: U.S. Department of the Interior, 1992.

Neely, Sharlotte. *Snowbird Cherokees: People of Persistence.* Athens: University of Georgia Press, 1991.

Perdue, Theda. *Cherokee Women 1700–1835.* Lincoln: University of Nebraska Press, 1998.

Perdue, Theda. *The Cherokees.* New York: Chelsea House, 1989.

Rossman, Doug. *Where Legends Live: a Pictorial Guide to Cherokee Mythic Places.* Cherokee, N.C.: Cherokee Publications, 1988.

Rozema, Vicki. *Footsteps of the Cherokees: A Guide to the Eastern Homelands of the Cherokee Nation.* Winston-Salem, N.C.: John F. Blair, 1995.

Speck, Frank G., and Leonard Broom. *Cherokee Dance and Drama: In Collaboration with Will West Long.* Norman: University of Oklahoma Press, 1983. Reprint of 1951 edition.

Ward, H. Trawick, and R. P. Stephen Davis. *Time Before History: The Archaeology of North Carolina.* Chapel Hill: University of North Carolina Press, 1999.

Wilkins, Thurman. *Cherokee Tragedy: The Ridge Family and the Decimation of a People.* Norman: University of Oklahoma Press, 1986.

GENEALOGICAL RESOURCES ON CHEROKEE HERITAGE TRAILS

People with roots in the southern Appalachians often find a Cherokee connection in their family genealogy, several generations ago. These ancestors can be hard to trace because of reluctance on the part of earlier generations to identify themselves as Cherokees and reluctance of other family members to discuss this. In addition, census records beginning about 1900 recorded only "black" and "white" races. Materials do exist on Cherokee ancestors, and several genealogists have made the history of families of the Eastern Band their area of expertise. Along the Cherokee Heritage Trails, several places offer more information on Cherokee genealogy.

OFFICIAL CHEROKEE TRIBES

Those tracing their ancestry should understand the legal aspects of tribal membership. Three groups have been federally recognized as Cherokee tribes: The Eastern Band of Cherokee Indians, the Cherokee Nation of Oklahoma, and the United Keetoowah Band. Federal recognition was granted to the first two in 1868, because they had made treaties with the federal government prior to that time. Recognition of the United Keetoowah Band came about more recently, because of their shared language, history, and documentation of their group throughout Cherokee history. Each of these three bands has its own, specific, legal requirements for membership enacted by their tribal councils. These involve proving that you have an ancestor that was part of their band at a specific time, and having a certain degree, or quantum, of Cherokee blood. For example, the Eastern Band of Cherokee Indians requires that its members have an ancestor on the Baker Roll of 1924 and that the member today has at least one-sixteenth Cherokee blood.

ENROLLMENT RECORDS

A number of census records, or "rolls" exist for the Eastern Band and Cherokee Nation, recording the names of all enrolled members, such as the Baker Roll, mentioned above. Some rolls include additional family information. These rolls have been published and can be purchased at a number of locations. They are described below, along with selected titles that are also helpful in pursuing Cherokee genealogy.

GENEALOGY BOOK LIST

Cherokee Proud: A Guide for Tracing and Honoring Your Cherokee Ancestors, 2nd ed. By Tony Mack McClure. Chunanee Books, 2001. Softcover, 308 pp. Informative and helpful, this best-selling guide provides specific information for doing your own research and answers many questions.

Eastern Band of Cherokee Indians Genealogy Workbook. Softcover, 31 pp. "The purpose of this publication is to guide you in preparing your family tree as well as to see if you are eligible to apply for enrollment with the Eastern Band of Cherokee Indians."

Cherokee Roots Vol. 1: Eastern Cherokee Rolls. By Bob Blankenship. Cherokee Roots Publications, 1992. Softcover, 165 pp. This book reprints all the census lists from 1817 to 1924 for Cherokees living east of the Mississippi.

Cherokee Roots Vol. 2: Western Cherokee Rolls. By Bob Blankenship. Cherokee Roots Publications, 1992. Softcover, 374 pp. Official census rolls from 1851 to 1909 of Cherokees living west of the Mississippi River. Old Settler, Drennen, Dawes, and Guion Miller Roll West.

1924 Baker Roll: The Final Roll of the Eastern Band of Cherokee Indians of North Carolina. By Bob Blankenship. Cherokee Roots Publications, 1998. Softcover, 286 pp. plus three appendices. The official base roll, which defines membership in the Eastern Band today. Also includes all contested applications. Family names, birth dates, and more information.

Guion Miller Roll "Plus". By Bob Blankenship. Cherokee Roots Publication, 1994. Softcover, 275 pp. The 1909 Guion Miller Roll plus 1898 Dawes Roll information. Includes all applicants for the Miller Roll, Dawes Roll Number, Census Card Number, Degree of Cherokee Blood, and surname in 1989.

Dawes Roll "Plus" of Cherokee Nation 1898. By Bob Blankenship. Cherokee Roots Publication, 1994. Softcover, 217 pp. The entire 1898 Dawes Roll plus Guion Miller Roll information for those on both rolls. More than 36,000 Cherokee citizens included.

**SITES FOR GENEALOGICAL RESOURCES
ON THE CHEROKEE HERITAGE TRAILS**

GENEALOGICAL RESOURCES IN CHEROKEE, NORTH CAROLINA

Gift Shop of the Museum of the Cherokee Indian, Highway 441 and Tsali Blvd., Cherokee, NC 828-497-3481, <www.cherokeemuseum.org>. While the museum does not assist in genealogical research, materials for genealogical research are for sale in the museum gift shop and online.

The Qualla Boundary Public Library, in the Civic Center, Acquoni Rd., Cherokee, NC 28719, 828-497-9023. Genealogical library materials are available for use.

Church of Jesus Christ of Latter Day Saints, 26 Cattle Dr., Whittier, NC 28789, 828-497-7651.

Genealogists: Bob Blankenship and Pam Blankenship, P.O. Box 265 Cherokee, NC 28719, 828-497-9709

GENEALOGICAL RESOURCES IN FRANKLIN, NORTH CAROLINA

For more than two hundred years, people of Cherokee and Scottish descent have intermarried, since the first Scottish traders of the eighteenth century to the Scots-Irish Appalachian folks of today. For information on Scottish genealogy, clans, and tartans, go to the Scottish Tartans Museum. Staff there will help you determine your clan affiliation and your official tartan; they also can provide a color printout of your tartan colors. Many books on Scottish genealogy as well as tartan items are for sale in the gift shop. Scottish Tartans Museum, 95 East Main St., Franklin, NC 28734, 828-524-7472, <www.scottishtartans.org>.

GENEALOGICAL RESOURCES IN EAST TENNESSEE

The East Tennessee Historical Society in Knoxville contains many genealogical records for Cherokee and white Appalachian families in their facility adjacent to their museum in Knoxville. East Tennessee Historical Society, 600 Market Street, P.O. Box 1629, Knoxville, TN 37901-1629, 865-215-8824.

ACKNOWLEDGMENTS

The Cherokee Heritage Trails project is one of four heritage trails projects of the Blue Ridge Heritage Initiative, a partnership between the states of North Carolina, Virginia, Tennessee, and Georgia. The other projects also focus on cultural resources that reflect the region's unique identity—music traditions of the Blue Ridge, mountain crafts, and the area's agricultural traditions. Together, these trails constitute a network of sites and venues that allow residents and visitors to explore the authentic living heritage of the region. In addition to education, the goals of the Blue Ridge Heritage Initiative are the conservation and perpetuation of cultural traditions and sustainable economic development.

The Cherokee Heritage Trails project is a collaboration between the Eastern Band of Cherokee Indians and interested agencies, organizations, and individuals in the states of North Carolina, Tennessee, and Georgia. The National Endowment for the Arts provided initial funding for the project. Other major funding partners were the North Carolina Department of Cultural Resources, the Appalachian Regional Commission, the American Express Company, the Z. Smith Reynolds Foundation, and the North Carolina Folklife Institute. Additional support came from the North Carolina Arts Council, Cherokee National Forest, Southeast Tennessee Resource Conservation Development Council, the Southeast Tennessee Development District, and the Tennessee Department of Transportation.

Planning and implementing the Cherokee Heritage Trails has been a partnership involving the Folklife Section of the North Carolina Arts Council, the Museum of the Cherokee Indian, the Eastern Band of Cherokee Indians, the Tennessee Overhill Heritage Association, the Blue Ridge Parkway, and the Tennessee Arts Commission. Through a collaborative planning process, members of the Eastern Band of Cherokee Indians have been actively involved at every step. Several members of the Eastern Band supported the project from its beginnings. These include Mollie Blankenship, who helped conceive the idea, former Principal Chief Joyce Dugan, former Cultural Resources Director Lynne Harlan, and Cultural Resources staff member Garfield Long Jr., who helped in the early stages. Principal Chief Leon Jones and Cultural Resources Director James Bird have continued to encourage and support the project.

Following approval of the project by the Tribal Council, a task force guided its development. Task force members included Ken Blankenship, Bob Blankenship, James Bowman, Jackie Bradley, Linda Caldwell, Pat Calhoun, Roby Cogswell, Margie Douthit, Barbara Duncan, Lynne Harlan, Gary Johnson, Marie Junaluska, Lewis Kearney, Mary Jane Letts, Garfield Long, Wayne Martin, Freeman Owle, Beverly Patterson, David Redman, Katherine Reynolds, Brett Riggs, and Russell Townsend. Many helpful suggestions for the project have come from Sarah Hill, who met with the task force on several occasions and helped organize a meeting to introduce the project in Georgia. The Museum of the Cherokee Indian, which is the project's main interpretive center, hosted most of the planning meetings, greatly facilitating local participation.

The task force developed criteria for including sites in the heritage trails. Especially important was that "all sites on the trail should contribute to an understanding of Cherokee history and culture." The task force also organized the sites around strategically located "hubs" at Ken Blankenship's suggestion. With the Museum of the Cherokee Indian in Cherokee, North Carolina, as the main interpretive center, the interpretive hubs in North Carolina became the Junaluska Memorial and Museum in Robbinsville, the Scottish Tartans Museum in Franklin, and the Cherokee County Historical Museum in Murphy. For Tennessee, the task force selected the Sequoyah Birthplace Museum in Vonore and the Red Clay State Historic Park south of Cleveland. The interpretive hub for Georgia is the New Echota State Historic Site in Calhoun. Using this system of hubs, the task force decided, visitors will be able to find interpretation, information, and access within easy driving distance to all the sites on the Cherokee Heritage Trails.

Research for the project began with an inventory of Cherokee sites, using published materials, primary historical sources, and fieldwork. Folklorist Barbara Duncan and Eastern Band member Freeman Owle carried out the research and prepared the report for North Carolina sites. Archaeologist Russell Townsend, a member of the Cherokee Nation in Oklahoma, did the same for Tennessee and prepared that report with assistance from Julie Wilkerson Townsend.

The Museum of the Cherokee Indian has taken a leading role in developing the Cherokee Heritage Trails. Ken Blankenship, executive director of the Museum of the Cherokee Indian, helped direct the planning process, and he has quietly helped keep everything on track. Under his direction, museum staff members have helped coordinate production of this guidebook, have supervised development of the project website, and have scheduled training sessions for Cherokee people to serve as guides for tour groups. Sharon Littlejohn, administrative manager at the museum, helped arrange meetings of the task force and site representatives at the museum, and James "Bo" Taylor, archivist at the museum, has participated in many ways, from advising the task force and making presentations on Cherokee culture to searching out historical maps and photographs for the guidebook.

Because the initiative also focuses on Cherokee artists, a concurrent research project created the *Cherokee Artist Directory*. Building on an earlier speakers' bureau sponsored by the North Carolina Arts Council and Qualla Arts and Crafts Mutual, this directory includes fifty Cherokee individuals and groups who demonstrate crafts or perform storytelling, music, and dance. These contemporary artists carry on the living traditions of the Eastern Band: carving wood and stone; making baskets from river cane, white oak, and honeysuckle; making pottery; creating finger woven sashes and beadwork; making blowguns and darts; singing gospel songs in Cherokee and English language; performing traditional Cherokee dances with drum and songs; storytelling; and lecturing on Cherokee history and culture. Some of these artists and their work will be participating in events along the trail.

Over the several years this project has been in the making, many other people have made contributions and suggestions that influenced its course. These include Ginger Abernathy, Becky Anderson, Alex Aumen, Julia Autry, Lucy Banks, David Batley, Libby Bell, Tyler Blethen, Mary Burke, David Brose, Alice Carson, Jeff Chapman, Richard Clark, David Crass, Jan Davidson, Ann Davis, Chris Deming, Kathy Dugan, Betty DuPree, Robert Emery, Brian Ensley, Maryanne Friend, Wanda Galloway, David Gomez, Agnes Gorham, Deb Grant, Sanford Gray, Linda Harbuck, Charlie Harshman, Rob Hawk, Grace Hawkins, Dr. Ed Henson, Barry Hipps, Teresa Hollingsworth, Teresa Hughes, Betty Huskins, Diane West Hutsell, Pete Jennings, Gary Johnson, Sharon Johnson, Mary Jumper, Duane King, Will Kinton, Joe Kitchens, Patty Lockamy, Annie Loggins, John Henry Maney, Barbara McRae, Chip Morgan, David Moore, Kaye Myers, Bob Newsome, Matt Newsome, Jamey Nicholson, Phil Noblitt, Lois Osborne, Reverend Steven Phillippi, Winton and Marjorie Porter, Max Ramsey, Mary Regan, Charlie and Mia Rhodarmer, Larry Rose, Laura Rotegard, Ron Ruehl, Glenda Sanders, Allen Smith, David Smith, Cheryl Smith, Janice Smith, Kathy Sprouill, Wanda Stalcup, Jeff Stancil, Ruth Summers, Leesa Sutton, Helen Talley-McRae, William Tanner, Danny Tatum, Mary Ann Thompson, Carey Tilley, Julie Townsend, Nancy Trovillion, Steven Turk, Fannie Watson, Debbie Wallsmith, Jeff Wells, Barbara White, Ann Woodford, Sam Yates, and Will Zakroski. We are deeply grateful to all of them and to photographers

Cedric N. Chatterley, Roger Haile, Murray Lee, and others who contributed illustrations for this book.

This project has received national recognition thanks to the leadership of Linda Caldwell and the Tennessee Overhill Heritage Association who, with assistance from Roby Cogswell and the Tennessee Arts Commission, submitted a successful nomination for the Unicoi Turnpike to be designated a National Millennium Trail. This award paved the way for the North Carolina Arts Council to include the Cherokee Heritage Trails in a successful nomination for a Millennium Legacy Trail.

Special thanks are due to those who contributed to this book, especially the Cherokee people who shared their thoughts in interviews and allowed their words to be quoted here: Tom Belt, Robert Bushyhead, Walker Calhoun, Marie Junaluska, Freeman Owle, and Jerry Wolfe. Thanks to Jody Adams for permission to quote two of her poems. Sarah Hill and Linda Caldwell made valuable suggestions that improved early drafts of the manuscript. Sandy Brewer developed driving directions for some of the more remote drives in Tennessee, and William Lewis did the same for some of the North Carolina sites. Betty Duggan's research in Turtletown and work with the Tennessee Overhill Heritage Association provided information and perspective for the southeastern Tennessee entries. For helping to create and sustain the project, thanks to Wayne Martin, director of the Folklife Section at the North Carolina Arts Council, to Beverly Patterson, folklife specialist, and to Katherine Reynolds, folklife program assistant. William Lewis and Molly Matlock Parsons, folklife interns, assisted in verifying contact information for sites. Many thanks also to David Perry, editor-in-chief at UNC Press for his encouragement and his wise management of this sometimes unwieldy process.

Barbara Duncan would like to thank her family—especially her husband John and her children John and Pearl—for all their love and support. Thanks to all her Cherokee friends for sharing their wisdom, humor, and good company. Thanks to the Creator.

Likewise, Brett Riggs credits his family, Pan and Jake, for their love and indulgence through the many years of this project.

INDEX